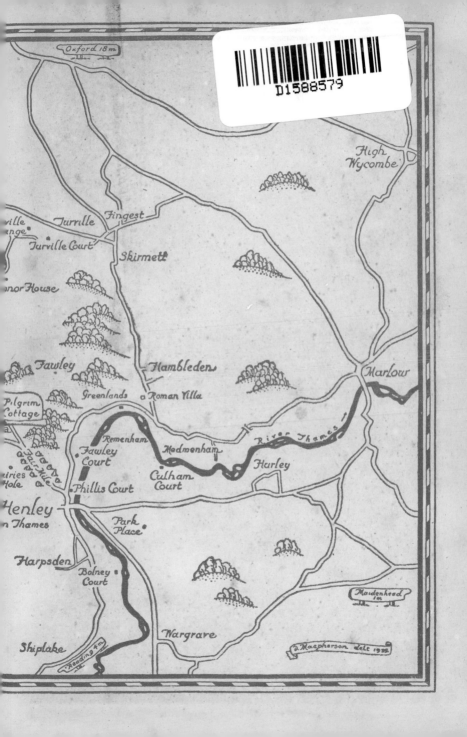

Oxford 18m.

High Wycombe

Turville

Turville Grange

Fingest

Turville Court

Skirmett

Manor House

Fawley

Hambleden

Marlow

Greenlands

Roman Villa

Pilgrim Cottage

River Thames

Remenham

Medmenham

Fairies Hole

Fawley Court

Culham Court

Hurley

Phillis Court

Henley on Thames

Park Place

Harpsden

Bolney Court

Maidenhead 1m.

Wargrave

J. Macpherson delt 1935.

Shiplake

Reading 4m.

# GONE RAMBLING

Frances Sprai

# GONE
# RAMBLING
## CECIL ROBERTS

HODDER·&·STOUGHTON
LIMITED·     ·LONDON

FIRST PUBLISHED . . . APRIL 1935
SEVENTH IMPRESSION . . JUNE 1948

*Made and Printed in Great Britain*
*for Hodder and Stoughton Limited, London, by*
*Hazell, Watson & Viney, Ltd., London and Aylesbury*

# CONTENTS

5

# ILLUSTRATIONS

7

# CHAPTER I

## A PINCH OF SALT

WHEN I decided to go ' rustic,' I not only had to determine the kind of cottage in which I wished to live, but also the place where I would like it to be situated. All my life I have never known where to live. I grew up in a provincial city of the Midlands, and spent my early years reviling it, but when, later, I came to see other provincial cities, I decided that Fate might have placed me in a worse locality than that bordered by Sherwood Forest and the winding Trent. The city itself, with its natural amphitheatre, terraced with houses, its high castled rock, Acropolis-like, commanding the valley, and distant hills, possessed a simple beauty worthy of the English scene. But the natural discontent of youth made me rebellious and blind to my surroundings.

Perhaps I shall never be quite settled. There have been moments when I have shocked my friends by a sudden declaration that I would sell Pilgrim Cottage. A cow lamenting its calf in an adjacent field through the watches of the night, a car that would not start up on an urgent summons to go forth, a train service to town that seemed expressly designed not to be express when most necessary, an arbitrary Assessment Authority, certain of one's helplessness after much expenditure on the purchased property, all these things and many others have evoked a sudden decision to pull up my roots and go.

Yet such alarms are vain, I know. The tendrils of my heart cling to the walls of my simple dwelling. Through each low window the line of the hills, the colouring of the beechwoods, the quivering of my four poplars, the level gold of dawn and sunset, are so familiar to my eyes that to lose these things would be to miss much that makes life lovely. There have been perverse moments, when, stirred by trivial irritations, I have vowed I would build a new house, with straight walls and secure plaster, with no dark corners or waste space, with high ceilings and wide windows, with everything labour-saving, if charm-losing, that the modern architect and builder can command. For a few minutes I have proclaimed this heresy, to the horror of my friends who enjoy a cottage in the country, run by someone else, and there without trouble when they wish to escape from town.

For one such restless mood I was fittingly punished. The day had been disastrous. The oil cooking-range, which had served us nobly for three years, had emitted a monstrous stink at the very moment when the most distinguished guest had honoured my table. I had perhaps lost a little of my sense of proportion, owing to the exalted nature of my guest, which helped, doubtless, to increase the proportion of the smell. But there it was ; I could have rushed into the kitchen and have slaughtered ' Florence '—this being the name of my hard-working oil range.

In that humiliating moment I vowed I would not live in a house without gas or electricity. The very next morning a train to town was missed owing to the inexplicable caprice of a ' self-starter,' misnamed. Three blisters on my hand, a brow covered in perspiration, and a garage filled with ' language ' reduced me to raging impotence and the humiliation of telephoning for a taxi. It came too late, both for the train and my temper, since the car had started in the interim.

Moreover, a drought had wrung my heart, a young apple tree had died, two cypresses had withered, every bed had a casualty, so that the garden was like a field hospital, and, final humiliation, a neighbour's cat completely defeated my attempt to stop it making a hole in my privet hedge through which it took a short cut to its hideous amours.

All this was too much of the ' simple life.' I would go and live in the town, I vowed. I would take one of those *de-luxe* flats with eight lifts, a public restaurant, lock-up garages, constant hot water, steam heating, built-in wardrobes, and everything complete in one payment. That would be truly the simple life. I would take a cottage in the country for four months each summer, and let others have the expense of keeping the gardener for the other eight months. I would get rid of the car, it should go once and for all time ; I would cease to worry because it did not rain, or feel depressed because it did. I would no longer turn myself into an unpaid innkeeper with an inflow and outflow of guests who took the wrong train on Saturdays, and left behind, on Monday, slippers, pyjamas, razor strops, silk stockings, face-cloths, and, on one incredible occasion, a budgerigar in a cage, for me to wrap up, forward, and pay postage on. This business of going rustic was too nerve-racking. I would lead a quiet life in a London square, with Harrods ever ready round the corner.

It was in this desperate mood that I set forth to make a call in London. The call made, Fate took me down a street in which an empty house was being decorated. Obeying an impulse, I stepped in. It was my kind of house—a double drawing-room, seven bedrooms, a light staircase, good fireplaces, high ceilings, and a sunny basement. It needed a new bathroom, electric light, a new kitchen, and a general overhaul, but it had a pleasing exterior, for there was a long balcony on to which the drawing-room windows opened. I saw that balcony blazing with flowers in summer, with nice striped awnings. The house faced S.S.W., which is what one likes a house to do ; it was in a wide street, quiet, with a cul-de-sac at one end. It was within five minutes of St. James's Park, ten minutes of my club, and near to Victoria Station when I felt like leaving England, or going down to the sea, or into the country. It was just my kind of house, in fact.

I immediately rang up an architect friend. He seemed a little surprised at my sudden decision to quit the country. " But haven't you written a book about your cottage—two books, a novel and one about the joys of going rustic, and isn't it almost a world-wide fact that you're now Cecil Roberts of Pilgrim Cottage, completely gone rustic, a God-wotter in a lovesome thing, fern grot, cool plot, whatnot—as the poem goes ? "

I cut his banter short. He seemed to me just then to be very unprofessional, deriding his own chance of a job.

" This is exactly the kind of house I have always wanted," I declared. " Will you examine it for me ? "

He agreed to, and visited the house in the best professional manner. He tapped walls, stamped on floors, looked up chimneys, opened and shut windows. The workmen were rather annoyed. Did the house belong to us ? a foreman asked.

" It may do," I replied brightly.

" It seems all right—but we'll have to examine the drains," said my friend. " I'll give them a smoke-box test, if you're serious, and the price suits you."

" A smoke-box test ? " I repeated. It sounded as if he were going mole-catching. I told him I was serious.

Three days later I was in the thick of the business. The architect was joined by the house agents, the solicitors on both sides, the builders and decorators. Buying a house seems to involve employing half-a-dozen professions, and at the end, when one reads the Title, it isn't at all clear who really owns the property. I gathered that it was my house for thirty years, but the land was not mine. For this I paid a ground rent each year. Later I was commanded to pay income-tax on the ground rent, an iniquitous demand which completely baffled me, since I could not understand how anything which had to be paid out should be regarded as money coming in. But it was ' explained ' to me by the solicitors, the agents, and the collector. Experience has taught me that it is really a waste of time to ask for explanations when the Government demands money. It can always ' explain ' that you have to pay.

The ground was not mine ; indeed, it was now a

yearly liability, and it appeared as if the house also was not mine. Two brothers who were Esquires, and lived somewhere in Sussex, demanded that I must insure my (their) property. I must paint it outside every three years in an approved colour, and inside every five years. I had to admit their appointed agents at such times as desired, I must not add, alter, or divide the property, nor sublet nor use for any trade purpose my (?) house.

There was a moment when I almost revoked the transaction. I seemed to have no rights except to pay, but my solicitors assured me all this was customary.

The conveyance made, there followed a conference with the builders, the decorators, the water and electric light authorities. The house was to be ready in a month.

" What about selling Pilgrim Cottage ? " asked my architect. " When are you leaving ? "

The question seemed a little premature.

" I haven't settled anything yet," I answered, diffidently. " It won't be difficult to sell."

" Oh no, I'm sure not ! " he agreed, with menacing faith.

The next morning the telephone rang. It was Sir Philip Gibbs. He was going to motor across the Continent, from Paris to Prague—would I go with him ?

" Of course," I exclaimed eagerly. " When ? "

" Next Friday."

" Next Friday ! " I gasped.

It was now Tuesday. I was in the middle of house transforming. Men were sawing, hammering, and painting. There were washbowls and radiators to inspect, their positions to be settled, colours to be agreed on, switches to be located, and a bath to be selected.

" I propose going through Burgundy, to Lyons and Geneva, then down the Rhône Valley, over the Simplon Pass, down to Lake Maggiore, and on to Milan ; then to Bergamo, Brescia, Verona, and up the Brennero Pass, via Trento and Bolzano, to Innsbruck. After that we'll probably go, viâ Salzburg, on to Vienna and Budapest, and strike north for Prague. We'll probably come back through Nuremberg, Munich, and Stuttgart, and then through the Saar on to Verdun and Paris. The only condition I'll have to make is that you don't write about it ; I'm doing a book on the trip, and it'll be my copyright. We'll have time for a little sketching, and as it'll be spring I expect the——"

" I'm coming," I said firmly, suppressing the hundred reasons for not going. The house in London and the house in the country must wait, also the new book half-written. Paris to Prague, in spring-time, in good company, was too much for any man, however self-disciplined.

I went, and left the architect, the plumber, the carpenter, and the interior decorator to get on with it. Paris with its chestnuts in flower ; forest-bordered Barbizon with its memories of Millet and Stevenson ; Moret-sur-Loing, so peaceful with its gateway, its mill, its stream, that we halted to sketch it ; Sens, with its great *bourdon* tolling for the feast of St. Jehanne d'Arc, its vestments worn by Thomas à Becket; Auxerre, with its ninth-century crypt; and smiling Burgundy, with the young vines shooting—what a pageant they provided! Evening fell golden on the ramparts and donjons of Sémur; and in Autun, with its Roman gates and the cathedral built by a Duke of Burgundy for the body of St. Lazare, more famous as a station than a saint, we sought in vain for a record of that profligate young bishop, Charles-Maurice de Talleyrand, whom Napoleon called to his face a liar, a cheat, and a heathen. Then Lyons and the mountains of Jura were left behind, and Geneva, ablaze with flowers, welcomed us, and, hugging the lake-shore of Haute Savoie, through Evian we came to Bouveret and entered the long valley of the Rhône.

How strangely are our wishes fulfilled! In the centre of the Rhône valley, baked on its plain between the high alps, there is a small town with romantic castles on twin peaks. They dominate the plain where the Rhône races, and, seeing them so often on the familiar route to Italy, I had often expressed a wish to stop one day and visit these alluring castles. Little did I know that I was destined to stop in the town of Sion, not for an hour, but for a fortnight. For my companion fell ill, seriously ill. I had nursed him on a memorable occasion at the close of the war. We were entering Brussels in the van of the armies advancing to the Rhine when my friend's car was telescoped on the gun-limber-churned road by Waterloo. Inflammation followed a severe abrasion of the arm, and, while Brussels deliriously cheered its returning King and Burgomaster, my friend lay feverish and in the hands

16

of an amateur nurse. And here we were again, in the same sad relationship, sixteen years later.

The days passed, and a crisis was reached which necessitated a summons to his family. Meanwhile, I studied Sion. I climbed to its castles, I drew them, I pondered over the singular physiognomy of these Valais peasants spraying their vines, and knew I had found the solution when I stumbled over the fact that this place had been a Roman town, as witnessed a stone in the *Hôtel de ville,* translated " A l'Empereur César Auguste, Fils du Divin Jules, Consul Pour XI Foi, Tribune pour la XVI, Père de la Patrie, Grand Pontife, La Cité de Sion à Son Protecteur." Spring was in the lair, and inadvertently I surprised a bronzed peasant lad, naked to the waist, rapturously embracing a laughing girl.

I rose at six, awakened by a squealing of pigs, lowing of cattle and braying of mules, to look down from my window on all the animation of a country market, with peasants truly leading their pigs to market by means of a string tied to the hind legs. Meanwhile, I massaged, measured medicine, listened to the verdict of doctors, and with an artist-companion made fitful excursions in ' off ' hours. And sometimes in the vineyards I thought of Pilgrim Cottage, amid the perfume and gold of lilac and laburnum. And, watching building operations as I sat in the *Café du Grand Pont de Rhône*, I suddenly bethought me of the house in London, wondering whether the bathroom was finished and the electric-power plugs were in the right positions.

Then, despite amateur nursing, the patient recovered, and we pressed on, through Brigue and the ice tunnels of the Simplon, to that high plateau where the old yellow and black diligence still runs from the Hospice to Iselle. And now the sunny plain of Piedmont stretched below us, and Italy, with its red tiles, white campanili, palms, and vines spreading from tree to tree, greeted us as we sped through scenes of haymaking in May, to gay Baveno embowered in flowers on Maggiore's shore. Italy, Austria, Bavaria—we scarcely tarried, but in Munich how near we were to tragedy! On June 1st, in Hitler's headquarters, the Brown House, a handsome young officer spared no effort to advocate the Nazi faith. On June 30th, at dawn, without a trial, he was put against a wall and riddled with bullets, stigmatised a traitor in the cause that evoked his infectious enthusiasm.

In Stuttgart my thoughts flew home again to Pilgrim Cottage, and the winter nights, when, in the low oak-raftered room, before a log fire, the radio broke on the country stillness with the midnight chimes of a clock. It was always the town clock of Stuttgart that called me to rise from my chair, turn back the half-burnt log, and put out the light. And here I was, standing in the fine old Platz at Stuttgart, looking up at the clock in the Rathaus tower whose chimes I knew so well, chimes that belonged even now to a cottage in the English Chilterns more than to a city of Württemberg.

It was at that moment there arose in me such an intense longing for my country home that I felt like chartering an aeroplane on the spot and fleeing from these alien skies. The thought of a long car journey back to Paris depressed me. Poor young Wyndham Tennant's lines came to mind :—

# A PINCH OF SALT

*I saw green banks of daffodil,*
*Slim poplars in the breeze,*
*Great tan-brown hares in gusty March*
*A-courting on the leas ;*
*And meadows with their glittering streams and*
*silver scurrying dace ;*
*Home, what a perfect place !*

But which home—the cottage in the country or the house in town ? I had almost forgotten that second purchase ; the idea of living in it now filled me with dismay. I wanted to get home to my corner of the Chilterns, to open the green gate, stand between the lavender bushes that guard the path, and look on that crazy old roof with its weathered tiles and triple dormer windows that watch the seasons pass in the beech woods above and the garden below. I now saw that awful London house as part of an evil conspiracy to entrap me in the futile littleness of social life. There would be cocktail parties to go to and give. I should always be on the point of escaping, and would never escape, for the town telephone entangles one in its wires like a Laocoön, and engagements for five to-morrow, eleven the morning after, and seven the next evening make the departure for the country seem like Macbeth's sad moan—to-morrow, and to-morrow, and the next day.

Fool that I was, to have been snared again by that agglomeration of numbered boxes, tied together by telephone wires, built on a labyrinth of pipes and bombarded by a cannonade of traffic ! London. Of those eight million inhabitants, desperately striving to preserve individuality while bolting from sleeping-box to office-hole, like nervous rabbits, long-eared to every alarm of the penny Press, fully three-quarters craved for green fields, a garden, and a view. I had these, and, perversely, was now papering and painting a little rabbit-hutch for myself, there to sit and munch the bran and lettuce of a social appetite.

One, two, three, struck the Stuttgart town clock. "No! No! No!" it cried, chiming with my inner voice. I looked around the lovely old Platz. There was a post office. In a few minutes I was inside, and had telegraphed to the London house agents telling them to sell the house.

Now, cautious, level-headed people, with only a drop of Scotch blood in their veins, will sneer at my instability, but I have observed that people who pride themselves on knowing what they want are always dilatory in confessing what they do not want, when they have made an error. They are firm in decision, but infirm in revision. It is a peculiarity of British quality. It makes us laugh at the Americans, who cannot bear to remember what New York was like, and, as soon as they have finished the belvedere on the sixty-second floor, begin to survey the foundations for the next building, more solid and insolvent. Of all the Rights I am prepared to defend stoutly, the right to change my mind is foremost, and, so long as I have only myself to consider, no harm is done and the expense is mine. And I am now reconciled to the fact that I belong to the second of two categories of mankind, those that sell at a profit and those that sell at a loss. Things have always cost me more than I get for them, but since I get a lot of pleasure making money in other ways it is only reasonable that I should lose it in this way. Things have a trick of balancing themselves.

Pilgrim Cottage has proved an exception to most of my possessions. Each year I like it better, each year I grow more and more convinced that it is in the kind of country I like best. I do not deserve such good fortune. Considering the impetuous haste with which I went rustic, the manner in which I almost broke into this untenanted cottage while a friend of mine mended a puncture on the highway, it should have developed serious defects. I was warned that the roof would fall in. The whole of the upper floor rests on a single oak beam. The beam had been spliced and bound with iron. The cottage had no damp-course. The floor was six inches below the level of the ground. It was near the Thames and would be flooded. It was between two roads and would be noisy. It was in the track of a mysterious spring that always flowed before a war, and all Europe was arming. It would be a preposterous price and would want a fortune spending on it. It had no gas or electricity and would probably never have them.

It was astonishing, according to my cautious friends, what a pig-in-a-poke I had found. The only kind word I had came from my solicitor, who said, " Well, I expect you'll get a lot of fun out of getting tired of it ! " For he knew, of course, that almost everyone who lives in a city dreams of living in a cottage, as old and uncity-like as possible, and everyone living in an old cottage longs for a flat in the heart of London.

It happened that all the prophets of woe were wrong. The roof has not fallen in. Under the strain of much hospitality, storms, and steam-heating it has not revealed a crack, nor let in a drop of water. The old builder who looked at the dining-room beam remarked, " They'll be able to hang your great-grandson from it, sir," which was meant to be a reassuring prophecy concerning the roof-tree, if not the family tree. The threat from the Thames proved the falsest of all woes. Actually, I discovered later, the Thames would have to rise a hundred feet before it crossed my floor, and I should get ample warning from London first ; for an ingenious friend worked out the fact that the portholes of the *Mauretania* would be level with the hands of Big Ben before I was in danger of having my carpets ruined. Locally, there is a legend that we live level with the top of Henley-on-Thames Church, which can be seen rising beyond the far end of the Fairmile, a noble elm avenue that wholly justifies its name.

And that missing damp-course ! So fearful were the results to be upon my bodily health that I foresaw the insurance company revoking my life policy, and no company, inured to the menace of fire, flood, storm, and act of God, being prepared to insure any man who dared to live in a house without a damp-course. Even now my friends look at me covertly, when I mention this fact, as though they expected to hear my joints creak, or see me begin to warp with rheumatoid arthritis.

I had a shock, let me confess. Soon after decorating I noticed that a corner of my study began to exude a salty substance. I brushed it away, but a week later it came again. " Ah ! " said my friends. " You see, you've no damp-course ! " " Neither had the Parthenon nor the Palace of Agamemnon. Solomon, in all his glory, knew nothing about a damp-course ! " I retorted. " Well, you'll see ! " was the answer, in a voice that suggested a bath chair.

I was worried. There was enough salt on that wall to run a household. I repainted the wall, giving it two coats. For a few weeks I thought I had mastered the salt works, but in time the white powder reappeared. My obstinate nature would not admit this evidence of damp. Everything in the house was dry. Someone had told me that a sure test of dampness was to leave an old pair of shoes in a floor cupboard. I put in an old pair and waited a month, but they came out unblemished. Yet that wall went on salting. One day curiosity led me to taste the powder. It was salt.

Did the Elizabethans make bricks with salt ? I asked my builder. He was derisive, but surely there was nothing unreasonable in the query. The Egyptians apparently made bricks with straw, since the Jews complained bitterly of being asked to make bricks without it. No one seemed able to give me the slightest help. I painted again. The salt came again. Of course it was no use, repeated my friends. But I remained unconvinced, and dry. Besides, had I not conclusive proof ? Every housewife knows that salt is the first thing in the house to show signs of dampness. It cakes in the salt-cellar. I once stayed in the country mansion of a man who had made a million out of the manufacture of an undampable salt. How could it be the damp on my wall, if its salt was a dry powder ? No one could answer that question.

For almost a year the mystery remained. I showed no signs of rheumatism, the wall showed no signs of ceasing to salt. At that time I employed an octogenarian gardener. He was wise in the countless ways of the countryfolk. It was his grandfather's great-grandfather who had passed down the story of having seen Mr. Chaucer, the Poet Laureate, walk past my garden on his way to Ewelme. He was training my outdoor vine one day when he remarked that when he was a boy there used to be a shop window where the vine now grew.

This information staggered me. I had no idea my cottage had ever been a shop. " Oh yes, sir, it was the only shop in the village, a grocer's shop, and a chemist's shop, and a sweet-shop——"

" How do you know all this ? " I asked, critically.

" My mother kept it, sir, and I was born here."

I have a feeling, difficult to repress, that a man should own the house in which he was born. It is a part of him. It is the one piece of property to which he seems particularly entitled. I straightway invited the old gardener to come inside and describe the geography of the house in his day. He immediately made two cottages of it, and quite convincingly explained a curious low recess in which I had placed a bronze copy of Narcissus, so-called (actually the Dionysus of Praxiteles), whose upraised finger, we are told, used to caution Mr. Gladstone to be careful as he sat at his desk.

That recess, explained my old gardener, was where the copper used to stand. It at once became an obvious fact. But he was in doubt about the room in which he was born. All he was certain of was that it was in the end cottage, not far from the copper. He had no hesitation about the shop window. He also showed me the site of a door, long since bricked up. And, casually, he made a remark that made me jump.

" Ah, there's some of the salt, sir, from the flitches ! "

" The flitches ! " I repeated, as he pointed to the powdery wall. " What flitches ? "

" Why, bacon flitches, sir. We used to pile the flitches up there. You never get the salt out of walls after that ; they get imperganated with it."

The mystery was solved. It was a shop wall ' imperganated ' with the salt from sides of bacon. It was not damp. But the persistence of that salt. It was still exuding, after almost eighty years !

Later, I found how to cure that wall of the salt that had cured the bacon. An architect friend suggested a coat of bitumastic paint, a known protector against the rust of sea-corroded hulls. The salt struggled hard for survival, but after a third coat it vanished for ever.

# THE TORCH

Twin castles stand in Sion,
Above the icy Rhône,
And morning makes the mountains
Her shining throne ;
Who walks these streets of Sion,
The peasants of Valais,
Or the men who marched with Cæsar
  The imperial way ?

Two thousand years in Sion
Are shrunk to one tense hour
When Pierre, of the vineyard,
Jehanne, like a flower,
Mingle their strength and beauty,
Two peasants of Valais,
Passing the torch of passion
  That fuses clay.

How can we, foolish cyphers,
Believe our urgent hands
Shall guide the line Fate traces,
Delay Time's sands ?
Two thousand years of Sion
In Pierre's shining eyes
Light the undying passion
  And gird his thighs.

# CHAPTER II

## THE COTTAGE FLOOR

### I

As for my cottage floor six inches below the level of the ground, there must surely have been a reason for this. To-day we raise our floors, since they are of wood, and must be ventilated. Most cottage floors are solid, and sunk down into the ground. It was suggested, when I began to make enquiries, that the floor of the cottage was sunk in order to make the roof look low externally. But I have always believed that these old cottage builders were simply utilitarian in what they did, and beauty came from their honest labour, and the eye of the simple craftsman. Repeated enquiries only made the problem more perplexing. An architect suggested that they made the floor lower than the ground-level in order to save bricks. The walls would be lower.

" But the foundations would have to be deeper," I replied, unconvinced.

A friend had no doubt whatever of the solution. " It's perfectly obvious—the ground outside's been rising for three hundred years. You know how they have to dig down for Roman ruins. Look how we build roads on top of roads. That's what's happened. Your garden's risen and risen, but your floor's where it always was."

I shook my head. " If the ground outside's risen,

then you would have to step down to the threshold. It's obvious that the threshold has always been level with the ground."

" Perfectly simple ! " declared an artist to whom I propounded my query. " They built the floor lower in order to keep out draughts ! "

Perfectly simple reasons are rarely perfect or simple. This would not do.

" Cold air goes down, hot air rises," I replied. " Nothing could suit a cold draught better than to go down into a warm room."

The next day at my club I met one of those wonderful fellows who can immediately explain anything, from the reason why the Prime Minister is the most asinine man that ever misled a nation that has lost its wits, down to real truth behind the autumn manœuvres. I knew he would know why cottage floors are below the ground-level. He did, at once.

" Perfectly simple, my dear fellow," he said, putting down his glass, and looking at me kindly, like a schoolmaster of infinite patience. " It's a relic of ancient days. It's only very old cottages that have floors like that. It was an instinct for protection."

I looked at him blankly.

" It's a relic of very ancient precautions," he continued learnedly. " You see, in the days of cottages like yours, you never knew who was coming. You had to be ready for anyone—you couldn't call a policeman or anything like that. The floor was made so that you had to step down. Now, when you step down "—he left the bar and gave a short demonstration—" you have to look down, don't you ? "

" Yes—I suppose you do," I agreed.

" Well, that's why ! "

I looked at his red face, blankly. " What's why ? " I asked.

He gave me a pitying glance.

" Watch me," he said, and again made a step down on to an imaginary floor. " You'll notice, as I step down, I look down involuntarily to see where I'm going. That gives the fellow in the room a chance to see who's coming in, and if it's an enemy, he can hit him over the head in time. Perfectly obvious, I think, eh ? "

" Perfectly," I said. " Have another drink ? "

" Thanks, I will."

For a moment I wished I had caught him stepping down and applied his theory.

The problem had now become an obsession. I asked everyone, including the oldest inhabitant. His answer had divine simplicity—" Because the door 'ad to swing in, sorr, an' they wanted the door to cover the 'ole all over ! "

For a moment I thought I had found the solution. The bottom of these cottage doors is lower than the threshold, but some cottage doors do fit ' the hole,' and yet the cottages have lower floor-levels.

Miss Whissitt, who brought her niece to tea, and has a habit of saying *N'est-ce pas?* at the end of her sentences, because thirty years ago she went to school in Tours, was surprised that I did not know the reason.

" To keep out the insects, *n'est-ce pas?* "

I must have looked stupid. She explained.

" You know that insects always crawl up ?  They'd all come in out of the garden if they hadn't to go *down*."

" But wasps and bluebottles crawl down into my beer-trap," I replied.

" I am referring to crawling insects, not flying—such as earwigs and beetles and woodlice.  They're of a different genre, *n'est-ce pas ?* "

" Do have another piece of cake," I said hurriedly. I wanted to know where earwigs and beetles went to when they got to the top of the wall.  The largest ceiling must lead to a down wall.  But I liked Miss Whissitt too much to laugh at her.  I made pretence to accept the crawling insect theory.

After that I made a nuisance of myself in the village.

" Would you like to have some seeds from my——" began a kind neighbour who met me in the lane.

" Can you tell me why my floor is six inches below ground ? " I demanded, interrupting him.

" So's mine.  I've never thought about it.  Have you noticed how tall the gladioli are growing ?  I suppose the drought——"

" Isn't it strange how we live with things and never notice them," I went on, my mind still on the floor.

He looked at me keenly, and then said he must hurry. Those mad authors again, he probably thought.

The village could not help me.  The omniscient Mr. Harris, at *The Golden Ball*, who never fails me in a crisis with a mole on the lawn, a rat in the larder, the sudden need of a file, or a piece of wire or an extra bed, failed me this time.  We have much in common, for we have been partners in crime, and have committed felicide between us : he shot my cat, condemned for thieving and murder. He is marvellously equipped to deal with the strange things that happen in a village, for he has been a sergeant-major in the army and a member of the county police force. He can throw a dart as neatly as he can draw a pint. He is infallible with a gun and a ferret. He can tell you the customs of remote Indian tribes, as well as the most likely horse for the Gold Cup, or what is eating away the lupin leaves. But he could not, strange to say, offer any solution on cottage floors.

I was born with a thirst for knowledge, perhaps in compensation for the fact that I have never had a thirst for drink, though I have tried hard to cultivate it in order to rise in Mr. Harris's esteem. I am a shocking customer at *The Golden Ball*. In my most desperate moods I fall back on sherry, but generally I try to save my face by ordering a tonic water as if it were a large tankard. I have never been able to understand all this Belloc-ing about beer, or G. K. C.'s insobriety. He lives in my vicinity and has never been caught doing any of that rolling of the singing drunkard to which he ascribes the tortuous pattern of our English lanes.

Because of my thirst for information an unsolved question will cause me to lose weight. I have surrounded myself with every kind of dictionary, encyclopædia, and atlas. My shelves groan with books on ' How it Works,' ' Every Man his own Plasterer,' and other curious works designed for people with a passion for taking watches to pieces, unscrewing water-taps, mending roofs, and trying to make garden rollers silent. I love gadgets, but not idiotic ones such as musical boxes set to play at an embarrassing moment of toilet, which filled a host of mine, a doctor of science, and a world authority on calories, with indescribable mirth. Few things have given me more pleasure than a most ingenious instrument that measures miles or kilometres on a map. You spread out Europe on a table, run the little wheel over the map, and then read on the dial that it is 1,886 miles to walk, motor, or take train to Constantinople or 1,471 miles to fly there.

But to return to the pressing problem. The *Encyclopædia Britannica* could not help me. But, then, why should it know anything about English cottage floors ? That was demanding too much of its astonishing omniscience. It could equally well call itself *The Encyclopædia Americana*, for it is now an American property, and gives equal attention to the life and characteristics of the vast American continent, so that Paul Robeson rubs shoulders with Delius. For this once it failed me.

A book entitled *Everything You Want to Know* proved, as usual, to know nothing. In the index I found ' Cottage—nature of, purchase of, restoration of—page 172.' On page 172 I learned that a cottage was a small dwelling in the country, with thatched or tiled roof. It was important to examine the ' title ' in purchase, as this was often doubtful, and not to pay too much, as the restoration was often costly. ' It is inadvisable to live in a cottage without a damp-course.' I closed the absurd book with a bang.

There remained one hope of elucidating the mystery. A Saturday night at *The Golden Ball* would bring a gathering of customers with a wonderful array of rustic knowledge. How much unwritten history I had heard in between the click of shove-ha'penny and the ' phut ' of the dart-board ! So on a Saturday night I entered the taproom at the rush hour, and propounded my question.

The knights of the tankard were astonished. There was a long silence. Many of them lived in old cottages with sunken floors. For many years they had stepped down on entering the house. They all confessed they had never wondered why.

" You do find some questions, sorr ! That be a good 'un, that be," said old Reuben. " Now I comes to think of it, I've been stepping down for eighty years, an' I might just as well 'ave been stepping up for all the good it's done me ! "

The first astonishment having subsided, various explanations were offered, but I had heard them all before. Reuben's co-octogenarian, who suffers from an inferiority complex because he is just a month younger and thereby loses patriarchal pre-eminence, observed, as I departed, " That's what comes of eddication and living in London. I've lived in a cottage with a sunk floor, and the question's never bothered me. No, it ain't. And don't you let it bother you, sorr, as long as the water keeps out."

Disappointed, I returned to my cottage. In the kitchen the radio was ' on,' and I heard, as I hung up my hat in the cloak-room :

" . . . And it is called Rush Sunday, because it was the custom in the old days for the villagers to take new rushes to the church, which, after blessing, were put down on the floor, and the old rushes were taken by the villagers for use in their cottage houses. The procession that went to the church was headed by a . . ."

I stood transfixed. There was a flash of light in my darkness. I walked into the study and sat down to examine my discovery. Before me, on a side-table, was a mechanical singing bird in its cage, the present of Louis Tissier, my friend in Paris and former secretary. I liked that bird for many reasons. It sang when commanded, and could be stopped by a lever. It wanted no seed, no water, no sand, no——

Oh, memories of boyhood! I had once pined for a canary in a cage. Since no one seemed inclined to buy me a canary, I saved to buy one. I looked around for a means of making money, but money-making at twelve years of age is always difficult. I was a particularly unfortunate little boy. I possessed no aunts or uncles or grown-up cousins to dispense sixpences. My wealth was amassed by odd pennies in a scarlet tin box that was a copy of a street letter-box. It had a slit for posting, a table with the times of collections, and an ' E.R.' in black letters with an imposing crown above it denoting that Edward Rex reigned over us.

Where is that pillar-box bank now? Does it exist still on any mantelpiece, receiving the pennies of children brought up in the laborious, and I fear, false faith of ' Take care of the pence, and the pounds will take care of themselves '? There was perhaps a more subtle truth in this axiom than I knew. The pounds certainly did look after themselves. They never let me look after them.

The times have changed. There are now no penny-

saving pillar-boxes even in the houses of the poorest.
When I go to the post office now I see on the counter
home-savings banks. They are beautifully designed
in the shape of a book, with bright colours, and of a
strength that shames those former tinny boxes. I
observe, too, that the standard of juvenile wealth has
risen. Apparently the Saturday penny, increased to
twopence at the age of ten, would arouse derision in
young Arthur and Agnes to-day. These new home-
savings banks only take shillings !

Even the poverty of my resources did not prevent an
occasional raid on the bank. This was made with the
aid of a meat knife. The pillar-box could only be
opened with a tin-opener. It was then finished. As
it was designed to hold sixty pence, its life was considered to be long enough before a saving of five shillings called for the breaking of the bank. The meat
knife provided a less desperate means of onslaught.
You inserted the blade in the slot, turned the pillar-
box upside down, and endeavoured to withdraw a
penny balanced on the blade. It was difficult with a
full money-box because of the weight of the coppers.
It was easier with an almost empty box. *Facilis
descensus averni.*

I have seen pitiful domestic scenes around those
pillar-boxes. I have seen a harassed mother raiding
the bank, in a gloom that deepened as the gas went
out of the penny-in-the-slot meter. As she fished for
a penny, anxiously watched by a small boy, she made
a promise to restore it on Friday night, when Father
came home with his wages.

To-day the world, the nursery, and the post office

no longer think in pence. You can no longer stagger
a child by giving it sixpence. We live in a world from
which gold has disappeared, but where silver is a
commonplace.

I longed for my canary. I rattled my pillar-box.
It was getting heavier and heavier, but oh, how slowly !
I must search for some quicker means of wealth. I
must go into trade. When in need, keep a shop
seems the axiom of Englishmen. The homes, motor-
cars, and holiday cruises of my butcher, baker, and
grocer prove the reliability of this axiom. If, instead
of weighing words, I had spent twenty years weighing
tea or sirloins, I might now have a chauffeur to wrestle
with my abominable car, although my friends who
have admirable cars tell me they wrestle with their
abominable chauffeurs.

It is difficult for a boy of twelve to go into trade, as
I was to learn. In the city in which I lived there was
a custom for small boys to rise early on a Good Friday
morning, and with a basket of buns on their arms,
cry—

> *Hot cross buns !  Hot cross buns !*
> *One-a-penny, two-a-penny,*
> *Hot cross buns !*

The buns were not really hot, they were not one-a-
penny, two-a-penny, they were twopence each. They
had a cross faintly cut on them. My own memory of
these buns is that they were tough and tasteless, and
had at the most half a dozen currants in them. Small
boys obtained them from the baker's overnight, and

early on Good Friday morning, following very ancient custom, went into the streets crying their wares.

Now I was told that large profits were made by the hot cross bun sellers. They made one shilling on a dozen twopenny buns. I calculated that if I sold five dozen hot cross buns I should make five shillings. This would go a long way towards my canary. So I decided to go into trade. On Good Friday morning I would sell hot cross buns. My mother gave me an order for six buns, as also a neighbour. This seemed a promising start.

But going into business requires capital. The buns had to be paid for overnight. Five shillings was required. I asked my two customers to pay me in advance, which they obligingly did, and I raided the bank for the remaining three shillings. Thus my capital was raised.

Very early on a cold Good Friday morning, I arose, and with a basket of buns on my arm went forth into the chilly and deserted streets. Now I was a very nervous child, afraid of my own voice, or of being in any way conspicuous. The result was that I shyly slunk into the streets, and probably my voice was never heard by housewives rising to their morning duties. I encountered a number of extremely rough boys with baskets on their arms, who bellowed their wares, and did not hesitate to bang on the doors of the houses. Desperate, I hammered at one door. It opened, and a woman so glared at me and banged the door again in her anger that I shrank back almost in tears. I discovered, moreover, that other boys had

39

already thoroughly canvassed the district, and were delivering their orders.

The sun rose, the traffic began, the world sat down to its Good Friday bun breakfast. There I was, a wretched failure with a weight of buns. I had sold one twopenny bun. Dismally I returned home. I was almost on the verge of tears, for I was ruined. My capital had been sunk. The buns would go rapidly stale. My mother, on my sad return, said nothing, but an unfeeling elder brother could not resist pointing a finger of scorn at me. Why had I ever imagined that I could sell hot cross buns, or anything ? They were beastly buns, anyhow, and he supposed that now we should have to eat stale buns for a week. And then he made a monstrous pun at my expense. I was bunkrupt. At that I dissolved into tears, and choked over the buttered bun, one of six on the table, and forty-seven in the basket.

All this to procure a canary in a cage ! This was my last excursion into trade. It should have warned me for the rest of my life, for I have never, since that early disaster, sold anything for as much as I gave for it.

But what have hot cross buns and a canary in a cage to do with the floor of Pilgrim Cottage being six inches below ground-level ? There is a sequence in my narrative, nevertheless. A year after the bun tragedy I possessed a canary in a cage. I loved it dearly, though it never sang properly, and it had an annoying habit of shooting its seed over the receptacle, so that it wasted far more than it consumed. But that bird, or rather that birdcage, brought me into collision with my father. The floor of the cage, like a tray, had to be taken out, scraped, and re-sanded at frequent intervals. I hated this job, and recall to this day the mess and the grating of the knife. Moreover, I was made to do it outside the house, even in winter. By this time I was tired of the bird and wanted a rabbit, and had already interviewed the grocer about a spare box, to be converted into a hutch.

There was a scene one morning, following an inspection of the canary's tray, which ended in my father ordering me out of the room after calling me ' a dirty, ill-mannered brat.' These words deeply mortified me, for at this moment I was in a phase of dandyism, a passion for posing as the Beau Brummell of my age. I had pestered my mother to be allowed to go into long trousers. I had also insisted that the new suit should be an Eton one, since all young gentlemen wore Eton suits. I had bought for threepence, in a bookshop bin, a book called *Manners for Men, or Correct Behaviour for Visits and Social Occasions*. I had learned its contents off by heart. I already saw myself, in an Eton suit, raising a silk top-hat to a bowing lady. I was an imaginative child, and I was very earnest about being a perfectly well-dressed, well-behaved little gentleman. And now my father had called me a dirty, ill-mannered brat. No four words in the whole range of the dictionary could have distressed me more. And all this came from a canary's tray.

Now, this tray was shallow and flat. It was a container for the sand. The shape and shallowness of my sunk cottage floor reminded me of this tray. It, too, was like a container. One might have scattered sand over it. I had wondered for a few moments whether sand had been placed over the cottage floor, but even so, it would not account for a depth of almost six inches. But when, on entering the cottage, I heard the radio lecture on rush-bearing, I knew I had stumbled on the solution. The villagers took home the old rushes from the church. Why ? To place on their own floors. If rushes were strewn over the floor they would have to be contained. Feet would kick them away, the wind coming in at the door would blow them in all directions. Moreover, if these rushes lay to a depth of two or three inches, the door could not open inwards unless they were well below the level of the threshold.

The problem was solved. That is why one steps down into old churches, old cottages. Their floors were rush containers. The manufacture of carpets did not begin in England until the eighteenth century. Even in manor houses and the halls of the aristocracy, rushes were used for floor coverings as late as the seventeenth century. A few nobles had imported Persian and Turkish carpets, and the use of boarded floors was growing, but in the cottages and farmhouses, and in churches, rushes were in use until the eighteenth century, hence the lateness of the rush-bearing ceremony.

I have wondered whether those floors of rushes did not also determine some features of Tudor and Elizabethan furniture. Refectory tables, heavy chairs, and buffets of these periods had large and almost clumsy bases. The tables had broad bosses, the chairs had heavy feet, like inverted basins, and lighter articles were often railed at the bottom. A rush floor, even after it had been well trodden down, could not give a level hard surface such as stone, wood, or close-knotted carpets. A heavy, broad foundation for furniture would be essential. It is significant that the spindle legs of Chippendale and Hepplewhite only came in with carpets.

The Sunday when the villagers took new rushes to the church became known as Rush-bearing Sunday. There was considerable ceremonial, with the maidens in white and chapleted with flowers. On the Saturday preceding, when the rushes were removed, there was a holiday and festival. The old custom of rush-bearing is still observed at Ambleside, Westmorland, on the last Sunday in July. Even so, how completely the tradition of the rush-strewn floor has died out. None could tell me why my cottage floor was below the ground-level.

## II

After I had been in my cottage three years, during which time I had not developed rheumatism from dampness, nor been flooded by the Thames, nor been troubled by traffic, nor seen the main beam give, nor the roof fall in, nor even seen the rising of that mysterious stream allied to the activities of Mars, the services of gas and electricity both came with a rush. Thus all the prophets of woe were refuted. Strange to say, the call of an affable young man from the electricity company did not fill me with excitement. It is surprising what one can do without, if one has never had it.

I shall always regret having bought my first motor-car. It will now be difficult to live without one, although I find it difficult and irritating to live with one. Every year cars become more and more wonderful, more and more intricate, more and more an income for the garage keepers. And as they grow more intricate, and capable of letting one down at essential moments, they become of less and less use in the large towns. There are now so many restrictions, so many lights and signs to observe, that the driver has no time to see the person he must avoid killing. I used to be three-quarters of an hour's run from my London house. Now, with twenty-one sets of traffic lights, innumerable markings on the road surface, beacons, one-way detours, and by-passes that add considerably to the distance and dullness of the journey, the time taken to reach my cottage has been almost doubled, and the nervous strain considerably increased.

What have I gained ? Time ? Certainly not. On the whole I have lost it, in other ways. Without a car I should not accept an invitation to tea ten miles away, go to a garden-party eight miles away, or to a cinema eleven miles away. I should not know all these people living within a radius of thirty miles. They are very charming to know, but are we to believe that a man who had to rely on a horse, or his own feet, lacked charming friends within a radius of ten miles ? Are we unhappy to-day because we cannot call on friends eighty and a hundred miles away ? Not at all. But when every man flies his own aeroplane, he will maintain that an aeroplane is essential to social amenities, as it will be when his social circle has a circumference of five hundred miles. Already, thanks to the motor and the telephone, we all know too many people. Even in the country one cannot now give a garden-party to less than a hundred people, since to ask twenty would be to offend eighty within the radius. The result is a great crush, a great gabble, a queue of cars, a queue at the buffet, and a host, uncertain whether he saw Mrs. Blinks and Mrs. Stumer, gibbering half-finished phrases, while he keeps an eye on the four hired waiters and hopes the gin won't give out.

When the telephone rings in my cottage I am often afraid it means some friend who will bully me into accepting an invitation to lunch at some very expensive restaurant, where I feel ashamed of eating at such gross cost in such discomfort of noise and seating. When I demur, he exclaims, " But it's only an hour in your car ! " Only the car and the telephone have made it seem reasonable to ask a man to travel eighty miles, at a cost of two hours or more, to eat a lunch.

> *Getting and spending, we lay waste our powers :*
> *Little we see in Nature which is ours ;*

wrote Wordsworth. To-day, he might write " Motoring and telephoning." Every Sunday down the Fairmile near my house there is a procession of cars. They contain people taking exercise but not exercised. The motorists sit doubled up after lunch, until they can get out and sit down for tea, when they will again sit doubled up until dinner ; and the success of the excursion will be judged by the number of miles by which the tea was separated from lunch and dinner.

Do I sound a Methuselah ? Perhaps I am, yet I have been a great traveller. I know that the places I have enjoyed most have been those that I have come upon slowly. I traversed the St. Gothard Tunnel by train perhaps some thirty times before I walked down the Pass. Only then did I get the full measure of its grandeur. There is a curious mania seizes you as soon as speed is achieved, whether by road, train, car, or aeroplane. You are in a feverish haste to reach your destination. You are reluctant to break the journey, to step forth on the earth. How often, when motoring, I have begun with a resolution to break the journey and explore a little ! How rarely I have fulfilled it ! There is a demon that drives you furiously on to the final destination.

All things that quicken the tempo of life, all those amenities we so eagerly seize, tend to filch away our tranquillity. We are now distressed if we do not catch the evening postal collection. It is so essential the letter should be received in the morning. But it is only essential that your letter should be received because Mr. G.'s letter will also be received. One hundred years ago, when your letter took three days, Mr. G.'s letter also took three days. To-morrow, when you use the air mail, he will use the air mail, and you will still be neck-and-neck business competitors, with this difference, that you are both experiencing an increased nervous strain.

When the affable young man called with the offer of electric light and power, I saw in him another fore-runner in the advance of a complex civilisation. The mile drive to my house had been up a noble elm avenue. On wintry nights it was pitch dark and frightening to maid-servants, who have a curious obsession that innumerable men lurk in dark corners to waylay them on their evenings out. Now there is a row of lights down that avenue, placed on the wrong side so that it does not help the pedestrian and worries the motorist, and the avenue has been broken with a growth of houses plotted by the speculative builder.

When, therefore, the oil cooking stove went out and the electric cooker came in, and when no more the Aladdin oil-lamps shed their golden light, I had not only doubled the cost of cooking and lighting, I had taken another step towards making the cottage less a cottage. My housekeeper, of course, welcomed the change, though affection for ' Florence ' often led her to the garage where it was housed, and she still did a little slow boiling on it. It was pleasant not to have to strike matches and light lamps on entering the house, nor to have to carry them up to bed, but there is a romance in lamplight, and in the old lamp itself, which no switch-on-and-off apparatus can give.

I have now linked myself up with strikes and lock-outs. The forces of organised labour can stop me cooking my dinner or reading at my fireside. With a lamp and an oil-stove I was a self-contained unit. I could keep a supply of oil, if the oil man went on strike or went down with influenza. But now I am at the mercy of the magnates and the demagogues waging a war a hundred miles from my tranquil retreat. I am also at the mercy of accident. The complicated mechanism of the car in my garage can break down and throw my day out of joint. A defect in a generating station I have never heard of can cut off my power. I am linked up to the enormous ramifications and complexities of our civilisation. Only recently I read that the West End of London went without its Sunday lunch because of a failure at the Battersea Power-station ! So we have not said Farewell to faithful ' Florence.' We have boarded her out in the garage, where she can help to keep Morris warm in the winter.

III

Lastly, there was the menace of the mysterious spring that always flowed before a war. That it existed I could not doubt, though I had never seen it. It must still be a possibility, since our Urban District Council has cut a track for it alongside four miles of country lane, and after discontinuing the gutter in front of my cottage, so that I shall be truly swamped, in accordance with the prophecies of the dismal, it has continued the gutter into Henley town, where the spring ends in a mystery as deep as that in which it begins.

Now, although four years of watchfulness have never revealed a trickle along that bone-dry bed, I cannot doubt its existence. The first keeper of the Ashmolean Museum, the learned and ingenious Dr. Rob. Plot, as he signed himself, wrote of it in 1674, from the account of eye-witnesses. I am surprised he did not track it to its source, said to be under an oak tree near the village of Stonor, in the bosom of the Chilterns. He had such a passion for prying and poking, cross-questioning and deducting, that I wonder he did not go and stir up the spring, as he stirred up the Oxford-shire farmers, until in their resentment they were rude to him.

But one person at least had an underground know-ledge of that spring, and since she was carried away by it there can be no doubt it has flowed. " Some years before 1861," writes a Henley historian, cautiously, " a little child playing in the street by the side of the stream fell in, and was carried away with great rapidity, underground, the whole length of New Street to the river. Some men who saw the accident ran down to the river, and reached it in time to catch the little child, and rescued her from a watery grave, which appeared her inevitable fate. She sustained little injury, and lived to become the mother of a family."

New Street, which is one of Henley's oldest streets, and contains two perfect Elizabethan cottages and a lovely Georgian house, once the domicile of the Bishop of Ely, is almost a quarter of a mile in length. The underground journey must, therefore, have taken some time, and the child who made it in watery darkness, and emerged almost unscathed from a culvert into the Thames, must have had a tough constitution. No wonder she survived to be the mother of a family.

Is there an Assenden spring, and if so, will it ever flow again ? We live amidst rumours of war, ever since that war to end war, so that the spring, according to legend, must be in a constant state of mobilisation. I have taken precautions. The bedroom floor of my housekeeper is two feet below the garden level. She is very fond of her room, which has some fine oak beams and a dormer window that looks on to a green lawn, an apple tree, and a garden bed. If the spring begins to flow in the night, I shall not be overtaken by surprise. It will reach my housekeeper first, and give ample time for me to be warned ! She does not appear to be alarmed at the possibility of a wetting.

## SPRINGTIME IN COOKHAM DEAN

*How marvellous and fair a thing*
*It is to see an English spring,*
*He cannot know who has not seen*
*The cherry trees at Cookham Dean,*
*Who has not seen the blossom lie*
*Like snowdrifts 'gainst a cloudless sky*
*And found the beauty of the way*
*Through woodlands scented with the may ;*
*It is a rare, a holy sight*
*To see the hills with blossom white,*
*To feel the air about one flowing*
*With the silent rapture growing*
*In the hidden heart of things*
*That yearn, that flower, put forth wings,*
*And show their splendours one by one*
*Beneath the all-rejoicing sun.*

*Perhaps the joy of all the earth*
*Moved through us on that day of mirth*
*When, in the morning air, we trod*
*Hills sacred to the woodland god,*
*And heard behind us as we ran*
*The laughter of a hidden Pan,*
*Who dropped his flute because he heard*
*The artless cadence of a bird ;*
*And we, who love the southern sky,*
*One moment ceased to wonder why*

*A poet in his exile cried*
*To see an English spring, and sighed*
*Because a chaffinch from the bough*
*Sings and shakes the blossom now.*

*When Spring in her ascension fills*
*The chalice of the sacred hills*
*With blossoms like the driven snow,*
*And longing takes the heart, then go*
*On pilgrimage to Cookham Dean,*
*And through dim aisles of shadowed green,*
*Diapered with the light that trembles*
*Round each tree till it resembles*
*A maiden letting fall her hair*
*In cataracts of gold, draw near*
*The secret that brings Englishmen,*
*Faithful through exile, home again.*
*For whosoever has not seen*
*The cherry trees at Cookham Dean,*
*Who has not roamed its hills and found*
*Delight in that enchanted ground,*
*He cannot know, he cannot tell*
*Where Spring performs her miracle.*

# CHAPTER III

## A LITTLE PLOTTING

### I

UPSTAIRS, when I purchased the cottage, there was a wide landing. It was larger than the adjacent bedroom, so I took a strip off the landing and threw it into the bedroom, which is tiny enough even now. The bedroom has two small windows, one peering out through the long roof on to an apple tree embracing the dormer, with a view of a larchwood most glorious in Spring; the other window, cut into the landing partition, is made to slide open. It is placed so that it is in line with the landing dormer window, and it also has a view of a thick beechwood high above a steep green field, so that the browsing cows seem up in heaven.

Almost the first thing I did on entering the reconstructed cottage was to buy four large six-inch-to-the-mile Ordnance maps. These covered the area around my cottage. I pinned them up on the landing partition. I could now examine the domain in which I dwelt.

What pleasure and excitement those maps have provided! Our civilisation, with all its drawbacks, is rich in this : knowledge is within easy reach of all, it has been scheduled and indexed. No matter what the subject, one can make a rewarding pursuit through

53

dictionaries, encyclopædias, and atlases. I think atlases are perhaps the most exciting of all these guide-posts to the wonders of the earth. Followed in conjunction with Baedeker's guide-books, one can make, in the comfort of one's own arm-chair, the most exciting excursions. To read almost any book without an atlas at hand is to miss much pleasure and instruction. Experience has taught me that many writers, especially novelists, have never anticipated a geographical survey of their characters' movements. When you read an adventure story, with the hero escaping by the night boat, check up his movements with an atlas, a Baedeker, and a Cook's Continental Time-table, and you will be still more amazed at his ingenuity. He will arrive by train in Warsaw twelve hours sooner than the quickest express, or take twelve hours too long on the journey to Vienna, arriving at dusk instead of at dawn, with no explanation of his delay. It is a little disconcerting to find the motorist ascending the Rhône Valley to the Simplon Pass seeing on his right the mighty monarchs of the Bernese Oberland, when one's atlas, if not personal experience, informs one that the Bernese Oberland is on the left side.

One evening in the depth of winter my newspaper informed me that a distinguished politician was a great traveller, and knew everywhere ' from A to Z.' It is easy to say, but where would knowing places indicated by A to Z, ignoring the intermediate letters, have required the politician to have been? Curiosity made me open the gazetteer. Aabenraa, in Denmark, may have been visited by the much-travelled politician, but I doubt whether he had ever been to Zyzergana, in Mongolia ! I have been to Aabenraa, a pleasant little port, formerly Apenrade, in the renamed province of Slesvig, but I doubt if I shall ever see, or desire to see, Zyzergana, on the Siberian border of Mongolia.

Maps are revealing things, and a six-inch-to-the-mile scale will tell a man things he never knew about his own birthplace, or where he has lived for fifty years. Our strange education system may result in an advanced Form obtaining some idea of Mercator's Projection, though this was considered so much less important than French irregular verbs that I was never taught such a thing. I knew nothing of Gerardus Mercator, who freed us from the tyranny of Ptolemy, whose erroneous calculations had held geographers in bondage for fourteen hundred years. Mercator presented the Emperor Charles V with a superb *Cosmos*, a celestial sphere enclosing a terrestrial, together with a *Declaratio*, an explanatory brochure. It was a remarkable moment in the history of geography, for it marked an era in the observations of longitude by magnetic declination.

I like to think this Flemish scholar had contact with England. In 1564 he engraved William Camden's map of the British Isles, and four years later he produced for navigators his first map on " Mercator's Projection." We have gone confidently about the world ever since. A postal address is sufficient for most of us, but it does not help a ship crossing the Atlantic to find Southampton, Cherbourg, or New York.

Why are we not taught at school the art of map

reading, thus to discover all the romance that lies around us ? I have a postal address, but I have something much more important, without which that postal address would be almost useless. My cottage has a definite position in the geographical sense, and the first thing I did on opening the local survey map was to learn just where, on the vast globe, I was situated, in the latitudinal and longitudinal sense. The local authorities might alter the address, as they do sometimes, or change the spelling. Time plays strange tricks with names, as do wars and revolutions also. You can no longer go to St. Petersburg and Spalato, you go to Leningrad and Split ; and an untravelled person might think that Istanbul, Stamboul, and Constantinople were different cities instead of ancient Byzantium. But none of these places has changed in latitude and longitude since the time of Mercator, and never will.

Having discovered from the maps pinned on my landing the exact position of my cottage, I had a whim later, when in Rome, to test Mercator's projection. So I addressed a letter to myself, putting on the envelope my surname, and the symbols *Lat*. 51° 33·3′ N., *Long*. 0° 55·5′ W. I stamped the letter and posted it. Would it arrive ? The accuracy of that address, geographically, could not be contested. I had a vision of it sliding up the meridian line to Greenwich, on the direct route from Pole to Pole, continuing until it intersected the latitudinal line at 51°, and then slipping half a degree west, and falling through the slot of my garden door, its journey finished.

A sceptical friend assured me the letter would never

arrive. We left for home the day after posting it in Rome.

" And if it does arrive, it won't prove anything really. They'll have looked you up in *Who's Who*, and have found your address that way," he asserted.

" But I'm not a ' Who's Who ' in Italy, where it has to start from, so they can't trace me that way. And if it reaches England, my simple surname won't help much. Well, we'll see. I've great faith in Mercator," I said.

" You mean," retorted my sceptical friend, " you've faith in the intelligence of the postal authorities."

" In both, working in conjunction," I replied.

I received a pitying smile, and after that we forgot all about it. I was four days on the way back to my cottage. On arrival a pile of letters awaited me, and I began opening them with that quiet excitement letters always arouse in me. Suddenly my sight was arrested by an envelope. There it was ! *ROBERTS*. *Lat.* 51° 33·3′ *N.*, *Long*. 0° 55·5′ *W.*

Across the envelope someone had written in red pencil " Inghilterra." In one corner an English postal clerk had written in pencil " Try Henley-on-Thames," and the first try had succeeded. Now, whenever I pass a post office I feel like raising my hat. There must be brains in the post office at Rome, too. I felt a little guilty at having given them trouble, but perhaps they enjoyed the task.

The maps on my landing were bought for a purpose. I had settled on the western end of the Chilterns, and I wanted to study the surrounding country. I decided to do this at first on foot, and then, extending my radius, by car. But be not alarmed, dear reader, for the present we shall only undertake an eight-mile walk at the most. Hence these large-scale maps, from the Ordnance Survey Office, so amazingly accurate, so packed with information, and, considering the labour they entail, so cheap. These six inches to a mile maps cost two shillings each.

## II

All my life I have exercised a tireless curiosity. I cannot see anything without wanting to know how it works. I still remember the anxiety my first watch cost me, not because it would not go, but because I fought an overwhelming desire to take it to pieces. I took it to pieces, and despite scolding prophecies, put it together again. There was one wheel left over, but the watch went as before. This odd wheel so worried me that after a week, during which the watch kept perfect time, I took it apart again. The modern jig-saw puzzle cannot compete with the intense absorption aroused by that watch. Nothing I did would make the odd wheel fit in. Had it been a spare one tucked away by an exasperated watchmaker? I shall never know. I remade the watch and put the odd wheel in a drawer, ready for a breakdown. But it never broke down, until I behaved badly towards it.

The original cost of that watch was five shillings, though actually I had acquired it with a rabbit, a fine Belgian hare. The rabbit was the size of a terrier, and had a habit of coming into the living-room and stretching itself out on the rug before the fire, often displacing the cat. Here it would go to sleep. But as with the canary, a day came when my reluctance to clean out the hutch resulted in an order of banishment for the rabbit. So a friend gave me the watch in exchange.

It was called a Waterbury watch, and I remember it exercised a particular fascination because it was the first thing I had seen with the letters U.S.A. marked on it. There was a magic about these initials, never wholly dispelled in later years by six visits to America, because that country meant for me in those days the marvellous Mr. Edison, whose prodigious brain poured out inventions like the phonograph with wax cylindrical records, Buffalo Bill (Colonel Cody, who had also invented a flying machine), and Niagara Falls, where Captain Webb had perished in attempting to swim them. My heart bled for poor Captain Webb, whose face was so familiar to me on every box of matches standing on the kitchen gas-oven. In the picture on the box of matches named after him he had wonderful muscles on his arms, as befitted the first man to swim the English Channel.

In an evil moment a schoolfellow suggested that the watch was called a Waterbury because you could bury it under water and it would still go. The temptation to test this assertion was too much. One evening I took it with me into my bath. It stopped immediately, to my bitter disappointment.

Some twenty years later I found myself in Waterbury, U.S.A., a thriving town in Connecticut, where I was engaged to lecture. Recalling my first watch I told my host the story. " Why, that's too bad," he said, without a trace of a smile. " It shouldn't have stopped. I'm President of a large watch factory here. If you'll come round with me in the morning I'll show you watches going under water." And he did. But he could not explain that odd wheel.

My curiosity, of which I have given this early example, has never abated. I am always distressed at the thought that man is only allowed some seventy years on this inexhaustibly interesting planet. There is so much to learn, so much to do, so much to see, that it seems to me the body fails just as the brain begins to learn how to utilise its accumulations of knowledge. The slightest query will start me off on an exciting trail. Very often I am caught by my visitors, sprawling across the floor of the cottage, with half-a-dozen maps covering the carpets, and the place littered with various gazetteers, dictionaries, guide-books, and open volumes of the *Encyclopædia*. On the hunt goes, with note-book, pencil, and ruler, across the centuries and continents. Forgotten books on my shelves suddenly spring into use, and at last the quarry is run down. The problem of the cottage floor, for instance, was only one of many that sent me up and down my shelves hunting for a clue.

Yes, life is too short for a man who exercises a ceaseless curiosity. When I stepped into Pilgrim Cottage, a city dweller who had never possessed a garden, handled a rake, or tied up a clump of flowers, I started on an expedition of discovery that will be unending. I had ' gone rustic,' and within the walls of the cottage and the confines of the garden I was so absorbed by my discoveries and activities that I had no thought of rambling afar. But a day came when I pinned up the maps of my district and a new excitement rose up within me. A few walks had already shown me the enchanting vistas of my domain, but I had lived in Pilgrim Cottage a whole year before I came upon woods, valleys, heaths, stretches of forest and river, hamlets, old houses and inns, all within a morning's walk, that were a revelation of the untouched beauty still within forty miles of London.

The Thames encircling this area in a wide loop, a dead-end railway line at Henley, and winding valleys shut in by high hills, have fortunately preserved us from an overwhelming invasion of brick-box builders. The reluctance of water companies to supply the villages hidden in the Chilterns is not without benefits. A race of well- and roof-water drinkers lives without a cultivated need of running water and the daily bath. My old friends, Mr. and Mrs. Harman, the retired blacksmith and his wife, drinking rain-water in their eighties, can laugh at waterworks and water-rates. Two summers of long drought found them sending the bucket confidently down into the underground cistern by the potato patch. London was being frightened and fined. The flow of the Thames at Teddington Weir was being ' felt ' like the pulse of a feeble patient. Mr. Harman's water gauge was simple, an elm pole dipped into the brick cistern. After three months without rain it emerged wet to a reassuring height. Considering the very limited watershed provided by their cottage roof, the inexhaustibility of that cistern seemed like the widow's cruse.

The quality of the water ? I, too, have asked that question, but Eighty-four laughs at me, enjoying a pipe in the shade of the old smithy wall, and Mrs. Harman's rosy complexion and bright mind are proof enough of health in a tapless house. And what excitement in their lives that distant water company in a far-off valley has provided ! " They do say they're bringing the water next year," confides Mrs. Harman with a smile that derides this recurrent rumour. My old friend is not elated by the prospect. Neither am I, although it will increase the value of the Smithy, for a water supply will bring something worse than rates. The cottages will then be deemed ' livable ' by a horde of week-enders, and the ' unwashed ' village, as I have heard these waterless retreats called, will succumb to an orgy of plumbing, and go consciously ' rustic ' at the hands of Saturday-to-Monday tenants, complete with cars, dogs, brogue shoes, Harris tweeds, and antique furniture.

The great preference for tiled cottages rather than picturesque thatched ones, always shown by the villagers, was explained to me by Mrs. Harman. A tiled cottage meant a certain water supply off one's own roof. A thatched roof failed as a water-catcher and entailed a visit to the village pond. Charlie Sharp, looking back upon his childhood down a vista of eighty years, remembered his mother going daily to the village pond, shared alike by cattle and ducks, and cleaned occasionally at the vicar's expense. A downfall of snow in winter was always welcome. Old Mrs. Sharp then went to the door with the kettle and filled it with snow, thereby saving a mile walk to the pond. In her eighty-sixth year she was met by the squire, who, observing her bearing a yoke with a pail of water at either end, volunteered to arrange a supply. She expressed an opinion later that the pond water was sweeter !

The learned and inquisitive Doctor Robert Plot, after riding about Oxfordshire in 1670, devoted a chapter to the subject of water supplies. He starts his chapter with the surprising assertion " that Oxfordshire is the best-water'd County in England, though I dare not with too much confidence assert, yet am induced to believe there are few better . . . as for standing Pools, Marish or Boggy grounds, the parents of Agues, Coughs, Catarrhs, they are fewest here of any place to be found." Bogs, pools, and marshes are rare enough, but so unfortunately are rivers and streams, and the Chiltern uplands have presented a grave water problem to its denizens. I fear that dear Doctor Plot was not nearly as much at home on water as he was on land. He was ready to accept strange theories. He believed rivers began to freeze from the bottom up—" I find it the joynt agreement of all the Water-men hereabout that I have yet talk'd with "—and he has an astonishing story of a hatchet that fell into the Thames near Wallingford and was brought to the surface in an ice-floe !

### III

The maps on my landing show very few streams, but they are rich with interest, provided one knows how to extract knowledge from a map. Those published by the Ordnance Survey Office are covered with hieroglyphs which must be read and interpreted if their lore is to be fully extracted. Happy England, small enough to be walked over, so well charted and excavated over every inch of its surface, a palimpsest of the passage of Celt, Roman, Saxon, Dane, and Norman through two thousand years of history ! When I dig in my garden I wonder what villein or serf sweated above this patch of earth, while Cæsar's galleons grounded our shores, while Harold fought at Hastings, or Henry at Agincourt. And outside my gate, on the old Roman road, the feet of the village postman follow the track of Caius Quintius, soldier of the Eleventh Legion, who dreamed of the bright Roman day, as he marched to Dorocina (Dorchester), an outpost of Empire in a barbarian land.

Sometimes, when the moon rises over the crest of the hill, and the beechwoods lie dark along the slopes, I walk my Roman road, deserted and lovely in the white light. It is then that the Wheel of Time spins backward. These contours have not changed since the soldiers with Aulus Plautus came in A.D. 43 to force the crossing of the Thames, or to relieve the camp at Dorocina. Scarcely two miles from me, by a bend of the river at Hambleden Weir, they have found the site of four Roman villas. What brought the Roman builder here, to lay his tessellated floors, save the beauty of the scene as we see it to-day ? We are apt to think of these Romans as temporary visitors, but there must have been generations to whom Rome was only a magic name ringing in their ears, as London now rings in the ears of some youth on the Canadian prairie or in the African veldt.

A settled civilisation of over three hundred years must have evoked an illusion of permanence. These villas with their tessellated floors, their bathrooms, their hypocausts for steam-heating, their snug location and enchanting view, must have evoked affection in the hearts of their owners. Nearby, at Yewden Manor, the crowding gables of an Elizabethan house throw their peaked shadows on a smooth lawn, and long windows watch a green wave of yew trees that for three hundred years has seemed about to break across the roof. And yet this noble house, in point of time, can claim no longer permanence than those nearby Roman villas whose faint remains, stirred by the casual plough, are now so carefully hoarded in an adjacent museum. For, happily, a descendant of the W. H. Smith who gave so many bookstalls to the railway stations of England has preserved these stones and bones in honourable state by the place where they were found. But what puckish spirit has taken the skeleton of an elk's head, with huge eye-sockets, molars, and formidable tusks, and exhibited it as " W. H. Smith, 1850 " ?

The Roman, walking down my lane upon some moonlit night such as this wherein I think of him, may have returned from one of those hospitable villas at Hambleden, as I from the hospitable manor nearby. But he must press on up the hill to fortified Dorchester, or Dorocina as its postal address in Rome then ran, while I turn in at my green gate, and, at a step, traverse some nineteen hundred years. In the still, moonlit study, my fountain-pen gleams on the desk, beside a letter written but unstamped. In that museum at Hambleden I had examined with interest the bronze stylus pens found in the Roman villas.

What messages, human and trivial, had they engraved on the wax tablets for some relative in distant Rome ? I, too, had written on my envelope the address of a friend in Rome ; it goes on the same journey, with possibly much the same message. What shadows we are !

Then, switching on the light, I dismissed the centuries.

## NIGHT PIECE

The night enfolds us.   Not a leaf is stirred.
The ringing laughter of the sunny noon
Is stilled, the busy noise of bee and bird
Comes not again, and Night brings her soft boon,
For louder through the quiet now is heard
The silver weir beneath the rising moon.

Here in this garden dwell abiding things,
The green recurring pageant of the earth,
The lyric rapture of the bird that sings,
Dew on the grass, hoar-frost, the simple mirth
Of little insect lives, the peace that clings
To joys exalted by their common worth.

Now in the silence comes a space for thought,
A time to think, a quiet for the mind
To brood in ; and great influences wrought
By the enduring hand of Nature find
A healing mission in a world distraught
With all the greed and passion of mankind.

For silence is the wise man's true domain,
And Nature the great book whose wisdom leads
To tranquil days withdrawn from the world's stain,
And glut of idle gossip ; whoso reads
The language spoken by the wind and rain
Knows the one Truth behind the many creeds.

*The quest, the consummation everyone*
*Seeks for the dream he dreams, grows surer here,*
*Since little is so much, each moment spun*
*On looms of quietness.   Peace everywhere*
*Settles beneath Night's wings ; what we have done*
*Or what remains, loses its weight of care.*

# CHAPTER IV

## MAPS

### I

SINCE briefly we have walked the lawn of Yewden Manor, I must mention the Tree of Heaven before we go farther astray, on our six-inch-to-a-mile map. We were walking down a yew avenue that made a dark tunnel in the golden October noon, and, as I ruminated on how many hands for hundreds of years had kept this green avenue disciplined to such perfect shape, the voice of my hostess broke on my ears.

"Would you like a Tree of Heaven?" she said.

All through my childhood I was chided because I always said 'Yes' to everything that was offered me. "It isn't polite," scolded my Nanny; "you must say 'No' occasionally." I have always found it difficult to say 'No.' There are some things it is inhuman to say 'No' to, like an invitation to dine with a lovely lady, or "Have you any other source of income?" even when put to one by the Inland Revenue Inquisitioners.

Years and years ago I heard a poem that began, "Oh, have you joined the choir invisible?" I used to run about the house shouting the question, and answering, "Yes—I should think I jolly well have!" And again my Nanny would frown and say it was blasphemous.

69

" If I said ' No—I jolly well haven't ! ' you'd tell me it was wicked ! " I retorted.

Whereupon the poor tormented dear would smile at me and say, " Oh, Master Cecil, you are a tease ! "

So when my hostess asked, " Would you like a Tree of Heaven ? " I said ' Yes ' promptly, although I had not the faintest idea what a Tree of Heaven was. It might have been a bulb, or one of those little potted Japanese trees, or even a glass one such as they make so beautifully in the glass works at Murano.

The moment I had said ' Yes ' a sense of caution overcame me. " What is a Tree of Heaven ? " I asked.

" It's also called Ailanthus," explained my hostess. I thought it sounded like a Gilbert and Sullivan production, but I suppressed the idea. We had just arrived at the end of the yew avenue.

" That," said my hostess, " is the Tree of Heaven."

She pointed across the lawn, and I was speechless. There by the garden wall was one of the most enormous trees I have ever seen. It rose up to Heaven—hence its name, probably—with massive trunk and smooth gigantic branches. For a moment I felt like the famed Kubla Khan, in whose garden at Xanadu " blossom'd many an incense-bearing tree." If we are to believe that delightful Venetian explorer, Marco Polo, who saw the famous garden around A.D. 1280, " wherever a beautiful tree may exist, and the Emperor gets news of it, he sends for it, and has it transported bodily with all its roots attached to it, and planted on that hill of his. No matter how big the tree may be, he gets it carried by his elephants." But I had no elephants, and so I hesitated.

" I can't take one of those—you could put my cottage in the fork ! " I stammered.

My hostess laughed.

" Oh, you needn't take a grown one. Look, these are all shoots come up in the yew avenue. They travel hundreds of yards and come up all over the place. The gardener will cut you one."

I bore home the Tree of Heaven, and I searched for a place in which to plant it. A garden of a quarter of an acre does not encourage forestry. Moreover, wherever I turn I have pleasant views. Southwards, there is Lambridge Wood that rides level on the summit of a steep green slope, so steep that I sometimes think the cows will slide down into the cemetery in the valley. Westwards, I look up the hill that sweeps to Nettlebed and the golfer's paradise at Huntercombe. Northwards, a lovely larchwood lifts its feathery plumes to a cold blue sky, and there is never a day, summer or winter through, when some new gradation of tone fails to greet the eye on this keyboard of colour, from the gold bass of deep autumn to the fresh green treble of spring.

Now, a little eastwards of this wood there is a house. It is a nice house, belonging to a nice man, and so I do not greatly care that he overlooks me. He has said he enjoys overlooking me, my domain is so pleasant, and my cottage, like a lovely woman, seems to enjoy being looked at.

But the fact remains that an Englishman's home is his castle, and all proper castles are high on a rock or buried deep in a wood where they cannot be overlooked. That national instinct for privacy dwells in me, and at moments I have felt I could not bear being overlooked. There is a gap between my syringa tree and my chestnut tree. It was there, I determined, in no spirit of unneighbourliness, I would plant the Tree of Heaven. The small boy living across the road would be able to point to it in his old age, when it towered to Heaven, and say, " I remember that tree when it was only my height ! " and no one would quite believe him. For I was told it was a quick-growing tree, which came from India, and I was hopeful that I, too, in the course of years, would be able to stand in wonder beneath its massive branches.

And it gave me a virtuous feeling. The man who cuts down a tree is a wicked man. " They shall be cut down like . . ." the Psalmist's sentence of doom employs the right simile. Conversely, I feel that the planting of a tree is an act of grace. If I were one of those singular persons who like to found societies and sit on committees, I should found a ' Plant-a-tree ' society ; that would be much better than starting one of those hundreds of silly societies to promote this and prevent that, whose brass plates gleam brassily all over Bloomsbury and Westminster. What do these societies achieve ? There is always a secretary with cuffs and spats and papers, and a typist with a teapot and six tulips in a vase, and an annual meeting with Lord Snuff in the chair, and Brigadier-General Cough and the Hon. Miss Sneeze proposing and seconding the vote of thanks.

I have even thought of my epitaph as a tree-lover—

" Here lies one whose good deeds stand up. Rest in the shade ! " What a magnificent memorial a tree is, at what small cost—at no cost at all if you know a kind person to give you a Tree of Heaven !

At the end of my lane, connecting me with Henley town, there is an avenue rightly named the Fairmile. It is a glorious avenue of elm trees, one mile in length, with a road in the centre. It seems a terribly long road to the motorist, for it is a straight smooth mile, and takes almost a minute to get down it. But, for those who care to walk, it is twenty minutes of delight. Since my cottage nestles at the far end of it, I am impertinent enough to regard it as my own carriage drive, and I exhibit it to my friends with proprietorial pride. But I will not rob the really noble baronet who planted it of the honour due to him. He was one, Sir William Stapleton of Greys Court nearby. He was a Governor of the Leeward Islands, married an heiress, and had his portrait painted by Sir Godfrey Kneller, but nothing he ever achieved became him like the planting of the Fairmile, unsurpassed by any public road in the kingdom. It is his lasting memorial.

One day, wandering through the echoing rooms of Greys Court, a wilderness of falling plaster and wrong-headed building that a friend of mine had just bought with an heroic gesture, we came across a window of stained-glass with the armorial bearings of the Stapletons. Some dastardly vandal had deliberately torn down a wire guard in order to smash the window with stones. As I observed the splintered glass lying on the window ledge, and looked out on a ruined barn and a weed-grown lawn, I reflected on the decay of a proud

73

family ; half an hour later, driving down the Fairmile, ablaze with October's gold, I realised that Sir William's trees would outlive all the splendour of the family tree, and these leaves would give colour to the scene long after the heraldic glass lay shattered in the dust.

## II

As I planted my Tree of Heaven, it occurred to me there was one other aspect I might consider—an aspect that is likely to attract more attention in the future. It is the aerial aspect. In explanation of this let us return, after much wandering, to the Ordnance Survey maps in my corridor.

At first sight they require a little understanding. Two persons will look at maps. One will see nothing but roads, buildings, and fields, the other will read them like a history book, and surprise the local inhabitant of long standing with facts he never knew. Have you ever seen, on a stone, a pillar, a wayside cottage, this symbol ———? and if you have seen it, do you know what it means ? Looking at my map one morning I saw this sign pointing to a cottage at the beginning of my lane. Puzzled, I went and looked at the cottage. I looked so hard and so long that the housewife came out. She may have thought I had seen a crack down the front of the house, or that I suspected the children had measles. Or I may have evoked the just fear that comes into the mind of every occupant of a comfortable cottage when someone comes and stares at it—the fear that some heartless week-ender is going to buy it and evict the tenant.

# MAPS

When the housewife emerged the following dialogue ensued :

*Self :* I'm sorry I seem so rude, but I'm looking for a mark on your house.

*Housewife (surprised and suspicious) :* A mark ! What mark ?

*Self :* On a map I've got there's a broad arrow with the letters ' B.M.166·6 ' pointing to your house.

*Housewife :* What's it want to do that for ? There's nothing on this house, that I know !

*Self :* There might be —can I look ?

*Housewife :* Well, if you want to, you're welcome.

She opened the gate for me to enter. I wrote books, and wore no clothes in the garden. Nothing would surprise her concerning me. But she assisted in the search.

*Self :* I think it will be on the front of the house.

*Housewife :* An arrow ?

*Self :* Yes—somewhere, cut in the brick.

*Housewife (pulling aside some ivy) :* But whatever for ! Go in, Annie—the very idea, with no frock on and a gentleman looking at yer ! (*Annie vanishes.*)

*Self :* It's to mark the height above sea-level.

*Housewife (scornfully) :* Sea-level ! I know nothing about sea-level. We're well above the river. We've never been flooded except when the Assenden Spring ran.

*Self (starting with excitement at prospect of learning something about that mysterious spring, but suppressing the distraction) :* Do you mind if I pull back the chrysanthemums ? It might——

*Housewife :* Not at all—but I'm certain there's
nothing on the wall. I'd 'ave seen it if——

A triumphant gesture stopped her. There, a foot
up, cut in the brickwork, was the sign ———
↑

*Housewife :* Well, I never ! You might think it was a
prison sign ! What have they done that for ?

*Self :* It's a measuring point for the ordnance surveyor. It means that at this point we are 166·6
feet above sea-level.

*Housewife :* Well, to be sure. An' all these years, and
we've never seen it !

I left her, showing it to Annie, now in a frock.

England is covered with ' bench marks.' Sometimes, out walking, I begin to poke away with a stick,
pressing back shrubs or ivy, and my companion asks
if I've seen a rat. I explain that I am looking for a
bench mark which will give me the altitude above sea-
level. I astonished even alert Mrs. Harman up at
Fawley by discovering one on her house that indicated
a height of 489 feet.

The next question that arises, naturally, is, what is
sea-level ? Surely if there is one thing which is never
quite level it is the sea ? The problem is solved by
taking the mean sea-level. The reckoning has been
obtained for the ordnance maps from the mean of
hourly readings of the automatic tide-gauge at Newlyn
in Cornwall, during the six years from May 1st, 1915,
to April 30th, 1921. One would naturally assume
that the sea is level all round the English coast. But it
isn't. The datum was first fixed after observations at

Liverpool in 1844. Then new observations were made around the coast in 1859 and 1895, and it was discovered that the mean level of the sea at Newlyn is about eight inches above the mean level at Liverpool. Since Newlyn was chosen, the new reading has been adopted, but on all maps with the Liverpool datum the altitudes must be taken as starting from a point about eight inches below mean sea-level.

Back in my cottage I discovered that my map was based on the old datum. The cottage, therefore, was not, strictly speaking, 166·6 feet above sea-level. It was actually only 166 feet, but I decided to say nothing to the good housewife. When the New Calendar was adopted in 1752, people wrote to the Government protesting that they had been robbed of eleven days of life with the jump from September 2nd to September 13th. Similarly, the good housewife might complain that she was robbed of six inches of altitude. No one likes being lowered in the scale of living.

Trees play an important part in the ordnance maps. They are sensitively recorded. The maps show trees and trees; that is, there is a wide difference in their shapes. Examine the dots carefully, and you will find woods are not merely woods to the meticulous surveyor. Some of the trees are drawn round, and some are drawn pointed, thus differentiating deciduous trees and firs. A series of microscopic curves, like a flight of birds, denotes underwood, and trees in geometric formation represent orchards. The surveyors' ingenuity does not end here. These specks which seem alike are not alike. Closely examined, it transpires that the tiny variations denote furze, osiers, reeds, marshes, and rough pastures. And other dots are designed to show gravel, sand, and shingle !

Let us leave the vexed world of contours, marked by those thin red lines like lassoes over the map, often so difficult to follow. I remember a fierce argument between two men who had shot pheasants by a covert. One said the place was three hundred feet up, the other four hundred. When the map was produced, they almost came to blows as to which side of the red contour line should be taken for the altitude ! I, too, have trouble with contours, just as I have trouble with sea and land in ordinary maps. How often am I unable to dispel the visual fancy that the land is sea, the sea land, on those large world-maps, thus searching vainly for a city in an ocean !

But the ordnance surveyors are really as clear as they are accurate. With a little patience their hieroglyphs become readable. It is possible to identify a railway over a road, a road over a railway, a railway over a river, a road over a river, a canal or a stream, a level crossing, a sunken road, and a raised road. There are other astonishing little devices for imparting information. The small figures under a parish name in capitals denote the acres in that parish. There is a different type for the names of villages, parks, gentlemen's seats, bays, harbours, bogs, moors, mines, manufactories, locks, farms, workhouses, passenger railway stations, and mineral railway stations ! The antiquarian can tell at a glance where he may profitably tarry, for Roman remains, A.D. 43–420, are indicated in Egyptian capital lettering, antiquities prior to A.D. 43 in Old

78

English, and remains belonging to post-Roman times, A.D. 420–1688, in German text.

The markings of roads, bridlepaths, and footpaths are simple enough, but these engrossing maps have other symbols not so simple. My wonderful six-inch-to-a-mile map bears the legend " Heliozincographed from $\frac{1}{2500}$ Plans." One can read the map without understanding what that means, but a cryptic legend passed over is for me an untaken fort in the siege of knowledge. I am not happy to leave it behind, unsurrendered. So I worried myself about ' Heliozincographed from $\frac{1}{2500}$ Plans.'

Finally, since no one seemed able to enlighten me, I motored to Southampton. Why Southampton, you may well ask, since one usually goes to London in pursuit of information ? For some reason of economy or convenience or both, the office of the Director-General of Ordnance Survey is at Southampton. And why a Director-General ? Why not a Cartographer Royal, seeing the man in charge of the Heavens is the Astronomer Royal ? And, again, why a Director-General of Ordnance ? Ordnance is a term for great guns for military and naval purposes as opposed to ' small arms ' and their equipment.

In England, from Henry VIII's time, the Master-General of Ordnance managed all affairs concerning artillery and material of the army. In 1855 this office was abolished and its duties distributed. The department for making surveys and maps, once a subsidiary of the Ordnance Office, went eventually to the Board of Agriculture and Fisheries. Armaments, maps, agriculture, and fisheries, it is a queer jumble, but through it all, somehow, the chief map-maker has remained the Director-General of Ordnance.

To Southampton I went, and many mysteries were solved. The Ordnance Survey Department has grown prodigiously in the last twenty years. The Director-General directs an army of assistants, whose ranks are being constantly augmented, largely to satisfy the demands, among many, of the motorist. The roads of England have come into use again, and with their increased use and the growth of urban populations, necessitating area-planning schemes, the large-scale map and the small-scale map are in constant demand.

Heliozincographed from $\frac{1}{2500}$ Plans. What does it mean? The explanation was given me at once. A drawing on a scale of 1 to 2500 was made. "One *what* to every two thousand five hundred?" I asked. The answer bewildered me at first.

It transpired that a map on the scale of twenty-five inches to the mile gives the same picture as the ground would appear at a height of 2,500 feet. This altitudinal simile made me a little dizzy, and for our purpose we will take, later, another flight with a six-inch map. I learned that, the area of Great Britain being about 90,000 square miles, it required 60,000 25-inch sheets to cover it. Heliozincographed means that the map-drawing has been photographed, and from the negative a zinc plate has been made which is used for printing the plan. Is that clear?

Bear with me a little, for we are about to soar to great heights. We are going up to 10,560 feet, or two miles. What you see of the earth from that height, if you are not busy putting a personal possession into a little paper bag, is precisely the picture that a camera with a lens of 12-inch focal length would obtain of the ground below. To put it another way— I wanted it several ways before I could grasp these dizzy facts—when the eye is one foot distant from a six-inch map, the detail represented there will look the same size as the original object on the ground would look from a height of two miles, or 10,560 feet, hence the scale $\frac{1}{10560}$.

I couldn't quite believe this. I looked at the map with my cottage on it. I decided to make a test. Taking a ruler, I measured my domain on the six-inch map. It was one-fifth of an inch, from hedge to hedge. If what I was told was true, then ten thousand five hundred and sixty times one-fifth of an inch would give me the length of my house and garden from end to end. I snorted derisively. It seemed to me that any fraction of an inch measured over ten thousand times would give me a dwelling as large as Windsor Castle.

It happened at that moment that the men from the electric company were laying my cable. The foreman possessed a long tape-measure. I asked him to measure the widest reach of my domain. He did, and reported it was about 176 feet. Almost gleefully I went indoors to make the six-inch scale map look silly. I measured again with the ruler and found my property was a fifth of an inch. I began to multiply by 10,560, wondering whether Pilgrim Cottage would stretch a mile. In a few seconds I stared at the result. Then I multiplied again. The answer was the same— 176 feet !

I look now at the map with awe. I would make the Director-General a Field-Marshal—a much more appropriate title for a surveyor of our countryside.

One day it is my intention to ask a flying friend to take me up over the valley in which I live ; I want to look down at my house as an object $\frac{1}{10560}$ in the landscape. All that frightful labour in the garden to keep a ten-thousand-five-hundred-and-sixtieth of a place in order !

## III

You have been very patient through this dissertation. It will restore our conceit to know that the Director-General is sometimes not strictly accurate. He humbly confesses the fact. His 6-inch map does truly represent six inches to one statute mile, but his 25-inch map is actually on a scale of 25·344 inches to one statute mile, though he is careful to claim that every feature is strictly to scale. It is as though Mr. Philip de Lazlo produced a portrait with accurate features, but made the complete person a fraction taller than proportion warranted. If we could improve the features of some landscapes like Mr. Lazlo improves those of his portraits, we should not worry about a few inches one way or another. Flattery may be the mother of extension.

The Director-General also confesses to a little ‘ wangling.’ He has a simple way with congestion in crowded towns. He sometimes exaggerates the width of the streets to make room for the names, just as we exaggerate the portmanteau to make room for the contents.

# MAPS

This question of maps having been settled, we can now open the garden gate and explore a little. Our maps will be changed from time to time. When you buy property it is generally on a 25-inch scale ; when you are settled in you look around on a 6-inch scale, which shows footpaths and covers the surrounding fields. Then comes a day when the one-inch-to-a-mile map is useful. It will take us as far as we can walk. Motorists, of course, want smaller-scale maps, but since these are generally used for the purpose of getting ' there ' rather than seeing things we shall not need them.

## MORNING PIECE

The bright star pales before the dawn,
Dim is the garden, as a pool
Within the forest : from the East
The first flush spreads, the shadows melt ,
I cannot see you, O my love,
So gently breathing at my side,
But every line my fond heart knows,
Each silken curve and harmony
Music that wakes beneath the touch.

Now in the darkness, as I wait,
The first beam comes through dormer panes,
And in the half-light, sighing soft,
You turn with drowsy-lidded smile
To the known altar of my love ;
And from the chalice of your mouth
I take the morning's sacrament,
While day streams down the eastern hills,
Dews glisten, and bird-music breaks.

# CHAPTER V

## MISS WHISSITT

AND now let's go into the garden, and wonder what we are going to do with all the apples on the trees. Every year I believe that the next year will see a poor harvest. It would be rather a relief. October is a month of strain, both on the trees and their owner, just as September is a month of danger to anyone reckless enough to sit under them. A long drought through an otherwise perfect summer had brought the menace of falling apples earlier. They were dropping already in mid-August.

I recall that lovely September afternoon when Miss Whissitt had found me having tea under the russet-apple tree. My admiration for her dates from that day.

" Oh, I've just come as you're having tea—what a shame!" she exclaimed, standing inside the garden gate.

I felt like asking her whether four-thirty was an eccentric time for tea, but instead, as she knew I should, I asked her to join me.

" How sweet of you! I'd love to!" she said. Then, glancing at the path borders as she came down—" How glorious your gladioli are! Such an air of *romanticismo, n'est-ce pas?* "

She pronounced the word *glaydioli*, though she calls dahlias *darhlias*. And she insisted on gladioli, not 'oluses, though she would never admit that she rode in omnibi in London.

*Fe, fi, fo, fum,*
*The nice precision of spinsterdom,*

ran a rhyme in my head. But my eyes were solemn. I like Miss Whissitt.

" You look tired," I said, sympathetically.

She did look tired. At times Miss Whissitt looks quite pretty, so that one catches a glimpse of the girl who infatuated a whole camp of young Air Force officers in the days when she was a V.A.D. One of these gay lads, the heir to an old title and a lovely property in England, had wooed and won her, just a month before he was shot down over the German lines. Three years later, when the war ended, she received from a stranger in Mannheim a long letter, enclosing a miniature of herself she had given to her lover, and a letter from her found in his breast pocket. The German had not returned them with the other articles sent across the lines, they had seemed too intimate ; he had kept them for the days of peace. Miss Whissitt never spoke of this, she never made a single allusion to the war. I heard the story from a cousin.

There were moments, but this was not one of them, when I saw how attractive that young lover must have found her. But to-day she was tired, and might have been fifty-five instead of forty-five.

" I'm worried," said Miss Whissitt, with an apologetic smile.

" Money ? " I asked.

" Oh no, not money ! " she exclaimed, as if she had ten thousand a year instead of the five hundred left her by her father, a doctor at Reading. " One

should never worry about money, should one ? "
she asked.

" One does," I replied, " though I've observed that
the people who have no money worries have a genius
for inventing others. Mrs. Sendall, for instance,
worth half a million, and just frantic about having to
pay a halfpenny a unit more for her electric light in
the country. And now she's got herself into a libel
action with the company. Well, here's tea."

Miss Whissitt was silent while my housekeeper
emptied the tray.

Why, I wondered, looking covertly at Miss Whissitt
—why did she make herself look so old and un-
interesting ? Women should not look old at forty-
five. They can still look attractive, with a good
modiste and an eye on the sugar bowl. But Miss
Whissitt had let herself go. She scorned a touch of
powder or lipstick, and her footwear was abominable.
Her hat was worse than her boots. Pretty eyes and
a good mouth could do nothing under that hat. Had
she won it in a village raffle, or was it one that had
been taken down and set up again, like a second-hand
car ? It was a round hat, made of brown straw, and
balanced like a basket on a Covent Garden coster's
head. In pursuance of the vegetable market idea it
was trimmed with fruit, the kind of unfruitful fruit that
milliners favour—glazed cherries with cloth stalks, and
luminous grapes that would gripe a goat.

I was trying to think of a smart woman who could
take Miss Whissitt aside and tell her a thing or two
about dress and making the best of oneself on five
hundred a year, when she spoke again.

" What's worrying me is——"

The sentence was interrupted. Something happened, so ludicrous in itself, that I wanted to burst into laughter. But Miss Whissitt killed that laughter, even as it rose in me, by an exhibition of stupendous sangfroid.

Just over her head there was a heavily burdened bough of an apple tree. A long drought had caused the apples to fall. One fell now, a small rosy apple, and it chose to fall right into the middle of Miss Whissitt's hat, in the middle of that trimming of glassy fruit, where it reposed, chief ornament of the milliner's cornucopia. Miss Whissitt must have felt the bang, for I heard the straw creak, but her hand firmly held the tea-cup, and, ignoring my astonished gaze, she finished the sentence :

"——why, unlike every other flower I know, doesn't the gladiolus turn to the sun ? "

And having put the question so violently interrupted, Miss Whissitt raised her disengaged hand, removed the apple nestling in her hat, and without a word put it sedately on the tea-table.

It took me a full minute to regain my self-control. Miss Whissitt had asked me a question. She was worried. For a moment I had thought it was money, or some physical ill, or a notice to leave her cottage, which she had found a nightmare and converted into a dream. But all that worried her, even while an apple hit her on the head, was the strange fact that the gladiolus seemed to ignore the sun.

" But are you sure," I began, having recovered, " are you sure they don't turn to the sun ? "

" Quite—I've been watching them for three years.

They flower just as it pleases them. I've gladioli, some facing the sun, some turned east, west, and north—all in the same bed."

" Now you mention it, you're right—look at those ! "

I pointed to some splendid crimson, salmon, and white gladioluses proudly trumpeting to the snapdragons, whose disordered ranks flouted the Marshal Ney. I saw now, to my surprise, that the blooms were turned in all directions, quite oblivious of the sun.

"How extraordinary!" I exclaimed, my eyes opened.

" *C'est incroyable !* " said Miss Whissitt, in her best Tours French. She wiped her nose on a Burano lace tea-napkin in her concentration.

" Do orchids turn to the sun ? " I asked, since these flowers always remind me of orchids, and the orchid is a little inhuman, if one may say that of a plant.

" I don't know, but gladioli are monocotyledonous plants," answered Miss Whissitt.

" They're what ? " I demanded.

" Monocotyledonous," replied Miss Whissitt. " But the orchid differs from the more general type in the irregularity of the perianth. The gladiolus is iridaceous, nor orchidaceous."

" I'm afraid you're taking me out of my depth," I said, really alarmed now. I had heard Miss Whissitt go off like this before. " I don't know the difference."

" Of course you do ! " protested Miss Whissitt ; " Iris means rainbow, Orchis means ——."

At that moment the postman entered the gate. He bore the afternoon delivery.

" The orchid has a six-parted perianth which springs from the top of the ovary, whereas the gladiolus has a curved perianth tube, funnel-shaped, and widening upwards. Oh, what a lot of letters, how I envy you ! " cried Miss Whissitt, as I stopped the postman and he gave me a bundle of letters tied with string.

" My ' fan ' mail," I said weakly, after the mono-cotyledonous monologue.

" Do you answer them all ? " she asked.

" That depends—if they're not rude."

" I'm sure they're never rude ! "

" A few are sometimes very orchidaceous," I said. " May I open them ? "

" Oh, do ! Read them to me ! " cried Miss Whissitt.

" That would be hardly fair. In my next book I shall put down all you've told me about gladioluses. Perhaps we shall then learn why they don't bother about turning to the sun. In " Gone Rustic " I said I was worried by woolly aphis on my apple trees. My woolly aphis seems to have worried kind people in Australia, Canada, Japan, and Siberia. They write from all over the earth, telling me how to get rid of it."

" How do you get rid of it ? Do they all give you the same antidote ? "

"Invariably," I replied. "Let's see if there's one here."

I began opening letters. One of them, with Chinese characters printed on the heading, caught Miss Whissitt's eye.

" Oh, look ! Is it from Peking ? " she cried.

I examined the letter.

" It's from Shanghai—China."

" How astonishing ! " exclaimed my companion. " Do read it."

I could not think why Miss Whissitt should find a

letter from China astonishing, merely because it was from China.    After all, they had been writing letters in China long before 500 B.C., when Confucius spent his time writing at Lu.    I read the letter.

> DEAR SIR,—
>
> *Having just reached that part of your excellent book ' Gone Rustic ' where you mention Chinese Nightingales, I feel that I must——*

" Did I ever write about Chinese nightingales ? " I asked, breaking off.

" Yes," said Miss Whissitt, whose memory is prodigious.    " Don't you remember, you wrote about three German boys who were on a walking tour ?    You met them returning from Italy.    One of them had a guitar, and you said the two sang like Chinese nightingales, in French, Italian, and English."

" You're quite right ! " I said, and resumed the reading.

> *. . . I must write to you and ask you where you have heard these sing ?    I have heard three German Scouts sing folk songs, they happened to be travelling round the world, and I happened to be Scout Commissioner for Shanghai, so I know what a Chinese Nightingale should sound like !    I have lived here since the war, but so far I have failed to hear one, so I'm seeking information . . .*

" But there are nightingales in China ! " exclaimed Miss Whissitt.

" How do you know ?    Have you been there ? "

" No,—but—— "

" I've never seen a Venetian blind in Venice, or a Madeira cake in Madeira," I said, and continued :

*. . . Wish we could see your cottage, sounds just what we would like to buy and settle down in if ever we are lucky enough. I have built three gardens here and am now tackling a fourth. It was a garden of a sort when we got it, so there is far more work in it than there is in starting from a cabbage patch . . .*

" *Vraiment !* " said Miss Whissitt, feelingly.

*. . . You can make one very much more rapidly here than you can at home, I should imagine. For instance, you can put twenty weeders on at once when you want to make a lawn, whereas in England they would cost a small fortune. Here they are four for a dollar a day— 1s. 4d. English money.*

A photograph fluttered down. I picked it up. It showed my correspondent's weeders at work. There were eight fat women in trousers, hair drawn back in a bun, crouched on the lawn. Behind them were deposited four swaddled babies with bullet heads.

" I wonder if he would send you a Phajus ? " said Miss Whissitt.

" A what ? " I exclaimed, feeling she was becoming monocotyledonous again.

" A Phajus—it's a special orchid that grows in China. I'd like one. They say a single internode of each shoot is swollen to form a pseudobulb."

" How painful," I said, feeling I could bear it no longer. I opened more letters, and read.

" Ah—this really pleases me. Do you remember

my story about the man who made a wooden leg for his fowl, after an amputation ? A lot of my readers were very sceptical. Here's a lady writes to say her brother also made a wooden leg for a cockerel that had lost its leg. Now listen to this. Here's a cutting she sends from the *Daily Mirror*."

> *Out of a consignment sent from Scotland, a sheep with a wooden leg was found at the Stanley Abattoir, Liverpool.*
>
> *Judging by its appearance, the wooden leg had been in use for some time. It measured from four to five inches. A cotton-wool wad was placed on the top of it, and it was attached to the animal's leg by means of a leather ' coat.'*

" What an extraordinary letter ! And the woolly aphis ? " asked Miss Whissitt. " Is there anything there about it ? "

I went steadily through the pile. Suddenly I gave a cry of triumph.

" Here it is," I said, and began reading.

> *Your book has cheered me through a dose of 'flu in sheer delight, but I was grieved on reaching the end of Chapter X to find that Tilly, who obviously has much garden lore, never told you how to cure woolly aphis. Half-a-dozen nasturtiums grown round a tree is all you want—why, I know not, and your gardener will laugh me to scorn, but I have done it. Hope you don't mind an absolute amateur butting in.*

" How nice people are ! " observed Miss Whissitt, pulling on her gloves. " So that's why you have such a wonderful crop of apples. It's the simple things that are the most wonderful, *n'est-ce pas* ? "

" Actually I haven't tried the cure yet. But I shall. Tilly laughs at it, and says I must try a witch-ball," I said. " I must ask her about these gladioluses——"

" Why do you say gladioluses ? " asked Miss Whissitt firmly, in the middle of the garden path. " Surely they're glādioli ? "

" They may be—but the Oxford dictionary lets me say it. The name is derived from the Latin ' gladius,' a sword, hence the name ' gladiator.' Would you call him a glaydiator ? " I countered.

Miss Whissitt pulled at her gloves.

" The English language is *incroyable, n'est-ce pas* ? " she said, as she reached the gate. " Good-bye ! "

When the gate had closed, I looked at the gladioluses. It was perfectly true, they were turned in all directions, indifferent to the sun. Why ? Was it the way one put in the bulbs ? It could hardly be that, for plants turn their stems. Some of these gladioluses had turned themselves, in some cases it seemed, deliberately from the sun. There was one advantage in this eccentricity. They made good central plants, they could be viewed from all sides.

But I decided that I would cut the gladioluses that had turned their backs on me along the front of the house. I had little compunction in doing this, not because of their surliness to the sun, but because they are a lovely decoration for a room, and also they keep fresh for some days when cut early in the morning or late in the evening. The undeveloped buds will open in succession and go on blooming for a considerable time if their stalks are long and kept in water.

I cut a gladiolus that had not bloomed on the first day of November, fearful that the frost would kill it. The stalk was two feet from bottom to top, and I put it in a narrow vase of water. It had thirteen completely sheathed blossoms, of which the top six were half developed. Five days later the bottom flower burst from its sheath, two days later there were four more blooms, and fifteen days later five more. The plant then died with three immature buds, having survived over a fortnight.

Cut flowers, and gladioluses that ignore the sun, bring to mind the pleasing habit of grape hyacinths when gathered for indoor decoration. These lovely steeples of blue blossom have a sturdy uprightness in all circumstances. Even when their backs are weak, their heads are proud. When their stems droop, then the spear-head of blossom has a habit of bending upwards, insistent upon a vertical display of beauty. They are therefore ideal for display in bowls, where they make a delightful fringe of blue as a trimming to other contents.

Interior flower decoration is full of disappointments unless one is wary. The evening primrose refuses to have an evening out if you cut it and give it an evening in. October generally witnesses an orgy of beech-leaf decoration. The Chilterns are never so glorious as when they stand in russet and gold, particularly at that five-o'clock hour when the westering sun earns a hundred-per-cent. interest on his gold deposits in the beech banks. There is a field, not half a mile from my door, and 300 feet above my village, where an evening vista of such burning glory greets the eye that it seems as if the world below might suddenly burst into fire.

It is in the month of October that the chemists' shops of country market towns experience a demand for crude glycerine—to dilute with water to stop beech leaves withering, and car radiators freezing. But a few beech leaves go a long way, as I am reminded when I call on Mrs. Dingle. In October her drawing-room becomes a forest of beech leaves. They bury the piano, embrace the Empire clock, soar to the ceiling from immense Chinese vases, and tickle the ample posterior of the marble Venus brought back from Pisa after the Dingle honeymoon. And there, in her bushy bower, sits quick-eyed Mrs. Dingle, long-nosed and grey-faced, looking like a squirrel after the nutting season.

A few beech leaves, therefore. There are other October devices for decoration. Whenever I visit a lady whom her friends call 'Mrs. Cherry,' I am inclined to wonder what's in a nickname. I entered her Georgian drawing-room one October evening, and for a moment thought I was in a cherry orchard. It seemed to break into blossom all round one, and had she started singing the Flower Duet (*Shake that cherry tree*) from *Madame Butterfly*, I should not have been surprised. I paused like Pinkerton on the threshold. Then I looked again, and admired the artfulness of it all. It was a *décor* of black sycamore branches supporting that desperate October frivolity, the white, starry Michaelmas daisy—an enchanting decoration.

## MISS WHISSITT

Will no one love Miss Whissitt?
The time is getting late,
The roses in her cheeks are wan,
The winter will not wait;
Ten years ago, five years ago,
She hoped she would not be
Left lonely on the barren bough,
A sere leaf on the tree.

Will no one love Miss Whissitt
So gentle and so kind?
The summer tints are fading fast,
The Spring is far behind.
She smiles and still her lips are red,
And lovely are her eyes,
But no one seems to notice how
The hope within them dies.

Will no one love Miss Whissitt,
Recall a far-off day
When such a golden, laughing lad
Tumbled her in the hay?
Then every bird sang merrily,
The day was at the noon;
Oh, sorrow! when he marched away
To drill in Death's platoon.

Will no one love Miss Whissitt ?
Still winsome when she smiles,
With lovely lines about her mouth
With which she Time beguiles ;
Late Summer, and the autumn fruit
Comes crowding on the tree,
But oh ! the fruit she longs to bear
And place upon her knee.

# CHAPTER VI

## IN HENLEY TOWN

### I

IT is high time we went for a walk. We have gone round the garden, depressed by the convolvulus that clings and riots like a weak nephew supported by a rich aunt. In England it is a despicable plant, an *arriviste* clambering up anybody's back, determined to be in high society. Yet I have seen it, in conditions abroad, where it has appeared almost noble in its Tyrian purple. I shall never forget the gorgeous display it made on an immense baroque gateway of the Villa Pisani at Stra, on the Brenta Canal. This colossal villa, built to the glory of one of the richest merchant princes of Venice, seems to epitomise the fabulous wealth of the *settecento* patrician. Having built a vast palace on the Grand Canal, Pisani built his vaster *plaisance* on the mainland, where even the thirty-six stalls in his stables had bronze ornaments. Triumphal arches opened on vistas of chestnut avenues, ornamental waters, orangeries, shady lawns, box mazes, and garden towers. The gates of wrought iron had a flowery delicacy, and it was over the arches of these that I saw the purple cascades of convolvulus. It was so lovely against the azure sky that I forgot its vulgar bindweed brother.

We are at a gateway now, neither wrought iron nor

splendid stone, but simply two trunks of hawthorn to which a plain wooden door has been attached. My cottage gateway has a canopy of ivy that has an annoying habit of scattering raindrops on one as it is shaken by latch-raising. Nevertheless, I prefer this rough garden door to the lych-gate that, together with crazy paving, a stone bird-bath, and a pseudo-antique doorknocker, seem Everyman's outfit for an oldey-worldey cottage. A kind friend once offered me a splendid oak gateway. He had seen some made by a clever master carpenter in a nearby country town, oldfashioned gates at the new-fashioned price.

"Thanks very much, but I'll keep this until it falls down. You see, it's not a question for me only," I said.

He looked a little surprised. We were standing at the dining-room window, after breakfast, looking up the garden path.

"I don't think *he* would like it," I explained. "He might go off in a dudgeon."

My friend looked out and saw who ' he ' was. On the top of the old green door, exactly in the middle, perched a robin. That it was his favourite rustic seat no one could doubt from the liberal whitewashing he had given it. He sat there and sang cheekily, turning now this way, now that, to keep a lookout on either side of the gate, or to equalise the whitewashing.

"How very odd ! " said my friend.

I agreed, though I think he was referring to me and not to the robin. He said no more about the gate. Neither will I. Let us go through it out on to the Roman road, where Mr. Chaucer, Cardinal Wolsey,

King Charles I, John Hampden, the Duke of Marl-borough, Dick Turpin, Dr. Johnson, Boswell, General Blücher, and other distinguished travellers have passed on foot or horseback, or rattled in a coach or post-chaise.

There are certain things one should not say, such as—" You must take us as you find us, we live very simply "—this is often the rich bounder's prelude to a staggering dinner, with cooking aforethought ; or " You should have seen my garden last week " ; or " I don't want to boast, but I don't think you'll find a nicer spot anywhere "—which may refer to the view down a cobbled mews from a groom's converted hay-loft, or to the Battersea Power-station's chimneys seen through a November fog. Beauty is in the eye of the beholder, and myopia is often the mother of mirage.

Despite the danger, I want to boast. There may be places of equal beauty, but I do not believe there are any of more varied and greater beauty in this lovely England. From this garden door, within a radius of five miles, we shall walk upon a palimpsest of history as well as through scenes as varied as the eye can desire. Within our survey is the loveliest reach of the Thames, gliding through woodlands and meadows, past islands and backwaters haunted by the swan and kingfisher, with silver reaches, sparkling weirs, and rayless waters in the green gloom of overhanging woods. And by this river, high up on commanding slopes, or set back on emerald lawns, are some of the loveliest houses designed for this English scene.

This same waterway has known the coracle of the Celt, swirled about the legs of invading legionaries of Rome, and been forded by Saxon and Dane. So short a stretch of the river as that we shall traverse has been a cradle of history, yet it remains little changed. The Roman villa, steam-heated, with vineyards and kitchen gardens, looked on it, as at Hambleden. The abbeys and priories of the Middle Ages were built by its marge, as at Medmenham and Hurley. The State barges of Henry VIII and Elizabeth glided on this smooth highway, as also the cargoes of timber and corn from Henley's busy wharves. And after King Charles's supporters and Cromwell's Parliamentarians had bombarded each other across its water, from Phyllis Court and Greenlands, after the wild blades of the Hell Fire Club at Medmenham had brought it a brief notoriety, and the lavish spectacles of play-acting Lord Barrymore at Wargrave had given it a vogue, a longer fashion of the houseboat made the Henley reaches a social centre, and the Regatta a Mecca of international renown for rowing men.

All this is concentrated in a few miles of river. The landscape is no less rich. In a few minutes one is deep in valleys even yet remote from traffic and human habitation. From these same valleys one climbs rapidly through dense woods of beech, lime, fir, and larch, to commons and heathlands 500 and 600 feet above sea-level. Churches and hamlets, parks and woodlands where the shy deer start, houses of Tudor, Elizabethan, Queen Anne, and Georgian origin, yield up personal records and legends that run like the warp and woof through the crowded tapestry of our social history. Here a King's mistress hides her jewels, a French general dies in exile, a great Duchess lies, her effigy above, her skeleton below. And elsewhere spreads the ceaseless pageant, with statesmen, soldiers, poets, bishops, murderers, highwaymen, and gallants, all pressing the ground over which we may walk in a day's pleasure.

And lastly, in these Chilterns, at whatever season of the year, we shall be continuously surprised by fresh beauty, by new groupings of hills, patchworks of fields and copse, the light of moon and the fire of sunset on horizons gentle or abrupt against the glory or menace of clouds. And even when Nature's last wonder has released us, there will be the living stalwarts of Buckinghamshire, Oxfordshire, and Berkshire, soft vowelled, kind-faced, encountered in inn, cottage, farmyard, and smithy, to entertain us richly with the small chronicles that, from century to century, vary so little and remain so appealing in their comic and tragic aspects. Long-lived, long-memoried fellows are these. In two square miles I have counted seventeen, all over eighty, with merry eyes and wagging tongues, perhaps not Miltons, but certainly not mute.

## II

The maps along my landing will show us all these things, although we will never go farther afield from my garden gate than five miles. I have marked on these six-inch maps twelve walks, which yield up, in a space between breakfast and lunch, or, since we may picnic in the warm sun, in a three hours' walk, the whole pageant of nature and history I have outlined. Between times we will rest in old inns, visit friends, linger in gardens, or within my own hedge indulge ourselves with small talk, no small part of a garden's delight. And at the end of it all I will brave the challenge of my boast concerning this domain where I loiter and garden and scribble a little. If you desire the fleshpots you can quickly desert. London is less than forty miles distant, but I warn you that our radius touches no towns except our own, although they stand just beyond our circumference at Maidenhead, High Wycombe, and Reading.

Will it rain? No. Beyond the high skyline of beechwoods to the south-west the sky is a clear blue. The wheel of the windmill water-pump on the ridge above the Deer Park is pointing north, a sign of good weather. The gardener has ordered me into Henley, to buy some twine for the Dorothy Perkins and the American Pillar, which the wind blew off the trellis last week. He insists that it shall be tar twine. That cheap green garden string is no good, it rots in a few months. Also my housekeeper, opening the kitchen window between yew tree and clematis-covered porch, tells me she wants some Venetian red ochre for the flags. She little knows what a stir there is in my head at that order. Venetian red ochre! Shades of Titian and Tiepolo, of old palaces in narrow canals, of gaudy sails on the lagoons at sunset, of old tiles in the Campo Cristoforo, and the crumbling wall behind the Salute where endless artists would vainly snare the elusive magic of the opalescent lagoon!

Two pennyworth of Venetian red. No, I will not forget it. It is now eleven o'clock, and the shops close at one. There will be a blithe air about the errand boys of Henley since it is early closing day, and it's warm for bathing. And all those boys, who wobble so menacingly on cycles with baskets, who gossip at the kitchen doors, and stand pensive by counters, will discard baggy flannels, frayed jackets, and bulging boots. Stripped, they will turn a Henley meadow into a Greek gymnasium with their cool, lithe bodies. Pretty Miss Snow in the hardware shop, deft in a tangle of hanging lamps, pitchforks, and flypapers, will go on the river in a punt with the youth from the estate office who surreptitiously writes poetry to her, between moments of writing receipts for silly little sums in payment of tithes to Queen Anne's Bounty.

The Fairmile, straight before us, is lovely this morning. July sees the full leafiness of this double avenue of elms. There is a slight mirage above the hot tarmac, but the sward on each side is bright and green. At the far end, in dead centre, rises the square tower of Henley Church. Wherever one goes, that tower is at the centre, like the hub of a cartwheel. Yet one knows the town twists away to the left, to the river and the bridge, by which the church stands.

On our left runs the long brick and flint wall of the Deer Park, with the woods rising beyond. It was built by a squire of Fawley in 1804, when labour was cheap and income tax non-existent. He proudly inserted a tablet in the wall to date his enterprise. Behind us, on the left, is a little discarded schoolhouse, with Gothic arch and pointed windows, not beautiful, but, tiled and flinted, it nestles into the landscape, with the wood at its back, and a fine view up the valley and down the Park. I bought it in three minutes at a land sale, mainly because an old gamekeeper feared he was going to be homeless. So far as I am concerned he is there for life, though numbers of my friends have suggested what might be done with the house for week-ends—" No ! " I answer, heartlessly or feelingly, whichever way you look at it. I have interloped myself, though the eviction was achieved by someone years before, and had an element of bribery. The gamekeeper's cottage is a salve to my conscience. Moreover, I like the burr on his speech, his side-whiskers, and his gamekeeper's leggings, to which he clings, although he's now a gardener.

Past his cottage runs a woodland lane, called ' Pack and Prime,' up to the Park, which was later a carriage road to Henley Park House, a large Georgian residence commanding a fine view. Why ' Pack and Prime ' ? Behind that singular name hides the menace of dark lanes in the days of highwaymen. If you were wise, before journeying up that lane you saw that your pistol was packed and primed in readiness for self-defence. Such is the local legend, but the name may have meant that the way was a primary one for pack-horses.

In the brick wall of the Deer Park there is an opening to a footpath. It was once a brick path going up to the summit of the Park and thence on to Fawley. The wall-building squire tried to do a little encroaching, as was then the habit. He closed up the footpath, but fortunately the sturdy townsmen took him into court, and he was compelled to make a breach in the wall, and open the footpath. It was up this path that Charles I, escaping from Oxford, in 1646, rode as a servant, ' Harry Ashburnham's man,' carrying a cloak bag behind him on his horse. The fugitive King wanted to avoid the town, held by the Parliamentarians, and reach Hambleden Manor for the night.

Each end of the Fairmile has an inn. My own end, alas! has lost a lovely old thatched inn, and a Victorian substitute marks the site. The taste of brewers has improved, architecturally, and nowadays their buildings are more inclined to suffer from 'antiquity' rather than the Diamond Jubilee. But we need not feel in any way apologetic for *The White Horse Inn*, unobtrusively guarding the south end of the Fairmile. This undoubtedly is the tavern " with a bush only, at the Bowling Green without the town in Oxford way " which Taylor, the water-poet, spoke of in 1636. He mentions two others by name, *The White Hart* and *The Elephant*, so that, if his knowledge of taverns was worthy of a poet, despite the water variety of his verse, Henley had only three taverns selling wine in his day. Why does he mention the bush?

An ivy bush, anciently sacred to Bacchus, was once the common sign of taverns, especially of private houses where travellers could obtain beer or wine. Hence the proverb, ' Good wine needs no bush.' The Roman centurion, marching to Dorchester from Henley, would have understood that sign, for his own race brought it to England, and even the proverb is of Latin origin. The sign was familiar till the middle of the eighteenth century, a reign of seventeen hundred years in Britain! Shakespeare knew the sign, as also Poor Robin, who wrote in 1778—

*Some ale-houses upon the road I saw,*
*And some with bushes showing they wine did draw.*

We will not call at *The White Horse*, it is too early, but we will pause at *The Bell Inn*, whose glories all are fled. It stands back from the road by the turning to Marlow, and gives its name to Bell Street, which now begins and conducts us through its narrow way to the market-place. The old inn is hidden by an elm tree and the bushes in the garden that front it.

We will look at that elm tree. When my old gardener told me that Chaucer's granddaughter became a Duchess, and lay buried at Ewelme, with the garter on her left arm, in a canopied tomb blazing with escutcheons, I hurried off to that lovely old village in a fold of the Chilterns. It was exciting enough to find the duchess, and linger in the church, and I went often, but not a little of the attraction was the sexton. He was the perfect sexton, not the buffoon of Shakespeare's *Hamlet*. He joked, but with an apologetic smile. He had a patient way of conducting one through the labyrinthine pedigree of the De la Roue family—" Hence the wheel, Madam, in those arms, ' roue ' being French for wheel. And this, Madam, will interest you ; it is an oak chancel door without a hinge—feel the wood, Madam, how smooth ! "

He knew me from frequent visits with my guests. " I'm told I'm in your book, sir," he said, once, as though assured that he was in my good books. This established a more familiar relationship. I came from Henley. Ah, he had once lived there, long ago as a boy, in a house opposite *The Bell Inn*. " I looked on to the tree where they hanged a spy," he said.

" Hanged a spy—what spy ? " I demanded.

" A Puritan spy, sir," he said, with the relish of a

sturdy Churchman. "He was caught by Prince Rupert, who was a rough-and-ready sort of man, especially with Cromwell's scallywags. So he hanged him from the elm tree in front of *The Bell Inn*, in December 1643. When I was a boy I could see the chain they did it with still there. It was a winter's day, sir, with snow on the ground, December 1643, and he looked like a crow dangling black, there, under the bare branches."

I was tempted to ask him whether he had been present at the execution, so vivid was his detail, so warmly did he seem to approve the event. Outside the church, I reflected this was only a sexton's tale. But, consulting the local historians, I find he was right in the essential details. Prince Rupert, then holding Henley for Charles I, did hang a spy from that elm tree. The Parliamentarians replied by hanging two King's Messengers who brought to London a proclamation and letter.

And here is the elm tree on which the deed was done. And here's a chain, embedded deep in the old trunk.

"The same chain?" asks my companion.

"That's a little unfair—you can't expect me to commit myself like that," I reply. "But I've seen things no more improbable, the tongue of St. Anthony, in a bottle in his church at Padua, for instance."

"Don't be gruesome!" exclaims my friend.

"But isn't this gruesome? 'As he rode by at midnight the chains clanked in the wind, and an owl flew out in the moonshine.' It's the very stuff of drama."

That chain fascinates me. I have been to look at it several times. The leaves hide it in summer, but you can discover it with a walking-stick. The Civil War was not lacking in cruelty and horrors on either side. The Parliamentarians in turn struck terror into the inhabitants. A poor Henley woman complained of the taxes levied, so they took her and forced out her tongue until it could be nailed to a signpost, with a paper fixed on her back, setting forth her offence. They left her there while three companies marched by. They took an old widow, Elizabeth Cary, and convicted her of carrying the King's Proclamation from Oxford to London. They condemned her to the gibbet at Henley, and to have her back broken. Her sentence was postponed and, after long captivity, she lived to see the Restoration, and was rewarded with an annual pension of forty pounds.

And now let us look at *The Bell Inn*. It has been an inn and a Royal Grammar School, and is now wondering what its fate may be. It is pleasant to look at, long and low. There is a rough lawn and shrubbery in front of it. Two cats are asleep in the sun, some wild antirrhinums and hollyhocks suggest a former garden. There was a day when the stage-coaches rumbled outside this weedy plot, when postillions and grooms and lackeys fussed while the gentry dined within.

Ten years before the tree was made a gallows, a young gentleman of twenty-eight, the son of the lord of the manor, attended on Archbishop Laud and his train putting up there on the way to entertain the King at Oxford. The young man urged the Archbishop's removal to his father's, Sir James Whitelock's place, Fawley Court, but the Archbishop declined.

Young Bulstrode Whitelock is destined to be very much on the scene in the next forty years. He will become one of Cromwell's Lords and go as his country's ambassador to the Court of Queen Christina of Sweden, where his shrewd mind will earn the confidence of that wayward, abdicating lady.

At the moment, however, he is in the King's notice. He served on a committee formed by the Inns of Court that staged before Their Majesties a stupendous Masque, at Candlemas 1633. The masquers, spangled in silver, with white stockings up to their trunk hose, and sprigs in their bonnets, approached Whitehall in chariots, with such lavish splendour of attendants that the populace roared its approval, and the King was so delighted that he asked the procession to pass again, before it entered the banqueting hall. The pleased Court seemed to hear nothing of the rumbling of the approaching storm. Mr. Bulstrode Whitelock and his fellow masquers received pretty compliments on their splendid entertainment.

But we must not linger any more by the sad old *Bell Inn*, no longer an inn or a Royal Grammar School, with its secret chamber in the roof, and stables that once held a hundred horses. We will return again later, on January 6th, 1777, in the company of vivacious little Mrs. Powys, when my Lord Villiers had a great party to which came all the nobility and county at the opening of such a week of fashion and gaiety as Henley has never known since.

How long Bell Street will keep its ancient beauty I cannot estimate, but not long, I fear. The cinema has dropped its seed of sex in a crevice, and has expanded, destroying a pleasant old shop with bottle-glass windows. Bow window after bow window vanishes with the spirit of Queen Anne and the Georges, giving place to multiple stores with uniform windows.

If there were time we would look in at *The Bull* and *The Bear*, where the pack-horses and broad-wheeled wagons used to halt. *The Bull* is a true example of 'crazy-paving.' There is hardly a floor on the same level, and windows and doors and cupboards are the real old thing. The yard at the back of *The Bear* seems to have been shut off from 'improvements' for a century. At the corner of New Street, which is very old, and was there when Henry VIII was kicking in his cradle, there is an old house that——

But this will not do. Down the street we go, and turn into Hart Street, the real high street, and hurry on to *The Red Lion*, which looks on to the river, the bridge, and White Hill opposite, where the road to London rises up through a woodland.

If the view from the bridge, with its stretch of the Thames, does not fill the heart with delight nothing will. There lie the boats at the wharves. On the right hand are Marsh Lock Island and the wooded heights of Park Place, where we shall call later on General Conway, Lady Ailesbury, and the Honourable Mrs. Damer, to whom Horace Walpole left Strawberry Hill.

Upstream is lovely enough, but downstream is almost flawless, with the church tower, the towing-path, Phyllis Court's lawn, and, in the distance, the classic temple on Regatta Island, against a massive screen of trees and the background of the wooded

Chilterns. Naturally enough, it provoked a local poet
who wrote a hundred years ago—

> *Bid your postillions roll the whirling wheel*
> *Where Oxford, Bucks, and Berks, their bounds*
>     *reveal ;*
> *For there lies Henley—if the heart be right,*
> *Its loveliness will yield unmix'd delight.*

Nothing is so tedious as a description of scenery, so
let us stop and have a drink at *The Red Lion*. To-day
we have not time to go across the road to *The Angel*,
which is bow-windowed, black and white, roofed with
old tiles and mellowed with age. Its parlour window
overlooking the river is the place where I take friends
who talk too much. That quietens them. " Oh, I
say——" they begin, and the rest is silence as they
watch the river. But we can't go in there now. We
must call at *The Lion* before getting that Venetian Red,
and some insecticide for the rose-trees, and a new
incinerator, and some tar twine for the trellis—who
said life in the country was restful ?

I feel slightly ashamed of *The Red Lion*. Apart
from a noble wistaria that covers it, the entrance is
terribly commonplace. It was ' improved ' about
fifty years ago, and might now be the head office of a
brewery company. But it is the genuine thing so far
as local history is concerned. No one knows when it
first opened its doors, but Charles I stayed there on his
way to Oxford in 1632, and again in 1642. One
wonders whether it wasn't then ' the latest,' as Archbishop Laud and other notables used to go to the old

*Bell Inn*. That handsome Bohemian, Prince Rupert, made it the headquarters in 1642 of his brigade at Henley. During some restorations in 1889, the royal coat of arms, with King Charles's monogram and the date ' 1632,' was discovered over the fireplace in an upstairs room.

It is claimed that Shenstone wrote his famous verses here.

> *Whoe'er has travelled life's dull round,*
> *Where'er his stages may have been,*
> *May sigh to think he still has found*
> *His warmest welcome at an Inn.*

This superb tribute to the inn-keeping profession was said to have been written on a pane of glass, and we are told that Dr. Johnson quoted them with relish after staying at *The Red Lion*. " We happened to lie this night at the Inn at Henley where Shenstone wrote these lines," wrote Boswell. I am very doubtful about that pane of glass—it has quite disappeared. And I am certain, despite local historians, that Dr. Johnson was not at *The Red Lion*. He lay that night at Henley-in-Arden, Warwickshire, on his way to Ashbourne. Shenstone lived nearby, and so far from liking inns, ruined himself in making a splendid estate !

*The Red Lion* had plenty of distinguished visitors without stealing Dr. Johnson, or Shenstone's verses. The Duke of Marlborough used to break his journeys there on the way to Blenheim, but he seems to have taken no risks with the beds, for he furnished his own room, complete with bedstead and bedding, to be at his command whenever he passed that way. The furniture remained over a century, until 1849. The inn must have been a very popular one, for its owner, Barrett Marsh, when he died in 1816, left a fortune of £120,000.

As for the beds, the Duke's slight seems to have been unmerited, for a visitor wrote, in honour of the landlady, " The mutton chops of my old friend Mrs. Dixon are altogether unrivalled, and she has the art of making all her guests happy and contented." The chops must have been good, for George IV, when dining there, as Prince of Wales, ate fourteen of them at a sitting ! The visitor then goes on to say :

" I always enjoy myself greatly at her house, not only with reference to the beautiful scenery which I see all around, but from the real comfort and cleanliness of everything about me. The sheets repose in lavender till they are wanted, and her beds are neatness itself ; added to this, a large and respectable Bible is placed on the dressing-table of each bedroom."

This conjunction of Bible, bed, and mutton-chops makes one wish Dr. Johnson had stayed at Mrs. Dixon's. He would have approved so heartily. No wonder the house prospered, so that her son enlarged the premises and took in the Grammar School, which had now emigrated to the defunct *Bell Inn*.

The great day in the life of *The Red Lion* must have been June 14th, 1814. England thought she had at last laid low her bogey, Bonaparte. He had been packed off to Elba. Trafalgar had been fought. The trouble seemed over. Waterloo lay unseen in the near future. On this June day all Henley was *en fête*. England was full of the great of the earth, previously to their gathering at the famous Congress of Vienna. The allied Princes were to receive academic honours at Oxford. On their way there they passed through Henley. This great company included the Tsar Alexander of Russia, the King of Prussia, with his nephews, one of them destined to be the first Emperor of Germany, the Prince Regent, General Blücher, and a host of minor stars. In approaching the town the Tsar had stopped at the lodge of Park Place to enquire after Lord Malmesbury, once Ambassador at St. Petersburg, who was ill.

To view this procession let us take up a position in the window of an upper room at *The Red Lion*. We are in excellent company, encountering Lady Malmesbury, who at Park Place has so often entertained the Prince Regent, Pitt, and Canning. It seems only yesterday that she presented the colours to the Loyal Henley Association in a field opposite her house, where a tent was erected, and the carriages set down, and the ladies were handed out by his lordship ; and the Rev. Jeston, headmaster of the Grammar School, preached from a drumhead. But that was sixteen years ago, and who knew then what might happen, with the rebellion in Ireland, and Bonaparte threatening India and seizing Malta and Egypt ? No wonder Mr. Wordsworth felt alarmed, and had a seizure of sonnets ! These alarming days are now over, and the madman of Europe is locked up on Elba. We can breathe.

Lady Malmesbury looks charming. She is dressed in a muslin flowered gown with a high waist. Her hair is frizzed, and she has a bonnet, modelled on a Grecian helmet, with a Hector feather curled up from behind, which is all the rage just now. Her long green gloves match the colour of her hat, and also the parasol. She has her ' indispensable ' with her also, in which are smelling salts and oddments. She is accompanied by her friend, Mrs. Scott of Danesfield. A number of county bucks are round her, quizzing the rabble below.

They have lined up some of those new mail-coaches that go so incredibly fast now Mr. McAdam has found a wonderful process of road-making, and are using them as grandstands. Everybody's out. The procession is coming down White Hill now ! It's a wonder the bridge doesn't break down. And here's the first carriage, closed, with the Prince Regent in it. There's not much cheering. He's behaving very badly to the poor Princess Caroline, and he's not popular. So he sits back, not showing himself while the band plays ' God Save the King,' which finished, his carriage goes on. All Henley thinks he might have had the grace to show himself and bow. But there's cheering now, for here comes the great Tsar Alexander, in an open carriage, with his sister. The lads have taken the horses out and are pulling them down the street. There ! he's standing up now. What a pleasing countenance ! He has taken his hat off and is bowing to us—no, to Lady Malmesbury and the ladies. Why, some of the people are actually shaking hands with him ! What's the matter ? He wants to stop and greet Lady Malmesbury, and they won't let him, those mad boys go on at such a pace. More carriages without horses—who's that ? The King of Prussia, with the princes ! How well they look in their uniforms— the nephew is very handsome.

What a noise, what's happened now? The crowd's broken through the bridge turnpike! Who's this they're pulling along? Why, it's Blücher—the great General Blücher! There he goes. What huzza-ing!

" Oh, Mr. Dixon," cries Lady Malmesbury, " do go down and ask Sir Charles Stewart to bring up the General. That mob'll pull him to pieces—and I do want to meet him! "

There goes Mr. Dixon. He's caught up with them half-way down the street. He's made them turn. The General's coming back.

We're all in the room again, with the noise of the cheering outside. Here he comes. What a splendid-looking old fellow! He's fair and quite handsome, and with scarcely a wrinkle, but he seems feeble on his legs. Bravo, General Blücher! That was great work at Laon, sir! (Have you heard—they've just made him Prince of Wahlstadt. He doesn't look seventy-two!) Listen—why, it's French he's talking—says he's fatigued to death with all this acclamation—had no sleep for three nights. Who'd be a hero? He's not going? Wish I could shake his hand. What's that? So he is? Look, Amelia—he's drinking a toast to Lord Malmesbury's health—and to her lady-ship's.

The General has bowed and bowed. Now he goes on to the balcony and toasts the crowd. What a noise, what screams of delight!

He's back now in the carriage. One wonders what time they'll get to Oxford. They're sure to be late.

And so are we if we go on like this. We'll leave the allied Princes proceeding down the road to Oxford.

We might, of course, have seen them pass my cottage door. The horses always slow up there as they begin the steep rise to Bix Common ; the highwaymen have found that a good spot, with spent horses and a thicket for their retreat.

We must now concern ourselves with less romantic things, with Venetian red ochre, garden twine, and a refuse incinerator. They can all be obtained at the ironmonger's near to Blandy House.

" Blandy House ? "

" Yes—that yellow-faced house there, with the door in the middle—have you never heard of Miss Blandy, who poisoned her old father with a powder given to her by her lover, a wicked captain ? Well, there's no time now. But that was Henley's greatest sensation. I'll tell you later. Now for the ironmonger's."

But we are fated to be delayed. Miss Arabella Mervyn-Morpeth, and her brother, Brigadier-General Poultenay Mervyn-Morpeth, of Page's Bottom, are in the shop. They are known locally as the A.M. and P.M. My district is rich in Brigadier-Generals. They are sown plentifully along the Thames and on the Chilterns, and the soil seems to suit them, for they are of sturdy growth and take a lot of uprooting. Some of them were potted out in India, Egypt, and Africa, and the gales of 1914–1918 played havoc with them, although some seemed to thrive and blossomed forth with all manner of decorations. These fortunate ones, of course, were tied to the Staff with ribbons, and thus escaped being buffeted like the others, who were often transplanted and uprooted in the most reckless fashion. One of our more delicate species, brought up in an

Indian hothouse, was despatched direct to Northern Russia. He was badly nipped by the frost, and has never properly bloomed since.

Our Brigadier-Generals are as various in size as they are in temperament. We have tall ones and small ones, and some have a double bloom. On the whole they prefer sheltered positions, and are to be found in old manors, enlarged Elizabethan cottages, and occasionally in vast Georgian houses. But when the houses are too large, they wilt a little.

They might be termed proud plants, and their roots strike deep down into national history. It is a common fallacy, among caricaturists and humorists, that they thrive on golf-courses, and do not require much water (in their whisky), but I have found them in all sorts of places and have noticed their readiness to bloom, with the slightest attention, in the most unpropitious circumstances, their nature being essentially gallant, even on the poorest subsoil. For this reason I observe with pleasure the many shoots they put out and somehow maintain in our most expensive social conservatories. May they flourish ! The English landscape would be the poorer without their weather-beaten faces and tweed-clad limbs.

Brigadier-General Poultenay Mervyn-Morpeth, the P.M. as we affectionately call him, is a worthy representative of the genus. He is well-rooted in the district, and with the A.M., his sister, lives in a large Georgian house, of which the wing is closed and the roof leaky. They are, for their position, very poor, but in no way proud. You will meet them in the autumn with a wheelbarrow collecting firewood for the winter.

I have even seen the A.M. in laced-up boots, and a thick ' pullover,' with a bucket and a small coal-shovel, sally forth on to the main road after the Hunt has gone by, to collect those precious deposits, in a horseless age, which gardeners covet. She was as insensible to passing strangers as she was to the indignant sparrows, watching her taking manure out of the mouths of the poor.

That enormous house, in four rooms of which they camp out, is run by an odd man, and the odd man runs because the A.M. is always behind him. When these hospitable souls give a little dinner-party it is like a performance of magic, with the A.M. disappearing and reappearing in the gloom of candlelight, conjuring up food in the rôle of kitchenmaid-cook-butler-hostess, and with the odd man doing very odd things in the dim background. But the grand moment comes with coffee on the terrace, if it is summer, or in the immense drawing-room, if it is winter. Then the scene is truly squirarchal, with a smooth lawn, and great beech trees in the park ; or a log fire, and booted generals and high-bosomed ancestresses on the walls. The odd man, transformed by a striped waistcoat and white gloves, appears with an immense silver coffee tray. One then has a brief sad vision of the A.M. and P.M. clutching Time by the tails, since they have been unable to hold him by the forelock.

But we are in the ironmonger's shop, which, on our appearance, is suddenly filled with Good morning ! Good morning ! Good morning ! a lashing of dogs' tails (four), and the P.M., in between greeting, suff-suffing with a garden syringe that he is about to buy.

Another blight on his rose trees ! One damn thing
after another—gardens are not worth the trouble, no,
sir ! And did I know anything about *Nymphæa
Candidissima*, which had been strongly recommended
to him by Lady Almina Lushington-Crowfoot ? The
A.M. seized on me at once.

" It's simply monstrous—you've heard, I suppose ? "
she said, putting down a lamp glass, upright, so that
the ironmonger had to rescue it from a crash. " Yes,
I'll have that—one and eightpence—*eightpence* ?
Surely they've gone up ? No ? Very well, thank
you. Yes, simply monstrous—we must make a firm
stand ! " declared the A.M., turning to me again.

" They think they can do what they like with the
place. Well, sir, they can't ! I'm writing to *The
Times* ! " said the P.M.

" But what about ? " I asked, bewildered.

" There—that's just what I said, Poultenay ! They're
keeping it a secret. Mr. Roberts knows nothing about
it. It's simply monstrous ! "

" What's simply monstrous ? "

The P.M. touched me with a leather-gloved finger :
he wears riding gloves. He also wears buff riding
breeches.

" My dear sir, you're the very man we want. You
understand these things. The Press can stop it,
I'm sure ! "

" I'm not the Press, anyhow," I replied defensively.

" But you write," said the A.M. firmly.

The charge is familiar to me. Whenever I am
solicited for some campaign and show a retiring spirit,
I am told that I write. There must be an idea current

in the minds of these good people that one practises a
form of necromancy, or black magic. A few passes
with the pen and the Urban District Council can be
stopped building a swimming-pool opposite Mrs.
Cram's boat-house, or be made to put a lamp-post by
the corner where the courting couples try to compress
themselves into each other.

" Publicity will stop it. There'll be an outcry ! "
declared the P.M.

" Against what ? " I asked again.

" A cinema ! A cinema, if you please ! " cried the
A.M., using a hard ' k ' as in ' crime.'

" But we have a cinema," I replied.

The P.M. expanded his chest, and looked triumphantly at the A.M.

" Exactly, my dear sir ! As if one of those brain-
rotters wasn't enough for a place like this. And now
we're to have another nit-wit palace! "

" I suppose there must be a demand," I said. But
the moment I had spoken I regretted it. The shocked
expression on their faces made me add hastily—" Or
isn't there ? "

" That's really not the point—it's where they're
going to put the thing ! " cried the A.M.

I asked where, and the P.M. led me to the door.

" There ! " he said, more in sorrow than in anger.

' There ' was an old Georgian house, flat-faced and
regular, which had been an antique dealer's shop, and
now stood empty. It was of no particular beauty,
but its quiet, well-mannered air conformed to the
character of the old street. I began to feel indignation rise in me. That façade would disappear. There

would be a pseudo-Tudor or near-Elizabethan palace plastered with sex appeal, the whole lit up with arc lights, selling passion to Henley lads and lasses. The small towns of England were littered with these dark drug-shops for time-killers.

" A syndicate's bought that dear old house for a cinema," said the P.M.

" An outrage ! " hissed the A.M., swaying with indignation.

" We must stop it ! Such vandalism ! " declared the P.M.

" You must write to the Press ! " cried the A.M.

" I ? "

" You ! "

" I only write for the Press, not to it," I said facetiously.

" We've all written ! We're determined to stop such an outrage on the beauty of Old England," declared the P.M.

" Surely the Town Council won't let——" I began.

The A.M. and the P.M. shouted at me derisively.

" The Town Council ! The Town Council ! Did you see what they did to the old Town Hall ? " asked the P.M.

As the old Town Hall disappeared in 1898, I could not be expected to know, and the way in which they referred to the incident suggested it was not quite nice to know.

" Well, surely, there's a Town Planning Committee, and there's the Council for the Preservation of Rural England—can't they control it ? " I asked.

" They can control nothing, my dear sir ! They can

only suggest. What we want is a Ministry of Good Taste ! " replied the P.M.

" We want a dictator ! " said the A.M., one of the most fiercely individual women I know. " Anyhow, Mr. Roberts, you are with Us ? "

" Yes-yes," I replied, now a little anxious about Venetian red ochre, garden twine, and the incinerator, for it was one o'clock, and a boy was taking in rakes and door-mats.

The A.M. and P.M. thanked me warmly and climbed into their car, almost in keeping with their Georgian house. It went off with a bad smell and a noisy manner.

I bought the twine and the incinerator. I was really upset with their news. Every day somebody threatened something. My neighbour was building a cowshed, and I waited with bated breath to see whether he would tile it or use corrugated iron. I was no enemy of progress, but I hated to think of the quiet of that lovely old street being broken. At night, when all the shops were shut, and there was only the lamplight, the old street slipped back into the eighteenth century, and the ghosts of Miss Blandy and the wicked captain took an airing. If a cinema were erected it might be blatant till midnight with platinum-blonde women swooning in the arms of he-men, all in four colours and few clothes.

And thinking of these horrors I forgot the Venetian red ochre, and was greeted with the polite reproach of my housekeeper.

# COUNTRY THOUGHTS

When I walk by Buckingham Palace,
Where the King works hard all day,
Does he long to live in a cottage, I wonder,
And dream the hours away,
And never see a minister
But only make decrees
Concerning new asparagus beds
And planting cherry trees?

When I walk by Parliament Houses,
Where the grey old Thames runs by,
Does the Speaker forget to listen, I wonder,
And dream in his chair, and sigh
To hear the cackle of the geese
Around the old barn door,
Forgetting all the garrulous flock
That fills the Commons floor?

When I walk by Hyde Park Corner,
By the trees of Rotten Row,
Guardsmen in red coats stand like tulips,
And quick the nursemaids grow ;
And little plants all potted out,
In prams well-bedded down,
Lift flowery faces, starry-eyed,
To brighten London town.

*When I walk by Piccadilly Circus,*
*Where the night in hideous rout*
*Roars with a thousand wheels, and flames*
*Like a fiery roundabout,*
*I close my ears to all the noise,*
*My eyes to all the glare,*
*And see a timid doe flit down*
*A glade by Leicester Square.*

# CHAPTER VII

## YUCCAS AND FIREWOOD

### I

THERE are times when I feel that I shall have to give up living in the country. It is fatal to one's career. I can get nothing done. April keeps one on tiptoe with expectancy. There are birds and buds and blossoms. The grass begins to grow quite aggressively and a long battle begins with the ironmonger, who had promised the mowing machine would be ready on Tuesday, and, although it's Saturday, one is still without the mower. To-morrow, when friends arrive, one will feel like the man who has had no time to shave before breakfast. Gardens with their grass long are as detestable as Bohemians with their hair long. One cannot be too Prussian with a lawn.

In May begins the pricking-out frenzy. If you delay until June you are lost ; the lobelias, the antirrhinums, the marigolds and all the small fry insist on attention at once. Then comes June, when there is a sudden and mysterious shortage of stakes in the untidy corner where the odds and ends have spent the winter. If all these children springing out of their beds do not get leg-irons at once they'll go crippled for the summer, splay-footed, bow-legged, bent-backed, a misery to behold. Useless to be kind to them in July. Their poor faces are twisted to the ground, and, staked, they look like victims of the Inquisition.

At times, looking at the garden and realising its outrageous demands upon my time, I feel rebellious. The worst criminal sees an end to his hard labour, the good gardener never. Every year he must begin all over again. Sometimes, with that nervous apprehension which is the bane of the imaginative man, I have looked up at my trees and been dismayed at the thought that in November all those leaves, millions it seems, will have to be swept up, and carted away, and somehow destroyed. And all those beds, so thick with stalks, leaves, and blossoms, they too must be cleared, the roots thinned, the earth dug over.

No gardener ever rebels, of course. A few make desperate attempts at freedom. They reduce the beds, or extend the crazy paving, but when the new seed catalogue arrives they fall miserably. I marvel most at those evening gardeners. By good fortune I am a day gardener. Since I am my own employer, I can work at whatever time I choose. Thus it is I spend the morning in the garden, saying I will do my writing in the afternoon. Alas, it is always lunch-time before the job is finished, and since one cannot leave a garden in a mess, for someone may call for tea, another start is made after lunch ! It is soon so near to tea-time that it is not worth stopping.

After tea there is just time to write that most urgent letter before the post goes. Why is it always such a desperate business ' catching ' the post in the country ? Mine does not go until six o'clock, but every day sees me desperately scribbling at five minutes to six, and running along the lane at a minute to six, trying to stick on the stamp as I run. Sometimes I have to get out the car to chase the postman, and now that a progressive Postmaster-General has supplied him with a motor-tricycle it has become a most desperate business.

Since life is so difficult for a day gardener, then what desperate people, what enthusiasts or slaves must these evening gardeners be. You see them best by train, by any train that runs on a high embankment out of a metropolis, somewhere around seven o'clock. You look down on miles and miles of narrow gardens, all with the open back-door of a house at one end and a summer-house or odd-job hut at the other. You look down on strips of green grass, earth beds, rubble paths, odd rose trees, a clothes line, a radio aerial, a garden ornament, or a rustic bench. Some of these gardens are pathetic, some heroic. One owner commands his domain from a tiny terrace, another hides in a bower of roses, and the Taj Mahal seems to have inspired the ambitious waterpiece of ' Sunnymede.'

But whatever it is one looks down upon at this hour, little Kew, or cramped Chatsworth, or pseudo-Sandringham, there in the middle, as likely as not in his shirt-sleeves, will be seen the cheerful prisoner, stooping, reaching, pulling, or merely grovelling. He has been at the office from nine till six, he has gobbled a high tea, and rushed into the garden, hoping it won't get dark too soon. For miles on miles this is the vista. A nation of shop-keepers ? What nonsense ! A nation of gardeners, without doubt.

*Breathes there a man with soil so dead,*
*Who never to his neighbour said,*
*     Soon after tea—*
*     " This is my own*
*     Home-grown*
*     Sweetpea ! "*

It is a stirring, touching sight, this great army of
evening gardeners on the bend.   How do they achieve
their miraculous parterres, their glorious blooms, their
svelte lawns, they who have written and posted hundreds
of letters before six o'clock, who scarcely know their
gardens by the full light of day ?   For Sunday is a day
of sleep and newspapers, and Saturday is sacred to
cricket and cinema.   They put me to shame.   They
earn their living, and garden in their spare time.   I
garden, and earn my living in my spare time, and these
' evening ' gardens shame my own.

Conscious of all this, I am provoked whenever it is
suggested I have ample leisure.   " Yes—it's wonderful to be situated like you are, between two of the best
golf-courses in England," says a friend.   " I suppose
you're always there ? "   And I answer, a little aggressively, " I've been here four years, and I've not yet
been there—I never seem to have time."

Then, since I live within a mile of the Thames, and
the scene of Henley Regatta, it is imagined that I row
in a skiff, a four or an eight, or I punt, canoe, or swim
every day.

" I suppose you live on the river ? " says someone
enviously.

" I live near it, but I've not been on it or in it ten

times in four years," I reply, and add quickly—" I never seem to have time."

Only a gardener will understand this strange absorption. Potting and pottering, we lay waste our years. Waste? If ever that thought assails me, I call to mind the monstrously rich stockbroker of sixty who once sadly remarked in the middle of my garden-path—" All this makes me wonder what on earth I've been doing with my life."

Being, apparently, a fellow of such infinite leisure, I am asked other questions as to the disposal of my time. I live near a magnificent golf-course, and I do not golf. I live near a splendid river, and I do not row. Then, perhaps, I fish?

" No—but I spend a lot of time on Henley Bridge," I reply. " I don't fish, but I'm a great bridgeman. I've stood on the London bridges, the Paris bridges, on Brooklyn Bridge, on bridges over the Rhine, Rhône, Tiber, Po, Vistula, Danube, Isar, Hudson, Mississippi, St. Lawrence, the Grand Canal, the Golden Horn, bridges all over the earth—but Henley Bridge satisfies me most. It spans over a thousand years of English history, and of all the places I have seen this is the most tranquil and satisfying in its beauty."

It seems that a great many people have wanted to fish from Henley Bridge. In the eleventh year of the reign of Henry VII they had to pass a protective law.

" Ordered that no foreigner or stranger fish upon the bridge in the water Thames there with angle, hook, or nets or any other instrument on penalty of forfeiting the said instruments or 2d."

Having quoted this ordinance, I add, a little mischievously, " And you mustn't catch salmon in Kipper time." Although this sounds quite preposterous, I am only quoting a petition from the Commons, praying the good Edward III that " no salmon should be caught between Gravesend and Henley Bridge, in Kipper time." Kipper time, it transpires, was " entre les Festes de l'Invention del Crois et le Epiphanie."

But in a garden there is no ' Kipper time.' As in a well-run hotel, the beds are never empty ; the early-rising tulips must give place to the late gladioluses, the soil is scarcely off the guests departing before the leaf-mould is off the guests arriving. One of my neighbours is a scientific gardener. I think he is a sadist at heart ; he enjoys being cruel to little bulbs. I have seen him pull them away from their parents with a fierce joy, around whom they cluster so thickly. He loves to dig down into the earth and exhume rotted bodies and bulbs. He is the Bernard Spilsbury of the subsoil.

No surgeon ever approached a rich patient with a malignant appendix with the joy that my friend approaches his victims for cutting operations. He has a cabinet of sécateurs, graduated and gleaming like that of a great surgeon. His grafting operations leave me dumb with admiration, but I cannot resist a suspicion that one day he hopes to produce a monstrous freak. For two years he has been trying to persuade a normal tree to give birth to a tomato-rose, which is to look like the offspring of a *mariage de convenance* between a tomato and a peony.

The operating-room in his garden-house has a gruesome fascination. Things hang from the ceiling and walls, spidery, fungoid, tortuous, bulbous, making the place look like an alchemist's laboratory. That warm, fig-odour of hot-houses pervades the place. There are masses of flower-pots, baskets, subdivided boxes, seed cabinets, bulb glasses, tin trays, and bunches of raffia. One March day I encountered him walking with a tall cane, at the end of which was a mysterious fluffy object. It looked like a rabbit's tail.

" It is a rabbit's tail," he said, reproving my levity.

He then marched solemnly towards the hot-house, bearing his wand, and I followed like a novitiate in the Eleusinian Mysteries. Inside the hot-house was a wall with a magnificent peach tree in full bloom. The beauty of this tree, spread along the wall, held me entranced with its blossoms. But my friend seemed unconscious of this frail beauty crucified on his wall. Raising the wand, like a thyrsus in a Bacchic rite, he proceeded to titillate each flower. Like a priest he went from blossom to blossom, and I wanted to cry *Hymen io Hymen!* as I watched him perform the marriage ceremony with a rabbit's tail. When he had finished this cross-fertilisation by transferring the pollen on the fur from anthers to stigma, I borrowed the wand and did a little fertilisation for myself. What could be more pleasant than leading peach blossoms to the nuptial couch, and then, six months later, gathering their luscious offspring, with all the bloom of adolescence on them ? A peach-like complexion. There is no higher praise.

## II

A few months later, at that vast Pisani villa at Stra, I was initiated into other mysteries in the marriage of flowers. A sheet of ornamental water attracted our attention chiefly because of the lotus-flower in bloom there. It is so often encountered in poetry, and so seldom met with in nature, that we regarded the lotus with delight. " Shall we gather it and eat it and stay here for ever ? " I asked my companion, in the bright Italian noon, remembering the lotus-eaters.

" You'll probably stay here for ever," he replied ; " but not as you think. You're confusing two kinds of lotus. The Homeric lotus-eaters, or *lotophagi*, ate the fruit of the *Zizyphus lotus*, a North African shrub. You'll remember that Lotis, Neptune's daughter, was changed into a tree when fleeing from Priapus——"

" It seems to me that most of our flora has come from over-sexed young gods chasing reluctant nymphs. What a time they must have had, when any bull or swan might prove to be a youth rampant ! " I observed.

" Had Leda been chaste——" began my companion.

" Do you spell it with a ' d ' ? "

I received a withering look.

" The sun has caught you ! " he said acidly.

" Then I shall scream and be turned into a lotus," I retorted. " But may I have a choice of fruit or flower ? You were describing the difference ? "

" The Greeks were concerned with the fruit, the Egyptians with a water-lily, the Hindus and the Chinese with a water-bean, the Nelumbo."

" The Nelumbo ! The Nelumbo ! " I repeated, memory stirring. All at once I recollected where I had heard that name before. I was once taken to a wooden house in Texas, where we ate roasted nelumbo nuts. The nelumbo lotus is one of the loveliest flowers in the world. When the flowers die away the seed capsules have a kind of corn-nut. It was these green nuts we had roasted and eaten with such relish. But I could tell my friend nothing of this, for he was still pursuing the lotus fetish.

" The Egyptians pictured God sitting on a lotus above the watery mud. Its towering up through the mud symbolises the triumph of Divine intellect over matter, and the Deity sitting on it implies His intellectual sovereignty."

My friend's intellectual sovereignty, inclined to be overpowering at the slightest provocation, this time stimulated me. He should not have it all his own way on this hot Italian day. I interrupted him firmly.

" You have overlooked a very important lotus tree," I said.

" How ? "

" Which," I corrected him. " The lotus tree discovered by Mahomet in the seventh heaven. It flourished on the right hand of the throne of God. The seventh heaven——"

" Of delight——" interrupted my friend.

" No—not of delight. You are confusing Mahomet's seven heavens with the Cabbalists' seven, each rising in happiness above the other, the seventh being the abode of God and the highest class of angels. Mahomet's is different and not so exclusive. It is formed of Divine light beyond the power of tongue to describe, and is presided over by Abraham. Each inhabitant is bigger than the whole earth and has seventy thousand heads, each head seventy thousand mouths, each mouth seventy thousand tongues, and each tongue speaks seventy thousand languages, all for ever chanting the praises of——"

" I really think we must be going ; we can't keep the car waiting for ever," said my friend impatiently. " Do you think we might pluck that lotus ? "

" No—we shall be locked up by the Fascists," I cried in alarm, well aware of his passion for picking. But already he had stooped towards the lovely flower floating on the water. Suddenly he gave a cry, and I thought he had been stung.

" Look ! There's a *Vallisneria spiralis* ! " he exclaimed, " in the very act of fertilisation ! "

I was not sure whether it was really nice to look. Flowers, like human beings, should be allowed a little privacy, but ' I just had to,' as the maid at the keyhole said. All I saw was a tiny ball that had got caught up on the bent stamen of a flower just above the water.

My learned friend explained. It was not so simple as it seemed. The *vallisneria* is a long, grassy-looking plant that wavers under water. The females send up their blossoms on lines, and they float like tethered buoys, with their triple stigma on the alert for passers-by. The males have grown in clusters down under the water, and their chance of meeting the ladies out on the lake seems very remote. Presently they leave home, and go up to the top, where they drift about, insignificant-looking fellows, in the hope of something happening. Something generally does happen to unattached young men seeking adventure. Presently one of them, drifting along, is entangled by Miss *Vallisneria*. The stamens of the drifter stick to the triple-lobed stigma, and fertilisation takes place. This achieved, Mrs. *Vallisneria* withdraws under water again, pulled down by her tether, and lies at the bottom, awaiting an interesting event.

I have no pond in my garden, so that I have no means of growing the lotus or the *vallisneria*. Moreover, the English climate is unfriendly to both. There is one plant, however, a foreigner in the land, whose fertilisation is as remarkable as that of the *vallisneria*, and much less haphazard. It depends neither upon people with rabbits' tails nor the drifting male. The yucca takes no chances. It has its own private chaplain attached for the ceremony.

The first yucca I ever consciously saw was in a garden by Hambleden Weir. The distant roar of the Thames invaded the small garden, and a millstream raced through it. In one corner rose a stately yucca, tall, spiky, and decorated with a hundred pendulous bells. I coveted the strange object at once, and must have leaned over the garden gate with a very yearning expression on my face, for a kind lady, walking in the garden, invited me inside and enlightened me upon the yucca.

It has its own special yucca-moth for fertilisation. The moth emerges at the time of the opening of the flowers and loses no time, for sometimes they only open for a night. The moth makes a ball of pollen, flies to another flower, lays four or five eggs in the pistil, and inserts the pollen ball in the opening it has made. This is a cunning contrivance, both for the moth and the yucca, for each larva, on hatching from the egg, requires about twenty seeds for food. As the fertilised plant produces some two hundred seeds, this leaves a nice balance of about a hundred seeds for propagation. No other insect can fertilise the yucca and faithfulness is further ensured by the fact that the larva of the yucca moth can only live on its own species of yucca. This is pure breeding indeed.

The kind lady gave me a yucca, and I bore it off in triumph. But she must have failed to give me a moth with it, for the plant never flowered, an obstinate spinster until it withered away.

III

We were having a solemn consultation on the matter of firewood. I was late getting in my store for the winter. Here it was November 6th, and I had no logs. Alarmed, I had sent a line to the man who keeps me supplied, and he had arrived from his farm, high in the Chilterns, with a whole cart-load of nicely sawn logs. He brought me, also, at my express desire, a few short lengths of trunks. Since I cannot go out into a park and cut down great trees, like Gladstone of old, I practise my strength on these three-foot logs. They are all the exercise I want, for I attack them in the most primitive fashion, sometimes with a beetle and wedge, sometimes with an adze.

The first time I bought these large logs the man asked me if I had a good beetle. " Beetle ? " I echoed, wondering what he could mean. I had yet to see an insect that I should be prepared to call a ' good ' beetle, though the entomologist may have his moments of excitement. Eventually it was explained to me that a beetle was that most ancient instrument, the iron-bound log hammer, such as one sees used for driving in taut pegs and stanchions. The beetle and the wedge, an iron one, provide a quick way of splitting up a trunk.

It is neater but more laborious to saw logs. My saw seems to take an enormous time to eat its way through one of these trunks, and I was never more conscious of this than when, one morning in Italy, I was watching a man and a boy sawing logs. It was on the mainland opposite Venice, and as we waited for the tram to take us alongside the Brenta, with its villas of the old Venetian aristocracy, I found myself watching these two woodmen. They had a crosspiece on which they supported the log, and were using a long, two-handled saw.

Two things about this performance delighted me. The saw seemed to slide without any effort through the thick log, and no sooner was the trunk on the crosspiece than it fell asunder. Even more fascinating was the play of muscles on the shoulders and torsos of the man and boy. They were naked to the waist and magnificently developed, the boy slim, the man powerful. Their skin, tanned a warm mahogany by the Venetian sun, gleamed and caught a hundred tones and facets of light as the muscles glided with cryptic strength beneath their satin sheaths. Set against a fresh green meadow, with a group of straight slender trees forming a leafy screen under the blue of a sunlit September sky, the man and the boy at their labour formed a panel of colour and life that might have come from the brush of Puvis de Chavannes.

For fifteen minutes my tram held me there, and every time a sawn trunk fell apart I expected the woodmen to take a rest. But no, a fresh trunk was swung up with no apparent effort and swiftly sawn. There was not a sign of perspiration on their superb bodies in that hot noonday, whose shade they spurned. Yet I, in the depth of winter, with a log one-fifth the thickness, perspired freely.

I have such a veneration for trees that I never order fire logs without misgivings. In the woods around me there has been a most cruel slaughter, so cruel that even the woodmen have cried shame on the owners. When the cart arrives at my gate with the logs, I am tempted to ask where they have come from, in order that I may go and see whether the tree felling that I encourage is spoiling the countryside. But I suppress the desire and keep a cowardly silence.

After all, if we ask too many questions about the things we command and consume, life would become unbearable. I will never again eat turtle soup, having once seen in the ' green room ' of a great hotel the living turtles crucified on boards, with nails driven through their fins, in which condition, to stop them crawling, they had been brought across the world. In the horrors of that chill dark room they awaited the release of a chef's knife.

No, we must not ask too many questions. The only counterpoise to man's cruelty to inferior species is in his cruelty to his own, to which he brings the highest flights of his inspiration and mechanical genius.

So I ask no questions as to the source from which my logs come. They are beech logs, of course, and for centuries these Chiltern woodlands have been famous for their logs. Leland, writing in 1545, said there was plenty of wood and corn about Henley, and until recent times the beech timber was brought to the wharf between the bridge and Phyllis Court, split and cut up into lengths, and sent to London by barges. The price of " wood, billet, fagot, coles, and other fuel " was fixed by act in the reign of Edward VI, " but not to affect the town of Calais," and the suitability of beech for fires is thus set forth by an ancient record. " These observations and my enquiries thereon relate more particularly to beech wood, which is said to burn sooner, cleaner, freer from sparkle, and to make a better coale yet will keep fire longer than those of oake, tho' oake last longer than ye burning of beach, the measure and price being ye same or near it."

Edward I. bought his faggots in Henley. He had 2,500 in 1299, and sent a clerk to buy them, and another to superintend their transmission by water from Henley to Westminster. One wonders how much of the Chiltern beechwoods has floated down the Thames in the course of history. And now I am assisting at this denudation.

My logs were about to be unloaded on this bright November afternoon when a black cloud darkened the sky overhead. I looked up, and saw that it was no cloud, but a dense, swiftly-moving flock of birds. Their compact mass must have consisted of thousands. I watched them pass overhead, and suddenly their general must have given word of command to halt. The next moment I witnessed an astonishing transformation. Across the road from my cottage, by the one where my old gardener lived, there was a large lime-tree. It had lost every leaf, and stood forth, a filigree of black branches, naked to the sky. But in an instant it was clothed with feathers, every inch of it, from the lowest branch to the highest, and there came from it such a chorus of screeching as deafened the hillside. What it was all about I do not know, whether a mere dispute or a council. But the din arising from this living tree was so great that I left the woodman and crossed the road.

It was four o'clock in the wintry afternoon, but the birds outlined on the topmost branches, with not a pin-space between them, were vivid in the golden upper light. I saw now that they were starlings. My approach, though cautious, must have been observed, for suddenly, with a loud whirring of wings, they rose in a compact mass, leaving the lime tree as stark as before, and without a moment's hesitation they passed from view on their line of flight. What a sudden commotion they had created in the quiet close of that November day !

Starlings are noisy birds. I have heard them so often at dusk as they gather along the cornice of the National Gallery, and not all the roar of traffic in Trafalgar Square can drown the cheeping overhead. But noise in London is a comparative matter. Here, in the hush at the close of a wintry day their conduct seemed sheer hooliganism.

" That means a hard winter. I'm glad you've got the logs, sir," said my housekeeper, as I came in. Strange, I thought, how at this time of year everything seems to foretell a hard winter ; the berries in the hedges, the blue flame in the fire, the tameness of the robins, the rise in the price of coal. Why are we so eager to prophesy discomfort for ourselves ? Anyhow, these forebodings leave me unmoved. Last winter was to be hard, and it was unbelievably mild and sunny. The previous winter had made my French friend wonder why we troubled to go to the Riviera, where winter seems doubly hard and doubly long because of the absent open fire.

There is a movement afoot, emanating from gas and electricity companies, builders of human honeycombs, and anti-smoke societies, to abolish the open fire. It is wasteful, it creates labour, and fouls the atmosphere. Yes, all this is true. And yet, when the open fire disappears from the English hearth, there will have vanished one of the chief delights of the English home. Let the makers of electric radiators, gas and anthracite stoves, steam radiators, and oil apparatus be as scientific and ingenious as they will, there is nothing that can approach the cheer of the coal fire. Its flicker in an unlit room is one of the friendliest sights on earth, and winter gains a charm that competes with all those of summer.

How often, on a December afternoon, when outside the red glow of sunset sinks behind the iron woods, and the ground mists rise, have I entered the old cottage, and, before the blinds are drawn, or the room is lit, have I paused to watch the play of rosy light on walls and ceiling. It flickers under the old rafters, and draws new colours from rugs and cushions. Now of all times can one indulge in reverie before that ruddy glow, a pleasure scarcer and scarcer in these hurried days. The comfortable old arm-chair, the feet on the fender, a cat, if you will, coiled up on a cushion, and a brass kettle singing on the bar, with a glint of light falling on bellows, toasting-fork, and chestnut-roaster—spoils of visits to the antique shops —these are the symbols of home, and induce that pleasant melancholy of the reminiscent mind. You cannot, however you try, catch the same spirit before an electric stove or a gas-fire ; and a room with only radiator-heating is a room without a soul. And when to an open coal-fire one can add the blazing log, with its bright crackle and swift glow, then human comfort seems complete.

All this, I am aware, shows a very retrogressive and unscientific spirit. But it is one of the joys of living in the country in winter that one can indulge in the old-fashioned pleasure of an open fire, with glowing coal and roaring log, and commit no offence against society. In large cities it is a crime to burn coal, to poison the thick atmosphere, and add to the pall of smoke and the falling blanket of dirt created by a multitude of chimneys. In London I deny myself the pleasure of a coal-fire—though, inconsistently enough, I am cheered by encountering one in a friend's house ! But it is his offence, his pollution of the air, and my own social conscience is clear ; I am making no contribution to those four hundred tons, per square mile, of soot that fall on London every year.

I never wish to see a more melancholy instance of the destructive effect of smoke than that of the Acropolis at Athens. The unhappy decision less than a century ago that made Athens the capital and the seat of Government, instead of Nauplia, has resulted in a tremendous enlargement of the city so that its streets are now thickly clustered about the base of the Acropolis. This is lamentable and costly enough, from a point of view of archæological excavation, but worse still is the havoc wrought upon some of Time's greatest treasures. There is now a continuous drift of smoke across the Acropolis from the city spread below, with disastrous results on the columns and bas-reliefs of the old temples. The degree of deterioration due to the smoke-polluted atmosphere is so great that in the last fifty years there has been more damage done to these glorious monuments of ancient Athens than by the whole of the preceding two thousand years of exposure. It is foretold that another fifty years' corrosion due to the chemical impurities arising from the city will partly obliterate sculptures that are the very pinnacle of artistic achievement.

In the country, with houses so scattered, the individual chimney is incapable of doing any damage either to nature or society. The friendly smoke curling up from my chimney into the bright air rather enhances than detracts from the scene. Wherefore I pile on the logs, stir up the coals, and watch the blaze without any misgivings. Similarly the chimney of my neighbour down the lane is a signal, not of offence, but of good cheer, for whenever I see an increased volume rising from his slightly tilted old chimney I have a vision of him sitting by his hearth in warm content, what time the gale roars through the beech-woods above and the leaves do a dance of death in the garden.

IV

Where flies go in the winter-time is a question entailing no great enquiry, even though we reject the suggestion that they go to the glass-blowers to be turned into bluebottles. But I have often wondered where perambulators go when they cease to perambulate with the young life for which they were designed. I know now. They all seem to go to the country in winter-time to be used for fetching firewood. All through October and November one encounters small boys and their sisters, and old women and their husbands, pushing perambulators along the roads, so heavily burdened with firewood that the under-carriage seems in danger of collapse.

There is a nice law about this collection of brush-wood. Landowners around me seem to raise no objection to the collecting of fallen wood, and the beech and larch-woods that surround me offer a rich supply. None of the cottagers with whom I am acquainted would dream of buying firewood, and the outhouses in any of the gardens will be found crammed with wood for the winter. It is obvious that some of these hefty branches have not fallen naturally ! Short of sawing and swinging on a branch, any tree weak enough to part with its limbs will be encouraged to do so, but happily there is a limit to the perambulator's capacity both for size and weight, and the keepers of these woodlands appear now to acquiesce in the perambulator-measure.

Nevertheless, I am afraid that the safety of the sturdiest forest depends upon the degree of necessity among the adjacent inhabitants. I shall never forget seeing a royal park at Vienna disappear piecemeal before the attacks of the population during that terrible winter of 1920, when a starving city was without fuel. Handcarts, barrows, perambulators, and home-made trucks were all pressed into service, and the military were powerless before a desperate crowd armed with saws and hatchets, which soon devoured the park.

In my lugubrious moments, when I speculate upon the possibility of the invasion of England and the terrible privations that would follow, I wonder how long the royal parks, and other woods almost on the fringe of London, would remain unmolested. Happily, we have never had to witness the destruction of our woodlands under a shell-fire such as devastated stretches of Belgium and France. Among all the horrors of that man-made hell, the sight of blasted trees, with gaunt, splintered trunks and grotesque branches, added to the Doré-like Inferno. These insensate witnesses of carnage were enduring symbols long after the bodies of men had sunk into the mud or been covered by an iridescent scum in the water-logged fields.

Our woods have suffered from a war of a different kind. However much they were cut down in the demand for pit-props during the time of the Great War, economic pressure on the large estates has quickened the ruin. The results have always been worst where the owner, lacking intelligence, or indifferent under the necessity of gain, has handed over his woods to the timber speculator, who simply cuts his way in swathes, leaving behind him a ruinous track, thick with the broken trunks of young trees that should have been spared.  When I walk abroad now I am always in sight of this vandalism, hence the misgivings with which I see the log dealer at my gate.

Beechwood, as the old chronicler recorded, is ideal for the open fire, but the resinous pine, both for blaze and odour, cannot be surpassed.  Nothing is so delicious as a room faintly odorous with burning pinewood, but, alas !  it is an extravagant, swift fire.  I once made the mistake of thinking that all wood was suitable for the fire.  There was a time when I was troubled by a bad smell that occasionally invaded my study.  I moved the lounge and the bookcases, wondering whether the cat had left a dead bird or mouse there.  Then, even as I searched, the smell would go—to come again later.  My housekeeper and I might have been discovered sniffing here and there, suspicious of everything and everybody.

I am ashamed to say I once suspected Miss Whissitt. The advertisements in American magazines, more ingenious than tasteful, have opened our noses to the menace of halitosis, pyorrhœa, and B.O. the enemy of S.A.—all from U.S.A.  The advertisement writer has long exceeded the licence of our psychological novelists, who spared us the physical if not the mental ills of their victims.

Every conceivable source—drains, dead bodies, and B.O.—having been considered, the problem and the smell remained in my study.  It was so elusive, here at two o'clock and gone at three.  Moreover, we were becoming mental, we were developing into sniffers.

Was it something in the brickwork, an entombed cat, or a nameless deposit under the roof ?  I was driven to getting a ladder and entering that foreign region of a man's home, dim and spidery and cistern-whispery under the tiles.  The search was vain.  Then, for a fortnight, the smell vanished, and we breathed again.  But on the very evening of a dinner-party, when I was most anxious we should smell our best, that unwholesome presence was with us again.

It was then that I bethought me of a device which had filled me with wonder when I first saw it applied. I was a guest in a French château, and one day a party of foreign politicians was to be taken over the house and then given lunch.  Shortly before the party arrived, I came down from my room and went into the chief *salon*, where I sat down and read the newspaper.  Presently the door opened and in came a footman, impressively attired in the family livery of green velvet breeches, green and gold waistcoat, white stockings, buckled shoes, and powdered hair.  Let anyone who imagines the French Revolution or eighty years of republicanism have changed the customs of the French nobility stay in one of the châteaux belonging to the *ancien régime*, and he will be strangely enlightened.

I contrived to show no surprise in the presence of this splendid figure, but a few moments later, after the footman had apologised for his intrusion, I sat goggle-eyed.  Going to the fireplace, he proceeded to withdraw a red-hot poker, and my attention was drawn by the sound of loud sizzling in the corner of the room.  Was the fellow actually burning some-

thing ?   I turned and saw that he was pouring the
contents of a bottle on to the red-hot poker.   A small
cloud of vapour arose, and he repeated his poker work
in different corners of the room.   Then, restoring the
poker to the fireplace, he withdrew.

Was the fellow crazy ?   I got up to investigate, and
at that moment the whole performance was intelligible.
A delicate odour pervaded the room.   He had been
pouring eau-de-Cologne over the red-hot poker !   The
*salon* was now sweet for the statesmen.

Recalling this, and almost desperate with the smell
now awaiting my guests, I resorted to a little poker
work.   It was efficacious, but it was costly.   Moreover, a bad smell, as with a bad cold, cannot be long
suppressed.   The eau-de-Cologne vanished, the smell
remained.

It was the omniscient Tilly who delivered me from
my menace.   She appeared one day for lunch, complete with film director, and a slight accent from six
triumphant months in Hollywood.   Appearances as
a nerve-racked woman, an abdicating Queen, a dope
fiend, and the harem favourite of a cruel Sultan, had
not added one line to Tilly's flower-like face, or a
single trace of sophistication to her ingenuous nature.

" Oh, I'm so tired, the new play's going to be
dreadful.   It won't come alive !   Six hours yesterday,
two hours this morning—oh, what a funny smell ! "
she said.

I looked at Tilly miserably.   Of course her sharp
nose found it.

" Whatever is it ? " she asked, her delicate nostrils
twitching like a rabbit eating lettuce.

" I can't find out ! " I said, removing her coat.

" Well, I should say this is the real thing ! " observed the director, with adenoids, from Hollywood.

I was not sure whether he meant the cottage or the smell.

Tilly went on into the study.

" Why, it's here, too ! " she said.

" It's everywhere—it comes and goes," I replied. " I can't get to the bottom of it."

But Tilly had halted, and a pitying smile came over her face, whose value had risen from three hundred a year to twenty thousand pounds in three short years.

" You goose—it's there ! " she said, pointing to the fire. " It's that log ! "

" Nonsense, my dear," I retorted. " I always burn logs, and the smell comes and goes, just the ——"

She interrupted me.

" You're burning laurel logs. That's the cause. Smell ! " she commanded, and catching my hand made me bend with her over the fire.

" It does smell," I admitted. " Do you think that's it ? "

" Didn't you know laurel wood is quite impossible on a fire ? How long have you been burning it ? "

As soon as she asked the question I knew she was right. Two years ago three of my laurel trees had mysteriously died. I had cut them down, sawn them into small logs, and thrown them in a heap, which had been mixed with the beech logs. From time to time a piece of this laurel wood had got on to the fire. Motto for the future : whatever your laurels, never burn them.

There is one article by my fireplace that puzzles my guests. Once, when staying at a country house, I came down just before dinner into the drawing-room, to find a grandson solemnly walking to and fro, swinging a long thin log from whose charred end arose a filmy smoke. A delicious incense pervaded the room, and then it was that I recalled a passage in Burton's *Anatomy of Melancholy* : " The smoke of Juniper is in great request with us at Oxford to sweeten our chambers." When I left, I was presented with a log, decorated by the butler with a scarlet ribbon, brass-studded at one end, to prevent it being thrown on the fire. It sweetened my study for a year.

And while we are round the fireplace let me show you another article that has puzzled my visitors. It stands in a recess, and looks like a pewter tankard. It has a lid, and from this lid protrudes something like the handle of a soldering iron. This is my invaluable ' Cape Cod firelighter.' I first saw it in the house of an American friend, who had built himself a delightful retreat on an estuary at Milton Point, Chester County, New York. The tankard was half-filled with paraffin, and on the end of the iron rod was a lump of porous stone saturated with the paraffin. When lit this made an excellent fireball that would start any fire on its course without the worry of firelighters, bellows, and that dangerous expedient, the newspaper spread as a draught-maker.

I have said that, without the open fire, the English home will lose much of its character. This was never more apparent than one winter's evening when I had dined with friends at Turville. Dinner finished, our hostess retired, and three of us were left with the port. Presently, wandering off by myself, I made my way to the sitting-room. There, on the threshold, I paused, arrested by a scene that might have been set a century earlier. In the grate blazed a log fire. The room was softly lit, warm with cushions and rugs. My hostess's back was to me, as she sat in a low chair, her gown slightly Empire, and hair drawn up from the nape to match. But what gave the scene its note of the late eighteenth century was the occasional-table on which was spread some dried lavender that my hostess was picking. Exactly thus, one hundred or two hundred years ago, the lady of the house had sat picking lavender, to put into bags and tuck away in the linen closet.

And when, later, I assisted at this pleasant task, I learned something. I had gathered up the picked stalks, and was about to burn them.

" No," said my hostess, " don't burn them. Make them smoulder and leave them on the hearth."

I did this, and the delicious scent of lavender filled the room.

# THE ENGLISH CREED

Lovely the roses of old Stamboul,
And the stars in Taj Mahal's dark pool,
The cypress dreams on Garda's shore,
Wild sunsets crimson Elsinore,
> But here, together,
Roses and stars and cypress meet
> In rain-sweet weather.

An English manor house, a pond,
Green fields that fall to woods beyond,
A level lawn, a porch where blows
White clematis—the wanderer knows
> There's no denying
Above all other lands 'tis best
> To live or die in !

159

# CHAPTER VIII

## MISS MARY BLANDY

ALL really old houses that wish to be held in veneration are expected to provide a ghost. A good ghost enhances the value of the property these days when we exhibit no real fear of such things. I have always been anxious to meet a ghost and get on to speaking terms with one, but they are elusive things. Whenever I have been staying in their houses, they have declined to walk. Are there such things ? Well, that is a question it is vain to ask. The countryside firmly believes in them.

Near me there is, or was, the famous ghost of the Nettlebed donkey. In some way it was associated with the old windmill that stood on the Common and was burned down by mischievous boys, to the great loss of the district, for it was a famous and lovely old relic. When the windmill disappeared, the ghost of the Nettlebed donkey seems to have been laid. It has not been seen again. But I had the most trustworthy witness to its existence formerly. For generations the ghost of a lame donkey had been encountered roaming the common and the woods of Nettlebed. It mysteriously appeared and disappeared before the eyes of wayfarers, and it was known, not only by its vanishing trick, but also by its walk, for it was a lame donkey and hobbled painfully along.

Now there lives near Turville Heath an army gentle-man, a practical man of the world, married to a very practical lady.  No one would ever suspect either of them to believe in nonsense or to admit the existence of apparitions.  They are a hard-riding, level-headed pair.  Judge of my surprise one day, therefore, as we walked across Turville Park, when he said, "And down there, in that field, my wife saw the ghost of the Nettlebed donkey."

I knew nothing then about the famous ghost of the Nettlebed donkey, and immediately asked for details. It transpired that one evening my companion's wife had seen a donkey painfully hobbling along a path through the field.  Moved to compassion by the plight of this animal, she went towards it.  For a time the donkey allowed her to approach, and then proceeded to walk away in the direction of a thick hedge.  She followed, but to her amazement when the donkey arrived at the hedge it walked on and passed right through it, leaving her dumbfounded before a solid hedge !

Now, this was not hearsay, such as is the vehicle of most ghost stories.  It came from the General direct, and a few minutes later I was sitting at tea with his wife.  I have never been nearer to a ghost than this, although I am aware a donkey makes a poor show against an armour-rattling knight, or a spectre with its head in its hands.

I suppose the country everywhere is literally be-spattered or 'decorated' with horrors.  There is always a murder house or a fearful wood, the scene of blood-curdling crime.  My own district is not without these sites of bloodshed. Generally there is one grim house described as the place where ' 'e-chopped-'er-'ead-off.' On a road that leads up to Fawley there is a house pointed out as the scene of a dire tragedy. Fearful is the story of a man foaming at the mouth who, after shooting his wife, two children, and two servants, took to the woods with a gun and filled the whole neighbourhood with terror until he was found shot. The story is embellished by the country mind, though the tragedy was real enough. A most respectable and affectionate father in a delirium had shot his wife, children, and servants, and then, in the wood below, had committed suicide. The lane past that house is black at night, and with the wind moaning through the high elms it cannot be wondered at that the country folk scurry by.

Nearer, in the wood just above me, and almost in sight of my windows, there is a farm-house that is credited with a murder of the ' 'e-chopped-'er-'ead-off ' definition. Once, when the place stood vacant, I explored it. After a month in that lugubrious house, I would have been capable of chopping off anybody's head. In the dark dairy there was a kind of sunk pit that was a real incitement to murder.

But the murder story *par excellence* is located in Henley, the story of Miss Mary Blandy, who murdered her father by putting poison in his water-gruel, in the year 1751.

There is still *The White Hart Inn*, and there is still a Blandy House in Hart Street, the main thoroughfare leading to the bridge, and not yet wholly spoilt by modern ' improvements.' *The White Hart* has still the yard in which, of old, bear-baiting was watched from

163

the gallery, but Blandy House is a mid-Victorian erection on the site of the house where lived Mr. Francis Blandy, a much-respected elderly gentleman, who was an attorney, Town Clerk of Henley, and steward to many of the gentry in the locality. Mr. Blandy was renowned for his liberal hospitality, his sound sense, and his considerable fortune. What exactly that fortune was no one knew, but Miss Mary Blandy was considered a prize, and aspirants were not wanting.

In this house, where plenty and comfort, a good table, and excellent service were the order of the day, Mary Blandy grew up, idolised by her fond parents, a young lady in a circle of gentility wherein Mr. Blandy, by a wise marriage of his daughter, hoped to increase his social importance. On her mother's side Mary Blandy's ancestry was not negligible, for her mother's brother was Mr. Serjeant Stevens, of Doctors' Commons, and of Culham Court, a most respectable property just over the river; another uncle was the Rev. Stevens, the Rector of Fawley.

At fourteen Miss Blandy was highly accomplished in all the duties of the house, and later events proved her to be an able writer, though she cannot have profited much by a liberal instruction in "the principles of religion and piety, according to the rites and ceremonies of the Church of England." Fate was unkind to her in one respect—like so many unfortunates of that age she had been a victim of the smallpox, which had left her face pitted. Her figure, however, was good, her black eyes brilliant, her manner vivacious. Moreover, it was no secret that she carried with her hand a dower of ten thousand pounds.

Henley society could boast of a smart set in those days. The fashion was led by General Conway and his wife, Lady Ailesbury, up at Park Place, the Freemans at Fawley Court, the Coopers at Phyllis Court, and the lesser landowners and gentry, together with a sprinkling of military gentlemen and local bucks.

For a time the field did not seem promising enough for a father so socially ambitious and a daughter such a rich prize. So one fine day the little attorney left his house, and at great expense gave his wife and daughter a season in Bath, then an excellent marriage market. For it was still the Bath of Beau Nash, of George II, and the Prince of Wales, with whom Miss Blandy once had the honour of dancing.

The results of this visit, matrimonially considered, were poor. A young apothecary was snubbed for his temerity. There was a Mr. H., to whom it was conveyed in an elegant and friendly manner that his means were inadequate, also a Mr. T., a gentleman and a soldier who was frightened off by the demand for settlements, and Captain D., who for a period, such was his ardour and gallantry, as well as his family and fortune, seemed in favour. An engagement followed, and, delighted, Mary walked with her lover in the fields around Henley. Alas, the gallant captain was ordered abroad, and poor Mary was left to dream of her absent lover!

It was during this period that another suitor appeared. There exists to this day in Henley, ' Paradise House,' a house with a considerable garden behind, in which there is still the Judas tree beneath which Mary and her new lover mingled their sighs. For

Mary was now courted by and enamoured with a gentleman of fashion, Captain the Hon. William Henry Cranstoun. He was a Scots soldier, staying with his kinsman, General Lord Mark Kerr, who had taken Paradise House and extended his hospitality to the obsequious little attorney and his family.

When the nature and the seriousness of Captain Cranstoun's attentions were known there was exultation in the Blandy household. Here was a true aristocrat, the fifth son of a Scots peer, the fifth Lord Cranstoun and his wife Lady Jane Kerr, eldest daughter of the Marquis of Lothian. Mr. Blandy at once saw a bright opportunity for his daughter. To think he had wasted all that money at Bath while here on his Henley doorstep was a scion of such great breeding !

Captain Cranstoun left Henley for a time. Captain D. returned from abroad, but not to Henley. He let it be seen very plainly that he was no longer interested in Miss Blandy. For some reason he ended the affair. Happily, there was now Captain Cranstoun.

It would be difficult to imagine a man who fitted better the fashionable melodrama's formula for a knave and a villain, except that he was not dashing and handsome. Actually he was mean in face and figure, pitted, like his love, with the smallpox, sandy, and weak-eyed. He was thirty-three years of age and, as detail after detail emerged, he possessed every disqualification except that of birth. But as soon as this aristocratic wastrel declared his passion, he was welcomed with unbounded joy into the Blandy family. He took up his abode at Blandy House, and proceeded with his courtship.

The course of this affair could not possibly run smooth, but for a time the man of fashion enchanted mother, father, and daughter alike. Then one day a bombshell fell in the Town Clerk's office. Lord Mark Kerr, outraged by his grand-nephew's conduct, informed Mr. Blandy that his proposed son-in-law had a wife and child in Scotland ! Captain Cranstoun repudiated the marriage, legitimate in every detail, although he knew his wife was now seeking in the courts at Edinburgh a clear definition of their marriage.

Mr. Blandy forthwith exhibited his indignation, but his wily guest was ready with an answer. " As I have a soul to save I am not, nor ever was, a married man ! " he declared, notwithstanding the fact that his mother had invited her daughter-in-law to the family seat, and his own brother had held his child at the christening ceremony. Captain Cranstoun's explanation was at once forthcoming. He had been trapped by a former mistress, and the courts would dismiss her impudent claim. Lord Mark Kerr had acted in spite, recalling an old grudge. To men of fashion, as Mr. Blandy would well understand, these ' affairs ' were not uncommon. Plainly put, the lady's action savoured of blackmail. If he would only await the issue, Mr. Blandy would see his name cleared.

With misgivings, and importuned by his wife, now completely under the glamour of their high-born guest, Mr. Blandy agreed to wait and let the engagement stand.

At the end of his first visit, which closed in the spring of 1748, Cranstoun went to London. Mrs. Blandy and her daughter visited a friend, Mrs. Pocock, at

Turville Court, a house high up on the Chiltern heath, some five miles from Henley. While there Mrs. Blandy fell ill, and her constant prayer was, "Let Cranstoun be sent for." He came, and there followed another six months' free lodging under the Blandys' roof. There were times when Mr. Blandy was openly rude to his adhesive guest. As for the case in the courts, Captain Cranstoun was marked down for the scamp he was. The marriage was declared legitimate, he was ordered to pay an annuity of £40 to his wife and £10 to his daughter, and to pay the expenses amounting to over £100.

Nothing of this would have come to Blandy's ears had not Mrs. Cranstoun, aware of her husband's duplicity, written to him, enclosing a copy of the court's decree. One would have expected this to end the Cranstoun connection, but that plausible villain declared the court had erred, and he would win an appeal, an action which had been advised.

Captain Cranstoun was a peer's brother, and the ineradicable snobbery in Mr. Blandy's nature led him to base a hope on this new project, and he postponed breaking the engagement. But by this time he was both irritated and suspicious. On the last day of September 1749, Mrs. Blandy died after a brief illness. At the very end she pleaded for the noble captain. " Mary has set her heart upon Cranstoun. When I am gone, let no one set you against the match," she said to her husband.

Mary Blandy wrote to her lover, now in London, and urged him to return. He replied that he could not leave the house for fear of the bailiffs. Mary despatched fifteen pounds and released the Captain. On his arrival Mr. Blandy was not very gracious. He was rapidly losing faith in that appeal.

It was at this moment that Cranstoun stepped towards murder. While in Scotland, he told Miss Blandy, he had met with a ' love-powder ' highly recommended. But Mary at once declared her disbelief in love-philtres, and the suggestion was dropped, Cranstoun observing, " If I had any of these powders I would drop them into something Mr. Blandy should drink." Afterwards, at her trial, the court was to hear much about these powders intended to make Mr. Blandy ' kind to her lover.'

The peace of Henley was rudely broken one day by a dunning letter from the Captain's creditors. The lovers were in a state of alarm lest the Captain's financial position should get to the ears of Mr. Blandy, whose irritation was now plain to see. Mary contrived to find the requisite fifteen pounds, and her gallant was despatched to London to stop proceedings. One would have thought that this infatuated young woman had by now seen the man for the scoundrel and poltroon he was. But worse was to follow, and she remained obstinately attached to the ugly little creature.

Cranstoun returned to Henley in August 1750. " He must come, I suppose," said old Blandy, and when the Captain arrived he told the usual lies about his impending appeal in the Scottish courts. It was at this stage that the love-philtre was tried, according to Mary Blandy. Cranstoun put some of the powder in the old gentleman's tea. Its effect, Miss Blandy attested later, was miraculous. Mr. Blandy lost his crossness, and showed himself most affable to the designing sponger in his house.

One day, when the Captain was out, Mary indulged in a little prying among his papers. Actions of this kind are invariably bitterly rewarded, and so it was with Mary. To her consternation she came across a letter from a mistress the gallant Captain was keeping in London.

Confronted with this evidence, the wretched man grovelled at her feet, sobbing and beseeching forgiveness. Indignant, she ordered him to leave the house. Conjuring up the memory of her mother, and playing on her partiality towards him, the glib Captain succeeded in extracting a pardon. Poor, foolish Mary Blandy ! She had already faced a confession he had made, in a moment of intimacy, that he had erred and was torn with contrition. He had had a daughter by yet another mistress a year before he met Mary. Two mistresses and a child, a wife and child whom he basely repudiated, creditors on every hand, such were the liabilities of this half-pay Captain whose only asset was that he was an Honourable, though of the most dishonourable variety.

In November he was borrowing again. His mother, Lady Cranstoun, lay ill, and he had no money for his stage fare to Scotland. Mary again gave him money, and at six o'clock one November morning he set off in a post-chaise. Old Blandy rose to speed the parting guest. It was the last meeting of the trio. But before Cranstoun went, in a gesture of romance, he had made an assignation with Mary in the grounds of Park Place, and it is believed that their diabolical plot was hatched there. The favourite walk of the pair became known thereafter as " Blandy's Walk," and one may see to-day, as fair as it was then, the sylvan scene where the lovers pursued their disastrous courtship.

The Captain was gone, but not before paving the way for strange happenings. He had staged a nice little ghost-walking scene. Cranstoun had declared he could not sleep for rappings, bangings, footfalls, and strains of unearthly music. Then one morning he announced that Mr. Blandy's wraith had appeared in his bedroom, with white stockings, a coat, and a cap on its head. Mr. Blandy had no patience with this nonsense, and called his guest light-headed. But Cranstoun insinuated, through Mary, to the maids that all these signs were messengers of doom and Mr. Blandy's end was surely near.

It was, but it was most clumsily encompassed by his determined daughter. Mr. Blandy's health began to fail. He was now sixty-one years of age, a man of active life who was troubled with gout and gravel. He was worried over his daughter's affair, he had lost his wife, and now he was losing his teeth. But he was strong enough to take one step. Now that the wretched Cranstoun was gone, he told his daughter to write, breaking off her futile engagement. He would have had still more reason had he known what was known to the lovers, namely, that the appeal in the Courts had been peremptorily dismissed.

Mary's letter conveying her obdurate father's view seems to have stirred the lovers to action. She received from Cranstoun a letter saying he had seen the woman who made the magic powder, from whom he had obtained a supply, and that he would send it along with a present of Scotch pebbles.

All of us who have delved among the relics of our great-grandmothers will recall those monstrous ornaments known as Scotch pebbles. They were made up into weighty bracelets and fearsome brooches, sometimes they decorated workboxes and ' escritoires.' Around 1750 they were the very height of fashion.

The pebbles arrived, and with them a packet inscribed " Powder, to clean the Scotch pebbles."

In June 1751, Mr. Blandy began to suffer acute internal pain. Susan Gunnell, a maid, drinking the tea her master had left, was violently sick for three days. On another occasion an old charwoman who had also drunk some tea left by Mr. Blandy became so ill that she had to go home.

It became obvious that tea was an unsuitable vehicle for the powder. Cranstoun was consulted, and suggested a substance on whose surface it would not float. Accordingly, Mary mixed it in her father's water-gruel. Mr. Blandy was violently ill and the apothecary was called in. That evening she again carried up some gruel and Mr. Blandy was again sick. Unluckily, the next morning the charwoman ate up the remaining gruel, and was so ill that she did not recover in time to give evidence at the trial.

It was not long before Mary Blandy took up more gruel to her father, and the maids, now suspicious, examined the pan and discovered a white sediment. Susan, the maid, locked up the pan, which later was conveyed to the apothecary.

The Rev. Mr. Stevens, of Fawley, hearing of his brother-in-law's illness, called to see him, and Susan took him aside and stated her suspicions. On his advice she reported her observations to her master. As soon as the shock had passed Mr. Blandy asked Susan where she thought his daughter had obtained the poison, and she named Cranstoun, whereupon the old man cried out, seeing the whole plot—" Oh, that villain ! That ever he came to my house ! "

The next morning Mr. Blandy went down to breakfast, and Mary again passed him his tea. He tasted it, and then fixing his eyes on his daughter, remarked that it was peculiar, and asked if she had put anything into it. She denied the suggestion. A little later, now alarmed by events, Mary Blandy consigned her lover's letters and the powder to the kitchen fire, but she failed to notice that the maid, watching covertly, afterwards rescued some of the remains, and kept them as deadly evidence.

Mr. Blandy's condition being now so serious, a specialist, Dr. Addington, was called from Reading. He at once saw that Mr. Blandy had been poisoned. Promising to return, he took with him a specimen from the gruel pan and from the rescued papers. As he surmised, the powder was arsenic.

Events had now developed to a point at which Mary Blandy was forbidden to enter the sick-room. Later, sent for and confronted with the evidence, she fell on her knees at her father's bedside and implored forgiveness.

" I forgive thee, my dear, and I hope God will forgive thee, but thou shouldst have considered better than to have attempted my life," he cried, and later, responding to her entreaties, " I bless thee, and hope God will bless thee and amend thy life. Do, my dear, go out of my room lest thou shouldst say anything to thine own prejudice."

That evening, by Dr. Addington's orders, Mary Blandy was confined to her room and a guard set over her. The following day Mr. Blandy's condition was beyond hope, and after great agonies he died on Wednesday, August 14th, 1751. He was buried at night in Henley Parish Church, after an inquest had been held.

By now all Henley and the countryside were aware of the horrid facts, and when, the next day, Mary Blandy escaped from her room, and fled down the street and over Henley Bridge, she was followed by so hostile a crowd that she took refuge in *The Angel*, the old inn still at the foot of White Hill. An alderman escorted her back in a closed post-chaise.

The next journey was to Oxford Gaol, there to await her trial for murder. But being a gentlewoman, she made the journey in spirit and style, accompanied by her maid, and very privately escorted by two constables. To avoid the mob, now greatly incensed, they started out early in a landau with four horses, and reached Oxford at eleven.

On arrival Mary's chief anxiety seemed to be whether she was to be fettered, but she was reassured on this point. Indeed, her imprisonment for a time was more like a private retirement. She had taken with her, not only a maid, but also a supply of her favourite tea. The best rooms in the keeper's house were reserved for her. No one was allowed to molest her. She walked in the keeper's garden, and in the evening played cards with her maid.

The Blandy affair was now the sensation of the country. There was an outcry for the apprehension of Cranstoun, who, from some bungling in official quarters, had avoided arrest and gone into hiding. So incensed were " the Noblemen and Gentlemen in the Neighbourhood of Henley-on-Thames " that they sent a petition to the Duke of Newcastle, expressing their thanks for King George's " Paternal Goodness to his people " for directing a public prosecution, and asking that a reward might be offered for the apprehension of " the Wicked Contriver and Instigator of this Villainous Scheme."

It was too late, the bird had already flown, with the connivance of his noble relatives. He succeeded in crossing the Channel. Meanwhile the clamour grew, and a suspicion was abroad that Miss Blandy, a gentlewoman, might succeed in moving powerful influences to aid her escape. The Sheriff of Oxford was therefore instructed to make the conditions of imprisonment more severe. The fetters were riveted on her ankles and the garden exercise was curtailed. Terror was also struck into the heart of her maid and gaolers by threats of dire punishment if she escaped.

There were not those lacking who saw in Miss Blandy a poor innocent dupe of the villainous Captain. A tornado of pamphlets arose and swept the country. Lady Ailesbury, newly come to Park Place, bought after negotiations with Mr. Blandy, a trustee of the estate, was convinced of her innocence, as was also the prison chaplain, whose reputation was none too sweet.

Up to this point Miss Blandy had carried herself with dignity and coolness, but when the fetters were riveted on her the reality of her plight could no longer be ignored. " Immediately on my arrival," wrote an official assuringly to his Superiors, " I went to the Castle, where I found Miss Blandy with the very same Iron on her leg which I saw riveted on, myself, when last here, and which I now believe has never been off since, for her leg is considerably swelled, and the Red Cloth which was round the iron before has been cut off to give her room, but it is so close as renders it impossible to be slipt over her Heel."

She was tried on Tuesday, March 3rd, 1752, in the hall of the Divinity School at Oxford, the Town Hall being then in a process of rebuilding, and the University authorities having refused the use of the Sheldonian Theatre. The trial began at eight o'clock in the morning, and the case was tried before the Hon. Heneage Legge and Sir Sidney Stafford Smythe. After the indictment had been delivered, the Hon. Mr. Bathurst began his address for the Crown. He covered all the facts of the case, which might have rested there, but a frightful windbag, Serjeant Hayward, arose, and at great length added nothing to the knowledge of the jury, occupied the time of the Court with his rodomontade, and concluded an unnecessary performance with an exhortation to a section of the packed assembly. " But you, young gentlemen of this University, I particularly beg your attention, earnestly beseeching you to guard against the first approaches and temptations to vice. See here the dreadful consequences of disobedience to a parent ! "

Miss Mary Blandy in Oxford Castle Gaol, 1751

The long day wore to its close. Throughout, save for a few moments after her godmother had given evidence, Mary Blandy showed no emotion, and, as was the custom then, made the speech in her own defence. " I can assure your lordships," she concluded, " as I am to answer it before that great Tribunal where I must appear, I am as innocent as the child unborn of the death of my father. I would not endeavour to save my life at the expense of truth. I really thought the powder an innocent, inoffensive thing, and I gave it to procure his love."

But the evidence was too damning. After five minutes' consultation the jury gave a verdict of ' Guilty.' It was now nine o'clock in the evening. The tallow candles had long been lit, and in the gloom of that great hall the frail young woman of thirty-three heard the sentence of doom.

She was composed to the end, and in a level voice made a last request of her judge, " That your lordship would please to allow me a little time till I can settle my affairs and make my peace with God." The request was granted, and the execution was fixed for April 4th, and postponed later to Monday the 6th, as the University authorities observed that such an event in Holy Week would seem improper.

When Mary Blandy left the court she " stepped into the Coach with as little concern as if she had been going to a Ball," ran a contemporary account, and, finding her gaoler's family in distress at the news, exclaimed, " Don't mind it. What does it signify ? I am very hungry ; pray, let me have something for supper as speedily as possible." She may have said this, but the

Press from earliest times has never lacked an unscrupulous imagination.

She had five weeks before the solemn final scene, five weeks of considerable literary activity. A " Reverend Divine of Henley-upon-Thames " addressed to her an elaborate exhortation to confess her crime. Miss Blandy replied that she was innocent, and sent him her own version. The clergyman's letter and her own were published on March 20th under the title, " A letter from a Clergyman to Miss Blandy."

This started the pamphlet tornado. It was speedily met by " An Answer to Miss Mary Blandy's Narrative." A defender arose to pen " The Case of Miss Blandy considered, as a Daughter, as a Gentlewoman, and as a Christian." Miss Blandy's final shot was a longer version of the Narrative she had forwarded to the clergyman. It must have occupied her last days on earth. " Witness my hand, Signed by Miss Mary Blandy in the Castle at Oxford, April 4, 1752, in the presence of two Clergymen, members of the University of Oxford." It was not published until two days after the execution, and was such a solemn protestation of innocence on the verge of the scaffold that it moved large numbers to believe there had been a miscarriage of justice.

But criminologists have pointed out that murderers will lie even on the gallows, and last protestations are usually worthless. In her Narrative she complained of the noise in court during the trial, while paying a testimony to the fairness of the judge. " But most surprising treatment ! without going out of the Court, without being any time consulting, their verdict was,

Guilty ! God's will be done ! My behaviour at my trial, and when sentence was passed, I leave to the world." And after an exhortation to ' the Christian Reader,' she concludes, " Whosoever thou art, whose eyes drink  ı this sad and moving tale, indulge one tear. Remember the instability of sublunary things, and judge no man happy till he dies."

The final narrative was a document of over ten thousand words, and showed considerable adroitness in avoiding the most conclusive proofs of her guilt. Her conduct during and after trial certainly was above reproach, except in one instance. She never lost her spirit, and her bearing would seem an example of tremendous bravado were one not compelled to conclude that she was merely callous.

There was at the time another woman, Elizabeth Jeffries, who lay under sentence of death for murder. Mary Blandy read the trial, and agreed that the murder was barbarous, but observed, " Poor, unhappy girl, I pity her ! " which so shocked a lady visiting Miss Blandy that she left in indignation, whereupon Mary remarked, " I can't bear with these over-virtuous women. I believe if ever the devil picks a bone, it is one of theirs ! "

She wrote to her fellow-convict expressing sympathy, and the young lady replied. Finally, she confessed her guilt, and Mary, after some reproaches for the deception practised, concluded the correspondence, saying she would be her suitor at the Throne of Mercy.

The fatal day drew near. Not all the pamphleteering had shaken the evidence, or moved the Government to consider a reprieve. The evening before the execution, Mary Blandy asked to be allowed to view the gallows, so that, when the hour approached, the sight would not shock her to the extent of rendering her incapable of her last speech.

This request was accorded, and at dawn the next morning she went into the upper rooms of her prison, and looked down upon the Green, where the gallows had been made by laying a pole across from tree to tree. She observed that it was very high. At half-past eight the chaplain visited her, and after half an hour of prayers they went down into the gaol-yard, where the Sheriff's officers met them. She held two guineas in her hand for the executioner, which she took with her to the fatal tree. She was dressed in a black crêpe sack, with her arms and hands tied with black paduasoy ribbons. " Her whole dress extremely neat ; her countenance was solemn, and her behaviour well suited to her deplorable circumstances ; she bore up under her misfortune with amazing fortitude."

She addressed the crowd, affirming her innocence, and that she had administered the powders to her father without knowing they had any poisonous quality. Finally, she ascended the ladder.

Hanging in those days was a matter of strangulation. A humane executioner had not yet invented the noose and drop which cause instantaneous dislocation of the spine. A contemporary account records the gruesome finale.

" As she ascended the ladder, after she had gone up about five steps, she said, ' Gentlemen, do not hang me high, for the sake of decency,' and then, being desired to step up a little higher, she did two steps, and then turning herself about, she trembled and said, ' I am afraid I shall fall.' After this the halter was put about her neck, and she pulled down her handkerchief over her face, without shedding one tear all the time. In this manner she prayed a little while upon the ladder, then gave the signal, by holding out a little book which she had in her hands.''

The ladder was then snatched away, and, to use the phrase of the time, she '' was launched into Eternity.''

The next scene was the most barbarous. The crowd, now in tears, watched her dangling body for half an hour until the Sheriff's officer came to cut her down. No proper arrangements had been made. '' There was neither coffin to put her body in, nor hearse to carry it away ; nor was it taken back into the Castle, which was only a few yards, but upon being cut down was carried through the crowd upon the shoulders of one of the Sheriff's men in the most beastly manner, with her legs exposed very indecently for several hundred yards, and there deposited in the Sheriff's man's house till about half an hour past five o'clock, when the body was put in a hearse and carried to Henley.''

At midnight on Monday, April 6th, 1752, there was a great concourse of people inside and outside Henley Parish Church. It had been rumoured that the body of Mary Blandy was to be buried, at her own request, at midnight, in the family grave in the chancel, where lay her mother and father. Shortly before 1 a.m. the hearse from Oxford arrived, and in the dim chancel, by candle-light, was enacted the last scene in a grim drama.

Only by a few weeks had this interment been possible. Murder being rife, and a savage judicial system full of monstrous abuses failing to deter crime, a law was passed that same year ordering executions the day but one after sentence, and giving the body to the Surgeons' Company for dissection. Hangings could also take place in chains.

The new law was applied two months after Mary Blandy's execution. " It is shocking to think what shambles this country is grown," wrote Horace Walpole. " Seventeen were executed this morning, after having murdered the turnkey on Friday night, and almost forced open Newgate." To General Conway, of Park Place, he observed, " Miss Blandy died with a coolness of courage that is astonishing, and denying the fact, which has made a kind of party in her favour ; as if a woman who would not stick at parricide would scruple a lie ! We have made a law for immediate execution on conviction of murder ; it will appear extraordinary to me if it has any effect, for I can't help believing that the terrible part of death must be the preparation for it."

In connection with the hanging of Mary Blandy and Elizabeth Jeffries, there was another circumstance in common. The ancient manorial laws operated in respect of both of these felons, and by an astonishing coincidence they held property in the same manor. As early as 1337, in the reign of Edward III, a Sir John de Molyns held a charter to keep a Court Leet as lord of the manor of Henley. This entailed the right to have a gallows, pillory, and tumbrel. In ancient times the man was hanged, the woman drowned, after a death sentence by the lord of the manor, and the charter was granted *de furca et fossa*, " of the gallows and the pit, for the hanging upon the one and drowning in the other."

The lord of the manor was entitled to the chattels of all felons, fugitives, waifs, and strays. It was incumbent upon him to maintain his apparatus for punishment, and in 1421 a lessee of the manor of Henley was proceeded against because he " did not provide the pillory, ducking-stool and gallows, that he obstructed the way from Fawley Lane to Kings Mead, and that his pasture was kept closed between his Common at Assenden and Henley Park."

At the time of the execution of Miss Blandy and Miss Jeffries the Corporation were lessees of the Manor and farmed the revenues. Mr. Gislingham Cooper, then living at Phyllis Court, was Lord of the Manor. By an astonishing coincidence it happened that both Miss Blandy and Miss Jeffries died possessed of property, the one of two fields, the other of a house, within the manor of Henley, and by the ancient law of escheat these became part of the Corporation's revenue from their lease of the Manor. In August 1752, Walpole, referring to this, wrote : " I have since been with Mr. Conway at Park Place, where I saw the individual, Mr. Cooper, a banker, and lord of the manor of Henley, who had those two extraordinary forfeitures from the executions of the Misses Blandy and Jeffries."

And what of the villain of the piece, Captain the Hon. Wm. Cranstoun ? He was safe across the Channel, and his family, who showed not the slightest conscience in the matter, made him an allowance. He was struck off the Half-pay Establishment, as an

absconder, and as an accomplice in the murder of
Mr. Blandy. On fleeing from England he escaped
to Boulogne, and sought out a distant relative, Mrs.
Ross. She persuaded him to change his name to
Dunbar, and for a time he thought he was safe. Unluckily he chanced upon some of his wife's relatives,
who threatened violence if he fell into their hands, and,
after hiding for a time, he fled to Ostend and then to
Furnes, a town in Flanders, then in the jurisdiction of
the Queen of Hungary. He stayed there, but in
November he fell ill, and after nine days' illness he
expired, fittingly, in " the most agonising torments,"
according to a contemporary pamphlet. He seemed,
to the very end, boastful about his conquest of
Mary Blandy.

" Nothing," said the Captain, " seems impossible
to Men of undaunted courage and spirits. . . . I am,
you know, the Son of a Nobleman, and consequently
have those high thoughts and ambitions which are in-
herent to those of noble Extraction. As a Younger
Son, my patrimony was too small to gratify my Passion
for those Pleasures enjoyed by my Equals. This put
me on contriving Schemes to answer the extent of
my Ambition."

His illness was said to be mysterious, and, according
to the pamphleteer, inflicted on him all the agonies he
merited—" he was swollen to that Degree that it was
apprehended he would have burst, and felt such
Torments in every Limb and Joint, as made him wish
for Death." Shortly before his death he became a
Roman Catholic. He died on December 2nd, 1752,
aged thirty-eight. His personal belongings, consisting

of laced and embroidered waistcoats, were sold to pay his debts, and his small fortune, already assigned by the Scottish courts, went to his wife and daughter.

The Holy Church seems to have made the most of its convert, for it gave him " a pompous funeral." The Corporation attended, and a grand Mass was said over his body in the Cathedral Church, which was finely illuminated.

Cranstoun's letters were all sealed in a box and sent to his brother Lord Cranstoun, who was careful, despite challenges, that they should never be seen. Moreover, the wretch who assisted in smuggling him out of England, despite the most solemn assurances was never paid for his trouble, or his cash disbursements to the needy Captain.

One touch of irony completes this sad history. Poor Mr. Francis Blandy provoked his end by a pious fraud. In his overweening vanity and social ambition, and to enable him to sell his daughter in a higher market, he had enormously exaggerated the dowry that went with Mary's hand. So far from being £10,000, it transpired, on his death, that his total fortune did not exceed £4,000. Had the scheming Cranstoun known this, it is doubtful whether he would have played such a desperate hand. If poor Mr. Blandy had not been a snob his daughter might have married a respectable attorney or apothecary and have graced his old age with grandchildren about his knees. But perhaps this is too much to have hoped from so unnatural a daughter. Enamoured by a scoundrel whose true character was never hidden from her, she seems to have walked resolutely to a felon's grave.

The case was the sensation of the age, it produced some forty pamphlets, a number of engravings, and, with newspaper and magazine accounts, a considerable *Blandyana*. To-day, when I pass Paradise House and Blandy House, it would not seem strange to me if I saw Miss Blandy emerge, in a neat sack dress, escorted by her ugly little Captain " the Wicked Contriver and Instigator of this Villainous Scheme " as " the Noblemen and Gentlemen of the Neighbourhood of Henley-upon-Thames " so rightly called him.

## MASQUERADE

If the faces of old houses
Bore signs of what happened within,
Some would be set in a grimace,
Some in a fearful grin,
Some would have lines still more beautiful
Than those they now show to the street,
And a Queen Anne face still entrance us
With a manner demure and sweet.
But the Georgian house might affright us,
And its mask of grave dignity
Fail to hide the unfading stain
Of a shameful conspiracy ;
While the dark Victorian villa,
With a face of stucco and grime,
That looks so murderous is probably
Quite innocent of crime.

The manor house, pure Tudor,
Considering the horrors within,
Should bear on its face of ineffable grace
The foul ravages of sin.
And strange to believe, the bungalow
So monstrous to the sight,
If the life within took outward shape,
Would fill us with delight.

Who would think for a moment that ruinous hovel
Saw the birth of Beau Brummell the dandy,
Or that flat-faced house in the Henley street
Was the home of the poisoner, Miss Blandy?

No, you never can tell from the face of a house
The tense drama enacted behind,
Whether love makes a heaven or lust makes a hell,
Emotions, fine, sinister, kind,
Not one leaves a trace on the outward face
And, perhaps after all, it is well—
For what horrors we'd meet in a walk down the street,
And how difficult life might become
If the windows scowled, and the threshold throbbed,
And the walls were no longer dumb!

# CHAPTER IX

## FAWLEY COURT

AT the very edge of the wood that runs up from the valley in which my cottage lies, to the crown of Henley Park, there is a little gamekeeper's lodge. It sits pleasantly enough with the wood behind it and a windmill water-pump rising above the fir and larch. It looks south upon the Fairmile, east towards Henley, where the church tower rises, and west up the Assenden Valley. Whenever I say it is a gamekeeper's lodge my friends look at me curiously.

" Why, it looks like a chapel, with that Gothic door and those lattice windows ! " they cry.

They are not wrong. It was a compromise originally between a schoolhouse and a chapel. It stands there, by Pack and Prime Lane, a memorial of piety, charity, and shocking bad taste. When Hallam, the historian, father of the young man who inspired Tennyson's *In Memoriam*, left Henley Park House in 1842, a Mr. and Mrs. Birch took it. They were touched by the plight of my village, which had three inns, no church, and no school. So they built this Gothic schoolroom for the children of the poor in the locality, and supplied it with a mistress, and an evening service once a week, themselves defraying the expense. Then, other provision being made, it fell into disuse, and became a gamekeeper's lodge.

When, along with the blacksmith's cottage at Fawley, it came into the market, I bought it for the same reason, to preserve, not only the cottage, but also the old game-keeper whose breeches and cloth gaiters are an essential note in the colour of rustic life. He pays me his rent every Monday morning with a punctuality by which I could set my clock, and when Bank Holiday Mondays come round, in order that the payment should not be delayed until Tuesday, he pays the rent on the previous Saturday ! I hardly know which to admire most—his sturdy independence, his Oxfordshire accent, his cloth gaiters, or his grand beard.

There exists an admirable " Council for the Pre-servation of Rural England " which wages war on speculative builders, corrugated iron, soulless Urban District Councils, petrol pumps, and Philistinism in all its forms, but what can be done for the preservation of rural types ? A few of us may buy their homes to keep them *in situ*, but when the type dies out, whence will come the craftsmen that made the English village the thing it is—or was ?

I am sorry the lodge is Gothic. Happily, the old brick has weathered, and it is a pretty piece of Oxford-shire flint work. It was difficult for anyone building around 1850 to escape the baleful influence of Pugin's Gothic mania and Ruskin's chapter on the " Nature of Gothic." They started the craze for mock Gothic that pitted England's face with dreadful buildings, and resulted in a ' restorer ' ripping out of Winchester College Chapel a lovely oak screen and wall panelling by Wren.

The lodge is the kind of house one cannot live

in without side-whiskers. Nevertheless, like side-whiskers, it has charm. The background of fir, larch, and beech, the small sloping garden, and the lovely views, have made it coveted of many.

But let us hurry past the lodge, for we are out on a short ramble that will take us up the woody lane to Henley Park House, then down by the Deer Park, on to the Marlow Road, and thence back by Fawley Court and Phyllis Court to the old *Bell Inn*. These four places are all associated in the history we shall stir up. As for what one's feet stir up in this lane, be not deceived, it is not mud, but a compost made from fifty years' accumulation of beech leaves. My gardener's faith in the growing power of this compost surpasses anything in a hair-restorer's advertisement. But we have not brought a bucket and spade with us to-day. We have left a note for two pounds of peas at the gamekeeper's lodge, admired his wallflowers, and wondered whether we shan't have to have a little bit of painting done ; and now we are free.

At the top of the lane we reach a plateau. On our right is the Deer Park, with a natural beacon for the bonfire in celebration of Queen Victoria's Diamond Jubilee. Among the horrors this Jubilee provoked, this park is not one of them. It commands a superb view of the Thames Valley, with wooded steeps across the river. It contains a herd of deer and many noble trees. It also contains a curiosity in a plantation of oaks in the form of a Maltese Cross, and a number of zarebas.

Not zebras, if you please. What, I asked, when I first heard this word, is a zareba ? There are some words that one likes at sight or sound. I have always wanted to own a toucan, as much for its name as for its colour. To this list of odd things I want I must add a ha-ha, a gazebo, and a zareba. Strange to relate, I am near enough to them even if I do not possess them. A charming neighbour wrote to say her mother had owned a pet toucan, so one day I may do likewise, since they survive in our climate.

When Miss Blandy went to Paradise House, and met her fatal lover, Captain Cranstoun, there was a ha-ha opposite the house. I lament its disappearance, but there is a splendid one at Greys Court. What is a ha-ha, you may ask ? It is a ditch or sunk fence serving the purpose of a hedge without breaking the prospect. An eighteenth-century poet has paid it a tribute.

> *In front a level lawn is seen*
> *Without a shrub upon the green,*
> *Where taste would find its first great law,*
> *But for the skulking, sly ha-ha,*
> *By whose miraculous assistance*
> *You gain a prospect two fields' distance.*

And how is ha-ha pronounced ? I have always followed the pronunciation of the villain in the melodrama. This poem suggests the pronunciation of the haughty colonel.

A park wall by which I drive has a gazebo, and the deer park is full of zarebas—little plantations of trees protected by railings. How that word has travelled ! It comes from the Arabic *zariba*, meaning a containing pen.

# FAWLEY COURT

A ditch on the far side of my lane sometimes tempts me to say I have a ha-ha, and it occurred to me in a flash of delight that, since my sun-bathing platform is over the external garden wall, and commands a view of the road, it might be called a gazebo ! There remain now, for the completion of my ambition, the toucan and the zareba. But you cannot very well support a zareba in a garden which is only a quarter of an acre, and my tiny dwelling could scarcely house the enormous beak of the toucan.

But we must pass the zarebas and the fallow deer, and press on, leaving Henley Park House, down the lane again towards the river meadow, where lies Fawley Court.

My corner of the Chilterns abounds in courts, commons, bottoms, heaths, and chalk pits. Fawley Court, Greys Court, Phyllis Court, Culham Court, Bolney Court, Harpsden Court, Turville Court, Wyfold Court, so the list runs. All the old houses with any pretensions to size took this grandiose name, and visiting them one is often moved to exclaim, " How pleasant are thy Courts, O Lords ! " These ' seats ' are never where the ' bottoms ' are, and mostly they avoid the commons, which are generally high up. The commons and the heaths are often magnificent expanses of turf, covered with broom or bracken, some with ponds and fringed with old cottages, and they are generally elevated, commanding the countryside. But to-day we are down by the river, in the flat meadows where the Thames glides quietly under Henley Bridge, past Phyllis Court, Fawley Court, and Greenlands, on to Hambleden Weir.

There is one noteworthy feature of this district. The rambler is scarcely ever prohibited from following his desire in the satisfaction of curiosity. The Chilterns abound in footpaths, and these often cut right across private estates, following a route in direct view of the house. When a friend of mine bought Greys Court, she was distressed on discovering that anyone could walk across the bottom of the lawn. She was somewhat reconciled to this ancient right when she learned that almost every other estate was similarly intersected, and that her own privacy was guarded by a noble ha-ha.

It is a public right that is seldom abused and never so tenaciously defended as when it is threatened with withdrawal. We often hear talk of the intolerance of country landowners. In the matter of poaching they were often ferocious in their application of monstrous laws. But they were seldom offensive, and more often were very hospitable in the privileges they allowed to the walkers over their domains. These privileges are so long established that they have now become almost unchallengeable rights.

I know of no other country where a man may roam over private property with such freedom. In Canada and America the landlord is so newly conscious of his possession that trespass is often opposed with bodily violence. Nowhere did I ever encounter a right-of-way across the grounds or parks of a private owner. I still remember the notice on a wire fence in Florida— " Anyone Found in Here Will Be Shot." But gentle manners are not a feature of a country in whose public parks are notices " Get off the Grass ! " This ferocity of ownership is in singular contrast to the renowned hospitality of the American.

There is a public footpath down the side of Phyllis Court, along the river, and across the front of Fawley Court. It then continues along the riverside beyond Temple Island, with its noble clump of trees and classic garden house, across the grounds of Greenlands, to the Marlow road. As for the woods in the vicinity, they are latticed with footpaths, and avenue after avenue of noble beeches opens up with bewildering enticement.

The most eminent occupant of Fawley Court was Sir Bulstrode Whitelock, who played so prominent a part in the struggle of Charles I. with his Commons. He rose to high office under Cromwell, going as his Ambassador to the Court of Queen Christina of Sweden, and succeeded in making his peace with Charles II. at the Restoration.

His father, Sir James Whitelock, bought Fawley Court in 1616, and he spent the following summer repairing the house and replanning the gardens. Sir James was Chief Justice of Chester, and afterwards a Judge of the Common Pleas. Charles I. knew and valued him, and thus it was, doubtless, he looked with favour on young Mr. Bulstrode Whitelock.

There is a glimpse of old Sir James during the terrible year of the Plague, 1625. " Henley, next town to your grandfather's house," wrote Bulstrode Whitelock for his children, " was infected, and it was so violent in a village in Berks called Remenham, over against Fawley, that in some families there children and servants were swept away, scarce one left of a family. Your grandfather was careful to keep his people retired, and his doors shut, not permitting any but necessary recourse to his house, and when any money was to be paid (as some was that harvest time) a tub of water was set without doores, and the money first put into it, and then taken forth by the party that was to receive it."

Old Sir James died at Fawley Court in 1632, and by good fortune his superb monument in Fawley Church remains intact to this day. His son Bulstrode, born in 1605, succeeded to Fawley Court and estate, but he was destined to see stormy times. We meet him at *The Bell Inn*, in 1633, waiting upon Archbishop Laud, then on his way to Oxford to entertain the King, and begging him to accept his hospitality at Fawley Court. He was in the Long Parliament, and was Chairman of the Committee for the trial of Lord Strafford, who observed to a friend that, whereas two of the committee used him ' like advocates,' Whitelock used him like a gentleman, while leaving out nothing material to be urged against him. His whole career was marked by his temperate conscientiousness, and thus, in 1643, he seemed well-fitted to be one of the Commissioners sent to treat for peace with the King at Oxford.

When Charles I. had flung down the gauntlet by raising his standard at Nottingham in 1642, his supporters began to recruit for the Royalist Army. The Commons took up the challenge, and thus it came about that Sir Bulstrode Whitelock went under their orders to apprehend the Earl of Berkshire, and others, who had sent a letter to the Corporation of Henley, and other Oxfordshire towns, calling them in the King's name to meet at Watlington on August 15th.

Whitelock, with six servants on horseback, was joined by John Hampden, his Buckinghamshire neighbour, with a company of Foot, and off they set for Watlington, where the Royalists took fright. The Earl of Berkshire and some associates found refuge in a neighbouring house, which Whitelock and Hampden beleaguered. The Earl and his friends were taken, and conveyed that night to Henley. Whitelock observes: " Finding the Lord very proud and peevish, and sullen, and empty in his discourse, I would not trouble myself any further to bear him company but left him to the guards to be conveyed to London."

Empty in his discourse ! One wonders how talkative Whitelock felt at that moment. " In this business," he wrote, " I received the hurt in my mouth by pistol shot, and I have cause to bless God that it was not worse, and I concealed it from my wife."

But there was something else besides capture to make the noble lord peevish. He was that difficult person, the scorned inventor. Sir Bulstrode Whitelock, five years back, had declined to be duped by one of the Earl's inventions.

When I read Dr. Plot's learned treatise on Oxfordshire, I found that delightful old gentleman had not only been looking into every corner of the country, and rousing the farmers to anger by his inquisitiveness, but he had actually been looking into the housewives' ovens. What he found there I found behind my own study fireplace, a large oven built into the back, which may be seen obtruding on the outside of my cottage like half of a large beehive. This acted both as bake oven and malt kiln. " These malt kilns of

Henley are so thriftily contrived that the kiln holes are placed in the backs of their kitchen chimneys, so that, drying their malt with wood, the same fire serves for that, and all the other uses of the kitchen beside." When we remember that in Dr. Plot's days tea was unknown among the peasants, and that practically the whole country drank beer for breakfast and other meals, the necessity of home-brewing is apparent.

" The Earl of Berkshire," recorded Sir Bulstrode Whitelock, " hoping to repair his indigent fortune by putting on foot and engaging in new projects and monopolies, had gotten a patent from the king for the sole making of a new kind of kiln for making of malt, and laboured to bring the same in use, particularly in Henley, a great malting town ; and he was to have money of all those who put up the new kiln."

How familiar it all sounds ! These indigent Earls are still with us, lending their names to new projects and monopolies, just as some of their wives lend their faces to face-powders, soaps, and dentifrices. Let us see how the Earl went to work to push his project, remembering the year is 1637.

" The better to persuade those of Henley to make use of his new kiln, which he pretended would save them much money in expense in firing, he offered me a share in his project that by my interest in Henley it might have the better reception. But I looked upon such projects as dishonourable and illegal, and little better than cheats, the issue of them being seldom found in any measure answerable to the pretences ; and therefore I refused to join with him, but rather opposed his design therein ; at which his lordship's pride and disappointment conceived great disgust and ill-will against me."

No wonder the Earl felt peevish and sullen. He had sought to capture Sir Bulstrode, and now the wily knight had captured him !

Meanwhile, events were moving for the knight. In October 1642, the King decided to advance from Oxford on London. His army began to march on Henley, Reading, and the surrounding district. Prince Rupert quartered his brigade at Henley, and sent a regiment of horse to occupy Fawley Court.

" Sir John Biron and his brothers commanded those horse, and gave orders that they should commit no insolence at my house, nor plunder my goods ; but soldiers are not easily governed against their plunder, nor persuaded to restrain it, for there being about a 1000 of the king's horse quartered in and about the house, and none but servants there, there was no insolence and outrage usually committed by common soldiers on a reputed enemy which was omitted by these brutish fellows at my house. They had their whores with them, they spent and consumed two loads of corn and hay, littered their horses with sheaves of good wheat, and gave them all sorts of corn in the straw.

" Divers writings of consequence and books which were left in my study, some of them they tore in pieces, others they burnt to light their tobacco, and some they carried away with them, to my extreme great loss and prejudice, in wanting the writings of my estate and losing very many excellent manuscripts of my father's, and others, and some of my own labours."

This was bad enough. The rabble which either side was eager enough to enlist in the great struggle could not be expected to be nice-mannered, but what followed reads more like the Germans in Belgium and France in 1914 and 1915, soldiers invading foreign territory, than men despoiling the home of a fellow countryman.

"They broke down most of my park pales, killed most of my deer, and let out all the rest, only a tame young stag they carried away and presented to Prince Rupert, and my hounds which were extraordinary good. They eat and drank up all that the house could afford, broke up all trunks, chests and places, and where they found linen or any household stuff they took it away with them, and cutting the beds let out the feathers and took away the ticks ; they likewise carried away my coach and four horses, and all my saddle horses, and did all the mischief and spoil that malice and enmity could provoke barbarous mercenaries to commit, and so they parted."

In 1622 Sir Bulstrode's father had acquired Fillets Court, or Phyllis Court as it is now known. Sir Bulstrode had retired there after the pillaging of Fawley Court lower down the river. But the poor man had by no means come to the end of his troubles. Fillets Court was on the very edge of Henley town, and, when the Parliamentarians had flowed into the town after Prince Rupert's departure, they also decided to occupy Sir Bulstrode's new home. The Parliamentary General made a strong fort of it. "They did much mischief to me and my woods and houses," moans Sir Bulstrode, "tho' I was a parliament man, and the General himself and most of the officers my particular friends."

The house already had a moat round it and a draw-bridge in front. It was garrisoned with three hundred foot and a troop of horse. The purpose of all this was to command Greenlands down the river, which was held by the Royalists. Between these garrisons stood Fawley Court " miserably torn and plundered by each of them."

We can derive some idea of the manner in which family ties and friendships were torn asunder by the Civil War when we learn that Greenlands was held for the King by Sir John Doyley. Cannon-balls from Greenlands and cannon-balls from Fillets Court passed over or through Fawley Court, pommelled in between. Yet here, little more than ten years before, in his private chapel, Sir James Whitelock had gathered together his friends for the ceremony of consecration by the Lord Bishop of Lincoln. The guests included Sir Cope Doyley, whose son, Sir John Doyley, garri-soned and fortified Greenlands for the King, with a view to commanding the passage of the Thames from Henley and leading to London.

In May 1644, the Earl of Essex laid siege to this last stronghold of the Royalists in the district. By July he had almost destroyed the house. A few days later the garrison capitulated. There was additional irony in the fact that in 1651 Doyley was glad to sell the property to Sir Bulstrode, who now possessed the three badly damaged riverside houses !

A wily fellow, this Sir Bulstrode. As soon as Henley and the country around were firmly in the hands of his party, he obtained permission to dismantle the fortifications of Fillets Court. In August 1646, he enlisted an army of workmen with spades and pick-axes. He tells us gleefully of the sturdy work done by his neighbours, " who willingly came in to me. . . . I provided also stores of pickaxes and shovels for my soldiers, whom I encouraged to help in this work, allowing every one of them that would work sixpence a day beside their pay, which persuaded them all to work. In a few days, having many hands, I threw in the breast-works on two sides, and made two river-side walks—the one on the side next to the Thames, the other on the North side."

We will have a look at Phyllis Court on another ramble. For the moment we are on the river path in front of Fawley Court, which we have just left with the feathers flying in the bedrooms from poor Sir Bulstrode's slit ticks.

Like his friend, John Hampden, events and a sturdy sense of a man's rights had made a rebel of him, and like Hampden he would have welcomed the King back to his throne had the monarch confessed the error of his ways. But Sir Bulstrode, once the die was cast, did not look back. Cromwell found him a strong ally, as a commissioner in 1643 to treat for peace with the King, and as one of the three Commissioners of the Great Seal. He was nominated to the panel for trying the King, but he had no stomach for this, and declined to serve. At no time had he felt bitter towards Charles I., at whose escape across his lands he had probably connived when, attired as Dr. Ashburnham's servant, the King had passed through Lower Assenden, to Fawley and Hambleden Manor, where he rested a night.

Sir Bulstrode was made one of Cromwell's Lords, but never liked the title and abandoned it. He went, dutifully, as his country's ambassador to Sweden, to the court of Queen Christina, a risky proceeding, for some of Cromwell's ambassadors had been murdered. A more remarkable pair than the Queen and Sir Bulstrode it would be difficult to imagine.

Hollywood has given us a garbled and Garboed version of Queen Christina, who declared, in her memoirs—" I was born covered with hair ; my voice was strong and harsh." Nature played a trick on her, and Man was as unsympathetic to her as he is to all of Nature's misfits. She had the temperament of the male in the undistinguished body of a female. She parodied a man's attire, with flat heels, grey jacket, and flat cap.

With an insatiable lust for life, she had a quick tongue. She is probably the only woman who ever dared to visit the Pope in trousers. When she strode up the steps of St. Peter's, lined with Cardinals, on her way to an audience with His Holiness, she wore grey and gold breeches and a heavily plumed cavalier's cap. His Holiness carefully suppressed the shock he felt. After all, she had given up a throne and had driven across a continent in order to be received into the Church. He stood at the High Altar and received her while deafening cannon exploded all over Rome. She carried off the affair so well that, three days later, she was asked to dinner at the Vatican, where the Pope's table was a little taller, and the Pope's chair was a little higher, but where her own royal seat was surmounted by a canopy.

Sir Bulstrode took with him to Sweden two of his sons and thirty horses. On the way his ship was held up by contrary winds off the Nore, and he was thus able to learn, by special ferry service, that his beloved third wife had presented him with a thirteenth child, a son. The wind changed at once, and Whitelock, praising God, was borne across the North Sea.

That journey took seven days, the land journey from Gothenburg to Upsala fourteen. Outside Upsala a great coach was sent for him, accompanied by eighteen other coaches and a cohort of gentlemen. This display of State pleased the sturdy republican. He greatly incensed the notables who escorted him to his lodging by not descending the stairs to see them out, but he declared he was lame, and it was too painful. He shocked them again at a complimentary banquet by his flat refusal to drink a toast. He had not come to Sweden for nonsense of that kind.

Happily Queen Christina liked him. He was pompous, but he was trustworthy. He had a sense of style also, and at his first audience he had impressed Christina. His gentlemen were finely attired. They rode superb horses, the Ambassador himself wore a rich habit of black English cloth, a lined cloak, " both set with very fine diamond buttons, his hat band of diamonds answerable ; all of the value of £1,000."

At the second audience Christina walked him off his feet, so long did they talk and walk. She was more thoughtful afterwards. She delayed the commercial alliance he sought, and when Cromwell made himself

Protector, Sir Bulstrode had to wait for fresh credentials. She wanted to know how he sent his secret communications. He explained that he had invented an invisible ink. Two glasses of ' water' were left with the Secretary of the Council, one with which to write, the other for pouring over the Ambassador's letters when they arrived. Then the blank page suddenly appeared as a sheet of clear script.

He presented the Queen with a dog and a cheese. Finally, she had all his horses, but he had the alliance he sought. The fact that he was the first to whom she mentioned her plan of abdication shows she trusted him.

After Cromwell's death Sir Bulstrode supported Richard, and became Keeper of the Great Seal. At the Restoration he was not pursued vindictively, as many others. Charles II. is reported to have said to him, " Mr. Whitelock, go into the country—do not trouble yourself any more about State affairs—and take care of your wife and your sixteen children." He was buried at Fawley on August 6th, 1675.

The Fawley Court we are passing is not the house Sir Bulstrode saw pillaged. A new house was built, by a new owner, William Freeman, after the designs of Sir Christopher Wren, with a hall entered from an Ionic colonnade.

Sir Bulstrode spent his remaining years writing his memoirs for his children. This must have been a labour of love, unlike that of modern politicians, which is a labour of profitable annoyance to all their contemporaries. There is one passage describing the river at Henley, as he saw it flow past his windows, which is a mellow tribute to the beauty of the scene.

" These hills are richly adorned with pleasant woods and groves, consisting for the most part of beech, which crowne the topps of the hills, and att the foot of them gently glides the river Thames, offering to carry their burdens of wood and corne, to their chieffe citty, London. . . ."

No burdens of wood and corn go floating down to London now. Listen !

> *Oh, honey dewoo,*
> *I'm so blewoo*
> *Without youooo,*
> *Baby mine !*

In the drifting punt a gramophone carries the tumescent croon of a negro across the beauty of a summer's day. Naked limbs, contiguous, make a swan's neck arch in hissing disdain. I murmur some lines from Spenser to my companion :

> *Against their bridal day, which is not long,*
> *Sweet Thames ! run softly, till I end my Song.*

# JUNE BY THE RIVER

*Impulsive Sun, how well I know*
*The joy you feel this day of mirth*
*As, summer-flushed, you reckless go*
*Kissing each happy child of Earth ;*
*And I had thought the height of bliss*
*Was yours among those silver girls,*
*Sparkling and laughing in their fun—*
*But you have given a fiercer kiss*
*To that slim boy, the boatman's son,*
*Brown-limbed and crowned with wind-tossed curls.*

# CHAPTER X

## COTTAGE COOKERY

### I

WE are back in time for lunch, having taken a short cut
up through the Fawley Woods, along that high ridge
where the outline of the Hog's Back in Surrey cuts the
horizon, past the old square-towered church where the
Whitelocks lie, and later owners of Fawley are buried
in two monstrous mausoleums known as ' The Mustard
Pot ' and ' The Pepper Pot.'

Since it is so sunny and my housekeeper is so
sensible, the table is laid under the apple tree. There
are times when it is folly to dine out. As soon as the
wasps are abroad, I go in. Not that I fear them,
but they delay my meal, and killing them often proves
expensive in crockery. But on this June day I have no
fears.

Food snobs are the worst of all snobs. I once
attended the banquet of a society dedicated to eating
and drinking. Actually it seemed dedicated to speech-
making, and the food was the worst served, worst
selected, worst cooked I ever remember. The menu
looked like a culinary *Almanach de Gotha*. All the
crowned dishes and the nobility of chefdom seemed
listed there. A simple turbot appeared in what looked
like ermine sauce, and tasted of cheap sauterne.

The speeches were more indigestible than the food.

and I had a waiter who should have had tracheotomy performed upon him, so heavily did he wheeze over me. A very large lady on my right asked me, in a superior soprano voice, whether I knew Brillat-Savarin. Now, whatever I may be financially, I am intellectually honest. I have always had the courage to confess when I do not know. I replied, through a salvo of applause directed at some bore at the head table, that I did not know Brillat-Savarin. I had never been there. Where was it ?

I shall never forget the codfish stare that enormous woman gave me.

" You have never heard of Brillat-Savarin ? " she snarled.

" Never ! " I said, with a firmness equal to my veal.

" Really ! " she cried, meditating some withering comment. But my bland innocence was too much for this gorgon. Her mouth closed with a snap and she rotated towards her right-hand neighbour. For the rest of that interminable banquet she wholly ignored me.

Here let me say, in strict humility, I have been called a widely intelligent man. This may, of course, be very inferior to being a deeply intelligent one, but the particular dimension of knowledge I will not cavil over. I had never heard of Brillat-Savarin. Now that I have, I am impenitent, for he often wrote preposterous nonsense. Reaching home long after midnight—that orgy had lasted from 8.30 until 12.30—I turned to the *Encyclopædia Britannica*, and found that Anthelme Brillat-Savarin, who came immediately after ' Brill, a flatfish closely related to the turbot,' was a

French gastronomist, born, appropriately, at Belley, in 1755. He wrote various volumes on political economy and law, but he won fame with his *Physiologie du goût*, a treatise on the art of dining. In 1789 he was deputy, and in 1793, mayor of Belley. And now he seems to be the god of Belly, and the Encyclopædia, which so thoughtfully placed ' Brill ' on top of him, has put ' Brimstone' under him.

It must not be assumed, following this protest, that I do not eat with care or care for what I eat. The contention of the gourmets that a man is what he eats is a preposterous one. Eating is a necessity, it may be a pleasure, but it should never become a luxury. If we could get rid of our stomachs, life would lose half its slavery ; since this is impossible, let us try to keep the slavery within limits. The groaning tables of the eighteenth century now fill us with disgust. A similar disgust is evoked in me whenever I look at the menus of our City Companies on their guest nights. How can civilised men solidly eat their way down those crowded courses, with half-a-dozen wines, closing with port, cigars, and beribboned boxes of bon-bons ? The jowls and bellies of these hearties who sit guffawing at heavy admirals and sonorous bishops ! I have a vision of them all sitting in Turkish baths the next day.

I have never forgotten the comment of a famous surgeon who had operated on an emperor. " We couldn't get down to his appendix for the fat. My assistant had to hold it back like a wall ! " The gourmet will never confess to being the gourmand, of course, but I have never met a gourmand who did not pride himself on being a gourmet.

Since we must eat to live, let it be little, fresh, and good. The harvest festival held in our churches was originally designed as a thanksgiving to God for a good wheat harvest, by which famine was staved off. Nowadays we import most of our wheat and other foods. The church should really be decorated with tinned foodstuffs imported from the ends of the earth.

Life in the country has this advantage over life in the town—the food, even if less varied, is nearer to the sources from which it is derived. Milk from across the road must be better than milk that has travelled a hundred miles by motor lorry or train and has been frozen and de-frozen before consumption. Some will assert that it is exactly the same milk. But is it ? That the country table must be better than the town table is proved to me by one thing—the shop windows in which the word ' fresh ' is so overworked as an inducement to buy. Moreover, the food has not been ' got at ' by a trained chef, that expert who decorates to-morrow what should be destroyed to-day.

Cottage cookery, therefore, is one of the chief assets of country life. It should be simple and the food fresh. It cost me much vigilance and a stern eye to ban from my cottage the pressed housewife's boon—tinned food. The grocer's traveller was the chief culprit. My housekeeper, safely removed from shop displays, was seduced by this miscreant at the cottage window—all our ' shopping ' is done through a window opening between a yew tree and a clematis—and something had to be done about those surprising appearances of salmon, peas, asparagus, plums, and raspberries in off seasons. I caught the young man by the gate, and threatened him with a garden stake if he ever dared to bring his tinned population trespassing at Pilgrim Cottage.

" I shall examine the dustbin each week, and if I find a tin there, I shall charge you with culinary seduction of my housekeeper," I said. This frightened him.

" Yes, sir," he stammered, and then added, " What about bottled stuff, sir ? "

The wretch ! He had smelt the housekeeper jam-making.

" Bottles," I replied, evasively, " are in a different category."

## II

Something I saw on the lunch table as I entered the garden sent me back at once to Italy. Taste, quite as much as music and smell, can evoke memories. What I now saw were some thin sticks of bread, *grissini*, which I had bought in a Soho baker's shop merely because of their associations.

Down the narrow alley at the back of a dwelling in Venice, where two of us had kept house, with the aid of smiling Giuseppina, there was an odorous baker's shop. In the window they had those long pencils of bread called *grissini*, which snapped so easily in one's fingers and were munched so noisily between one's teeth. Their real home is Turin, where I have bought them hot from the oven. But in Venice, every evening, on returning through the dusky alley after a long day in the burning sun, I used to enter the dark little shop and buy my *grissini*, which were laid like cedar pencils across the pan of the scales.

A little black-eyed signorina called Maria used to sell them to me. Her father, her mother, and an elder sister all shouted to her from what looked like a dark tunnel behind the shop. I must always have called at the hour when there was a change-over at the *traghetto*, the gondola ferry, for by the doorway, in the white shirt, black trousers, and velvet slippers of the gondolier, stood a young man of twenty-two or three. He was always there when I called, always gave me a flashing smile and a " Buona sera, signore ! " I never heard him speak to Maria. He just stood there in the doorway, a lusty fellow, solemnly watching Maria weigh out my *grissini*. I had a feeling that he had been forbidden entrance to the shop, either by Maria or her parents. Perhaps they had quarrelled, or his attentions were not welcome, or it may have been just a form of courtship. But every evening for a month he leaned there with brown arms folded, brown-throated and bright-eyed.

There was an amusing incident when, one evening, in another part of Venice, on leaving a concert with some friends, we sought a gondola, and were immediately assailed by a chorus of " Gondola, signori ? Gondola, signori ? " For a moment we hesitated in our choice when, above the cries, came one—" Grissini, signore ! Grissini, signore ! " I looked, and it was the young suitor of the baker's shop. We took him.

I thought of him now, of Maria, of the little house with the walled-in garden, the balcony, the fig-tree, and the marble cherub's head spouting water. Our house stood behind the great dome of Santa Maria della Salute, and had an outside staircase from the garden-courtyard up to the first floor, where Giuseppina cooked in her kitchen built over the alley below.

The thought of Giuseppina, who had buried two husbands and was willing for another adventure, brought back memories of Venetian dishes. Alas, they will not translate ! *Scampi*, fat, succulent prawns, netted in the lagoon waters, so delicious when fried in butter. *Frutta di mare*, a sea mixture in which it is quite likely a little octopus will be found. *Fritto misto*, the Venetian mixed grill ; and, among vegetables, dressed *pomidoro*, *poppone*, and *zucchini*.

But there are things that translate, and since I liked *zabaione*, particularly at night, as a pick-me-up, I made Giuseppina copy out her recipe. It can be served as a sweet also, and its rich canary yellow looks splendid in green or blue ice-glasses. But serve it hot, and see the glasses are warm.

The broken yolks only of six fresh eggs placed in a basin. One tablespoonful of Marsala or Maraschino, in which are dissolved eight lumps of sugar. Boil the wine, and immediately pour slowly over the yolks, which should be whisked while the basin stands in a saucepan of boiling water. Continue the whisking while it rises and thickens for about ten minutes. Then serve.

The garden door opened behind me, and I started out of a world of *zabaione* and *grissini*. It was Miss Whissitt, looking young in a brown walking costume. I had quite forgotten that I had asked her to lunch. But my housekeeper had not. There were two covers.

" Oh ! *Grissini, n'est-ce-pas ?* " she exclaimed at once, picking up a bread stick.

I am always grateful for her unfailing intelligence, You cannot surprise Miss Whissitt either at a Bach recital or a dog-show. She had come to take me, after lunch, on a walk to Turville, and I knew I had the best possible guide.

"Now, how did you know that was *grissini* ?" I asked.

" I make it myself," replied Miss Whissitt at once.

My mouth must have opened as I stared at her.

" You make it ! " I repeated, recovering voice.

"*C'est incroyable, mais oui !* " laughed Miss Whissitt. " You forget I was once a nurse in a British hospital on the Italian front. For two months I lived with a baker at Belluno. He taught me to make *grissini*."

Her quick eyes noticed the salad in the bowl.

" Would you like me to dress it ? " she asked.

" Please," I answered, passing the cruet.

She sprayed castor sugar over the lettuce. Then she took a tablespoon and put pepper and salt into it. Next she picked up the vinegar bottle. There was one surprised glance, and then her face lit with a smile.

" Tarragon vinegar—tarragon ! How right you are ! Why do we kill salads with our beastly vinegar?"

" Miss Whissitt, there are moments when I think you're the wisest woman I've ever met," I said.

" *Vraiment !* " she laughed, delighted. " Yes, I do have my moments. I suppose you know Evelyn's recipe for salad dressing ? "

" No—do you mean John Evelyn, the diarist ? "

" Yes. You've read, of course, his book *Acetaria*."

" No," I confessed, watching Miss Whissitt sprinkling the dressing over the salad as she churned it in the bowl.

" Ah, then you don't know your Evelyn. I adore him, *je lis, je relis. Il est ravissant !* "

Miss Whissitt flourished a salad spoon as if she were conducting an overture in honour of John Evelyn.

" When Evelyn came back to England in 1680, after a visit to the Continent, he could think of nothing but salads, or ' sallets ' as he called them."

" The first of the vegetarians," I interposed.

" *Mais non !* Adam was the first, wasn't he ? "

" Of course, how stupid of me ! " I said humbly. " But go on, what about the ' sallets ' ? "

" This is a very good one," said Miss Whissitt munching.

" Your dressing is excellent," I replied.

Strange, I thought, here's Miss Whissitt, who can dress a salad to perfection, but has no idea how to dress herself. In this crazy world how many marriages are made at the costumier's and unmade in the kitchen ? So many women, expert with the lipstick, are clumsy with the suet. They can pluck their eyebrows, but they cannot pluck a fowl. As for the farmer's lass, she no longer singes the goose, unless it wears trousers. But Miss Whissitt was saying—

" He was so enthusiastic about his ' sallets ' that he even buttonholed Mr. London, the King's head gardener, and suggested he should cultivate seventy new vegetables."

" Mr. London—oh, what a grand name for a gardener," I cried. " It's as good as the night-watchman in a block of flats I go to—his name's Nightcap, believe it or not ! "

" Mr. London," continued Miss Whissitt, " thought that thirty-five ' sallets ' were enough, even for a King's table, and Evelyn had to be satisfied with that. Later, he published his *Acetaria, a book about sallets.* I've got a first edition—my father bought it. Evelyn appeals in it for a ' Pristine Diet,' as he calls it. When he talks of a ' sallet ' he means an uncooked vegetable. He gives a list of them which can be grown for every month in the year."

" That must be a marvellous list," I said. " In England there are lettuces and—and what ? "

" Nothing, in England. We stop there. No wonder Evelyn wrote *Acetaria.*"

" He doesn't seem to have reformed us," I grumbled. " By the way, since you seem to know everything—did the Brussels sprout first in Brussels or——"

" I detest conundrums," said Miss Whissitt, " particularly vegetable ones."

I was about to retort that it was geographical, but Miss Whissitt's face did not encourage me.

### III

On the evening following Miss Whissitt's salad lecture, I had two guests arrive very late. I do not encourage my visitors to arrive at half-past twelve at night, but for Tilly, motoring down after the theatre, I make allowance. It was a lovely moonlit night, and her brother Ralph motored her down. We actually sat in the garden for half an hour, so warm was the June night.

I was surprised therefore to be awakened early the next morning by a consciousness of someone in my bedroom. I opened my eyes, to find young Ralph standing there, in pyjamas and dressing-gown.

" I'm sorry to disturb you," he said ; " I thought you might be awake. I've had to get up—there's something funny about my room."

" Funny? " I said, half awake. " What do you mean ' funny ' ? "

To be aroused at seven o'clock and have the pleasant illusion that you are a good host shattered by a worried-looking youth in a green silk dressing-gown needs self-control.

" Well," he explained, " there're funny tapping noises."

I was wide awake now, and looked at my friend, astonished to find that he really was somewhat scared.

" Good heavens ! " I exclaimed; " you don't mean to say you've raised a ghost, and at seven in the morning ! "

" Oh no ! " he replied, in a manner that half suggested ' Oh yes.'

" What sort of tapping noises ? " I demanded.

He sat on the edge of my bed, and examined his bare ankles, bending down so that I should not see his face.

" Well—it's a kind of drumming—it woke me about six," he answered. " You don't think I'm being silly ; I'm not at all superstitious ! "

" It sounds as if you are," I said brutally. " Perhaps it's mice gnawing in the roof."

" No—it's not mice—I know mice," he replied, as though he spent his life with them. " Won't you come and listen ? "

" What ! " I said, " the ghost still walking in full daylight ! "

" I didn't say it was a ghost," he retorted, slightly annoyed. " It's a funny tapping noise. It woke me about six—it comes and goes. It's in the room, and yet it isn't—it——"

" God bless you," I said ; " there's one thing I've always felt this cottage ought to have, a well-authenticated ghost. Come along, let's be introduced."

I pushed my feet out of bed and fumbled for slippers. It was a radiant morning, with the sunshine streaming over the woods, and a woolly morning mist just curling off the top of the larches on the hillside opposite.

" Well, you'll see, whatever it is, it's funny," said my guest.

I suppose, had I been a nice host, I should have apologised for this visitation in my guest's bedroom. It is not pleasant to be awakened by a tapping noise of mysterious origin unless you are an active member of the Society for Psychical Research. My friend is a musician by profession, and I could not resist remarking facetiously that he should be familiar with plucking sounds.

" I said ' tapping,' " he replied irritably.

We arrived at his room.

" Now listen ! " he said solemnly.

We stood there like a couple of asses. Not a sound.

" That's funny. Perhaps it's gone," he said, after a long wait.

" Perhaps it's the cistern."

" Cisterns don't tap—they sizzle," he retorted severely.

" Then the radiator——"

I put my hand out to tap the radiator, when suddenly my friend said " Sssh ! " exactly like a cistern.

We held our breath and listened, goggle-eyed.

Tap-tap-tap-tap. Tap-tap-tap-tap. Tap-tap-tap !

He looked at me triumphantly.

Tap-tap-tap——

" It's very odd," I remarked.

" Odd ! I should think it is ! That's not mice ! " he exclaimed.

Where did it come from ? The sound surrounded us. The tapping had started again, soft but insistent, a kind of Morse code. I had heard of table legs doing this sort of thing, and had always been depressed by the thought that anything so unlovely as a table leg should be an instrument of spiritual communication.

" It comes from outside," I said when we had listened again. I moved to the window. It was louder there. I opened the window, but all I heard was a sudden whirr of birds' wings. Then a sound of someone chopping came on the morning air.

" We must take a long walk to-day," I said, scenting the fresh morning. There was dew on the grass, and one jewel of it scintillated in the leaf-cup of a lupin in the garden bed.

" You suggested going to Park Place," said my friend.

" Yes—that's an idea, we can go by boat. I've an invitation to——"

*Tap-tap-tap-tap. Tap-tap-tap.*

We looked at each other. It was there again. Quite unmistakably there, outside the window.

Cautiously I tiptoed up and looked out. Then that tapping made me look down. I drew back smiling. The ghost was laid.

" If you look down there very cautiously," I said, " you'll see eight birds standing on the bird tray in front of the study window. The tray's empty, and they're hammering hard with their beaks for breakfast ! "

He looked. There they were, all pecking on the bare board. His laugh was so loud that the birds rose in sudden alarm.

" I must confess I got a bit scared. It was so uncanny," he said.

" Anyhow, we're up early. It'll give us a long day," I answered. " Let's go out and feed them."

We went down through the quiet house. The garden smiled at us, bright as a child out of a bath.

" It's too wet for slippers," I said, shedding mine as I stepped on to the lawn. We left footprints in the dew. I emptied seed into the bird tray. How warm the sun was ! We stood still, drinking in the beauty of this morning world. A lark, a blackbird, and a cuckoo were all hard at work, making summer sounds.

" Do you know what I'd like to do ? " asked Ralph. " Roll in the dew ! "

" Then do."

He gave me a reproachful look, suspicious of a frightful pun.

" Will it seem quite mad ? " he asked.

" Quite," I replied ; " but at twenty, madness is your privilege."

" Here goes," he said, slipping off his pyjamas.

The rolling was most energetically done.

" Now I know what a foal feels like," he said, standing up, panting, covered with leaves and worm-casts.

" Foal or fool ? " I asked, unable to resist the retort.

" I look a mess, I suppose ? "

" You look like *le petit-déjeuner d'un faune*. You look at this moment as if you wanted to chase a nymph in the wood. I'm sorry, but I've no nymphs on supply. All I can offer you is the garden hose," I said.

" That's a jolly good idea," retorted that irrepressible youth. And forthwith I had to find the hose.

When a towel had been produced and he had dried himself, he looked at me with a glowing face.

" Isn't it funny how we enjoy doing anything different ? Last night I was all dressed up and dancing at the Berkeley, and here I am, like an old horse let out to grass, rolling in the dew ! "

" And hearing spirit tappings at dawn," I added.

" Oh, shut up ! You know you were taken in yourself at first," he cried. Then, snuffing loud : " Ah, I smell the British breakfast in the air ! Oh, isn't life good ! "

# COTTAGE DINNER-PARTY

At the oak table, in soft candle-light,
Sit my nine dinner guests, a pleasant sight ;
Young Peter, with his youthful, eager air,
And Ann his sister, delicately fair.


First on my left, the serious sloe-dark eyes
Of Mrs. Lane suggest my speech is wise,
While young June Trivett, wife at twenty-one,
Listens politely to the vicar's son.


First on my right sits happy Mrs. Dean,
For thirty years the County's reigning queen,
Intelligent, sweet-mannered, gay, despite
A husband who is well kept out of sight.


Lord Meaden, gourmand, holding up his glass,
Chuckles and works the jawbone of an ass,
Eyeing the brewer's widow, well content
To barter rank for unearned increment.


Brilliant, of course, as ever, Henry Hawke
Commands the table with his witty talk ;
Strange that a man so gifted wastes his time
Providing friends with dinner-pantomime.

*Good food, good wine, I hope, my table bears,*
*But as we eat and talk, four hundred years*
*Fade through the candle-light ; and in the room*
*Ten famished serfs shiver in rush-lit gloom.*

# CHAPTER XI

## THE CONWAYS AT HOME

THE steep hill that precipitates the motorist from
London into Henley, and at the foot of which he finds
Henley Bridge, guarded by two *Angels* and a *Red Lion*,
is bordered on one side by the grounds of an estate
known as Park Place. At the bottom of White Hill, as
it is called, one is asked to make, like Paris, a choice
of three beauties, of four, if we include Henley Town
itself among the attractions. Ahead of us, over the
bridge, lies Hart Street, the broad high street of the
town, with its church, its various houses and shops,
Elizabethan, Queen Anne, Georgian, Victorian, Ed-
wardian, and God knows what. It is still a beautiful
old street, perhaps not so beautiful as when Miss
Blandy looked out of the window, nor so lovely as
when Charles I. stepped out of *The Red Lion* and took
an airing with his ladies and gentlemen.

The great Duke of Marlborough would find much
that was familiar among much that was deplorable.
He would still turn right at the cross-roads, to journey
to his palace of Blenheim, and, if he had an eye for
beauty as well as for bloodshed, he would probably
linger on the bridge, as I often linger, wondering which
is the better view, up-river to Wargrave, or down-river
to Temple Island, at the foot of the Chilterns. The
views he compared would be much the same, but the

bridge on which he stood would be different. It would not, I think, be so beautiful. It would lack the sculptured heads from the chisel of the Hon. Mrs. Damer of Park Place, the daughter of General Conway and Lady Caroline, Countess of Ailesbury. Let us call on them at the mansion so superbly placed on the steep hillside commanding the Thames towards Wargrave.

Park Place had been the residence of Frederick, Prince of Wales, whose magnificent State barge in crimson and gold, for twenty oarsmen, built in 1732, can still be seen in the Victoria and Albert Museum. He lived there for twenty years, and after him came the Conways, to set their seal on the place for ever. The beautiful Lady Ailesbury was a good instance of the happiness that may come, despite the wiseacres, from being an old man's darling. When she was fifteen, and merely Caroline Campbell, her mother died. Since her father, a Colonel, was abroad with his regiment, it was decided to marry her early and solve the problem of guardianship. When she was eighteen, Lord Bruce, who was fifty-seven, proposed to her. It was monstrous, said everybody, except Lady Suffolk and Lady Westmorland, who said it was a great chance, for Miss Campbell had nothing but her face.

Lord Bruce had great expectations. He was quick-tempered and covetous. He married Caroline on June 13th, 1739, succeeded to the title as third Earl of Ailesbury, and died, with thoughtful consideration, while his wife was only twenty-six, leaving her very rich.

General Conway and Caroline, Countess of Ailesbury,
and their child Anne (later, Mrs. Damer)

The widow wasted no time. Within ten months she had married Henry Seymour Conway, brother of the first Earl of Hertford. One expects to learn next that she had married a *roué* and a wastrel. Actually she had married one of the most attractive and capable young men of the age, and there lay before her long years of unshadowed happiness. " He has the finest person and the handsomest face I ever saw," declared Horace Walpole, a kinsman of the Countess.

General Conway and his wife were just established at Park Place when Henley and the whole country were startled by the Blandy murder. Old Mr. Francis Blandy had handled the negotiations for the purchase of Park Place. All the actors in this sensational drama were neighbours. After a visit to the Conways, Walpole wrote : " The town of Henley has been extremely disturbed by an engagement between the ghosts of Miss Blandy and her father, which continued so violent that some bold persons, to prevent bloodshed, broke in and found it was two jackasses which had got into the kitchen."

Lady Ailesbury and General Conway, the moment they had taken possession of Park Place, proceeded to ' beautify ' it. There was then a passion for improving on Nature. It has not altogether died out, as anyone can see who visits gardens. On a hill near my cottage there is a rich man's dream of Heaven. He has gone, Heaven knows where, but has left behind him his monstrous spikey palace. Nothing would satisfy him but a miniature Matterhorn in the grounds. Often I have wondered if his chauffeurs yodelled as they came up the Zermatt-Henley Valley, bringing the guests to his *hôtel splendide*.

On a lesser scale there is the mania for decorating rockeries and gardens with dwarfs, goblins, and odious mannikins with long beards. I have never been reconciled to Peter Pan's invasion of Kensington Gardens, and have the warmest sympathy with the little boy who, after his mother's strenuous effort to awaken appreciation, exclaimed, very logically—" But, Mummy, why wouldn't he grow up ? "

I sometimes wonder whether that garden Matterhorn was not a piece of conscious rivalry with Park Place across the valley. The inhabitants of Jersey, having found a junior Stonehenge, presented it to General Conway, on his resigning the Governorship of the island. Did they feel there was already too much rock in the place ? With a courage only possible in days before excess luggage was known, General Conway transported and transplanted his Stonehenge to Park Place, forty-five granite stones, seven feet in height, in a circle of sixty-five feet. So far it has resisted American annexation, being neither chippable nor clippable. But one day it may cross the Atlantic, as a whole, numbered and orientated by a Harvard professor.

There was one activity of the gallant General's we must all applaud. He planted firs, pines, cedars, oaks, and elms. He was the first in England to plant the poplar pine, or Lombardy poplar as it is now called. A cutting was imported from Turin, and now, as one glides past the riverside lawns of the Thames, the noon is more lovely, the night more dramatic for these noble trees standing sentinel by the reflective waters.

There are three of the same species on the opposite bank of Phyllis Court, and on how many a still summer's night, when the river ran silver and the hills awaited the owl's cry, have I not watched the crimson moon climb to the sharp edge of their velvet screen.

Everyone came to Park Place in the days of the Conways. Royalties of many nationalities were often there. The French Revolution was preceded by Anglomania among the French aristocracy. They invaded England, they patronised the water fêtes on the Thames, for the State barge was still in vogue, being a more certain mode of travel to the riverside palaces than the stage-coach, the prey of mud, flood, snow, and highwaymen.

Lady Ailesbury was in Paris during the winter of 1774-5, where she attended the masked balls of Marie Antoinette. With her handsome husband she was a great favourite in French society. Her daughter, by her first marriage to Lord Bruce, had married, at seventeen, the Duke of Richmond. Later he was the British Ambassador in Paris, and this enlarged the Ailesburys' French connection. Many of their distinguished guests, the Duc de Biron, the Duchesse de Noailles, the Princesse de Lamballe, the Duchesse de Gramont, the Comtesse de Noailles, the Duc de Mouchy, were destined to perish by the guillotine.

Surely the most astonishing of these guests, had the true history been then known, was Mlle d'Eon, whom Lady Ailesbury found most entertaining and attractive. Little did she guess that the lady was the Chevalier

231

d'Eon. Twenty-five years earlier General Conway had commanded in an army that had fought the French army in which d'Eon had been A.D.C. to a general. The Countess of Ailesbury was not the only person to be completely fooled. The author of *Le Mariage de Figaro* had proposed marriage to the ' lady.' When d'Eon died, at the age of eighty-three, he could look back on thirty-four years of life as a woman, and forty-nine as a man.

The men of letters were often at Park Place. Was Rousseau ever there ? It is not improbable. Hume, the philosopher, was Conway's private secretary when he was Secretary of State. Rousseau came to England with Hume in 1766, and it was to General Conway that he owed his pension of £100 a year. Rousseau went to Oxford with Hume, and it would be almost impossible for them to pass by Park Place.

Gray, the poet, visited the Conways, and was somewhat grumpy about the society he found there. He wrote, after a visit, in 1760, " For me, I am come to my resting-place, and find it very necessary, after living a month in a house with three women that laughed from morning till night, and would allow nothing to the sulkiness of my disposition. Company and cards at home, parties by land and water abroad, and what they call ' doing something,' that is, racketting about from morning to night, are occupations I find that wear out my spirits, especially in a situation where one might sit still and be alone with pleasure, for the place is a hill like Clifden, opening to a very extensive and diversified landscape, with the Thames, which is navigable, running at its foot."

Gentlemen who wish to be alone for pleasure should not go to house-parties and stay a month. One suspects that even the author of the *Elegy* was a bore as well as doleful. Dr. Johnson said, " Sir, he was dull in company and dull everywhere, and Lady Ailesbury complained he never opened his lips but once and then only said ' Yes, my lady, I believe so.' "

The reputation enjoyed by Park Place suggests that Conway and his wife were ideal hosts. When the Princess Amelia, a born gambler, visited them, they gambled, and were as frivolous as she desired ; when the Lord Chancellor and a famous historian were there, card play was abolished and the conversation was intellectual. Conway himself was a man of considerable achievements. After a brilliant career in the field he became an important member of Pitt's Government, Secretary to Ireland, Secretary of State, and Leader of the House of Commons. He was enlightened, and sacrificed his position as Equerry to George III. and the command of his regiment, by voting against the Ministry that was prosecuting Wilkes.

" I passed all the last week at Park Place," wrote Horace Walpole, " where one of the bravest men in the world, who is not permitted to contribute to our conquests, was indulged in being the happiest, by being with one of the most deserving women."

This handsome couple was popular with all classes. Conway's kindness was notorious. One of Conway's secretaries set fire to their town house, to hide a theft of £900. The man confessed and was sentenced to be hanged. " When this man's condemned Conway will be teasing me to pardon him, but I am determined to hang him," said George III. Conway did try to save him, but the King kept his word.

Once, in Henley, in the winter of 1771, there was an outbreak of rabies, as it was thought. Forty people were bitten by mad dogs and cats in the town. There was a panic, and one of the women, who was bitten by a cat, " mewed like a cat and endeavoured to scratch and bite everybody that came near her." Conway at once prescribed a medicine, which filled all with hope. But it was in vain. " Mr. Conway has had a bad account," wrote Lady Mary Coke ; " the poor woman has mewed again and attempted to scratch everybody that came near her."

## II

While the old ladies were bitten by dogs down in Henley, the young ladies up at Park Place were bitten by amateur theatricals, gambling, and, of course, dress. Lady Ailesbury's daughters, the Duchess of Richmond and Hon. Mrs. Damer, were clever actresses. They knew the Garricks, and the fate of Sarah Siddons was bound up with them, for Garrick heard a little provincial actress at Cheltenham so praised by them that he sent down his agents to see her, and on their glowing reports he engaged her at five pounds a week at Drury Lane. Lady Ailesbury was the patroness of Miss Farren, too, and it was in her town house that the actress saw much of Lord Derby, whom she married.

As for fashion, Lady Ailesbury was in the van. She would not be out-feathered by anyone. When she found that the Duchess of Devonshire was leading the fashion because of her tall feathers, she tried to get some taller for herself. But taller could not be found, whereupon Lady Ailesbury brightly thought of the undertaker's splendid feathers. She sent round to him and he replied, regretfully, that all his hearses were out, but they would be back in a short time, and he would then try to accommodate her.

Her second daughter Mrs. Damer was quite as remarkable for her enterprise. She had not the beauty of her mother, but she had much talent. Her early childhood was spent with Horace Walpole, at Strawberry Hill, while her parents were abroad, and he watched over her education with great care.

Are we told the truth about these little girls of past generations who learned French, English, Italian, Latin, and Greek before they were in their teens, and were conversant with the literature of many nations? Were they infant prodigies, or were these legends from the pen of some obsequious scribe expecting substantial patronage? Little Anne Seymour Conway, for instance, was "thoroughly conversant" with several languages. Homer, Herodotus, Plutarch, Livy, and Cicero were her favourite authors. Walpole wrote of her, "We have by accident discovered that she writes Latin like Pliny and is learning Greek. In Italy she will be a prodigy."

When David Hume, her father's secretary, annoyed her by talking to a vivacious Italian street urchin who was peddling his plaster busts, and observed that the boy had produced work that she, for all the money expended on her education, could not create, this young lady of eighteen went off in a huff, and modelled a head that filled him with astonishment.

In pique she had discovered her gift. Henceforth, after some study, she found fame as a sculptress. George III., Queen Caroline, Nelson, Fox, Mrs. Siddons, and the Kembles sat for her. Her work is in many galleries, but the work most publicly hung is over running water. The loveliness of Henley Bridge is much enhanced by two large masks from her chisel. They are on the keystone of each centre arch. Father Thames, with fishes playing in wavy tresses, and bulrushes in the fillet bending his temple, looks downstream : upstream is the fair Isis, a nymph whose face was modelled on that of the artist's friend, Mrs. Freeman of Fawley Court.

As an actress she was in great demand for amateur theatricals, and the great Mrs. Siddons even considered her a worthy partner. She appeared with much success in the Duke of Richmond's company, of which a chronicler wrote, " They divide the attention of the town with the French commercial Treaty, Warren Hastings, and the Prince of Wales's debts."

Unlucky lady, she made a bad draw in the matrimonial lottery. Her half-sister was radiantly happy as Duchess of Richmond ; she was destined to be miserable. It appeared to be a splendid match. John Damer, Lord Milton's eldest son, was heir to a fortune of £30,000 a year. For the present he had an allowance of £7,000 a year, but he could not keep out of debt. A time came when his father refused to settle more debts, whereupon Mr. Damer supped at the *Bedford Arms* in Covent Garden, with four ladies and a blind fiddler. At three in the morning he dismissed his company, and told the fiddler to return in half an hour, which he did, to find Damer dead in a chair with a pistol at his side. It was Charles James Fox who, encountering Mrs. Damer as she came into London to join her husband, prepared her for the shocking news. The young rake of thirty-two left a wardrobe which fetched £15,000.

Mrs. Damer went abroad after this, and was captured by a French privateer, after a running fight of four hours. She astonished Rome with her sculpture, and was the first woman to wear black-silk stockings. She appears to have met everyone in Paris, the Talleyrands, Mme de Staël, Mme de Récamier, young Beauharnais, Bonaparte's mother, still a great beauty with dark eyes, General Lafayette, "a gentleman-like, sickly-looking man, in no sort of uniform, a plain blue coat, round hat, and cropped head." She went to the Tuileries and met the First Consul. Like so many other misguided ladies, she had a great admiration for Bonaparte. She found he had "a remarkable and uncommon expression of sweetness." Some years later she was destined to meet him in the rôle of Emperor, when she gave him a bust she had made of Fox, and received from Napoleon a snuff-box set in diamonds.

A woman so gifted, vivacious, and well-born naturally made contact with the most interesting men and women of the age. Park Place and the hospitality of Lady Ailesbury drew many of them into her ken, but she travelled and moved much in society, knowing Byron, Scott, Burke, and Moore. The great Nelson was a particular friend. He sat for her on returning from the Battle of the Nile, in the coat he had worn in the battle, and which he presented to her.

She inherited Strawberry Hill from Walpole, and lived there with her mother for some years after Park Place had been given up. Field-Marshal Conway had died at Park Place in 1795, and Lady Ailesbury thereupon sold it to Lord Malmesbury. The Duchess of Richmond died a year after her father, but Lady Ailesbury lived to be eighty-three, and died in Mrs. Damer's house in Upper Brook Street in 1803, " alert and beautiful to the end, the picture of what an old woman ought to be and so seldom is," wrote a friend.

Mrs. Damer was a great gardener at Strawberry Hill, as she had been at Park Place. " She chips away at her marble one half of the morning and trots about the grounds the other half, in all weathers," wrote a friend. Later, she sold Strawberry Hill and bought York House, Twickenham, from Prince Starhemberg, the late Austrian Ambassador.

Starhemberg was an old friend, frequently met with in the Henley set, of which Lord Barrymore, with his theatre at Wargrave, was also a shining light. His personal appearance was not remarkable for cleanliness. One night, playing *trente-et-un*, he kept exclaiming, " I am dirty ! I am dirty ! " At last, in his excitement, he embraced Lord Barrymore, crying, " I am dirty ! I am dirty-one ! " whereupon his Lordship retorted, " Damn it, so you are, but that's no reason why I should be dirty too ! "

Mrs. Damer lived at York House in the summer and in Upper Brook Street in the winter. Shortly before her death the Duke of Clarence made a request. She had already made a cast of Mrs. Jordan's leg, which H.R.H. well liked in life and still life. He now asked her to execute a bust in bronze of Nelson, and the remarkable old lady of eighty-two set to work at once, and finished it a few days before her death on May 28th, 1828.

She was painted by a great triumvirate, Reynolds, Romney, and Cosway, and also by her friend, Angelica Kauffmann, but her memory is best served by the masks on Henley Bridge, and the avenues, glades, and water-reaches of Park Place, where, one of a group of lovely women, she must have contributed to a Watteau-like scene.

Even now, for a moment, her ghost is evoked, when a boat is moored by the landing-place. She alights laughing, throwing a backward glance at courtly Mr. Walpole and grumpy Mr. Gray, as they help out the young Duchess of Richmond and elegant Lady Ailesbury. Farther down the glade she might encounter a fellow ghost, unhappy and dreadful, with the scar of the hangman's noose about her neck, that ill-fated too-fond lover, Mary Blandy, in the walk which once she frequented with her dark-souled Captain.

The lombardy poplar scarcely stirs in the evening breeze, the river runs coldly, and the light has fled from the Druidic circle of stones that General Conway so proudly imported. Higher still, crowned in the evening glow above the dark woods, Park Place stands hoarding great memories amid a scene that has not changed in its gentle English beauty.

# THE LONDON COACH

By the old White Hart, where the squire's post-chaise
Rattled on the cobbles in the good old days,
Where Lady Ailesbury stepped out of her carriage,
With her daughter, the Duchess of Richmond by marriage,
The big yellow coach from London Town
Pulls up and sets ten travellers down.

In the old inn yard where the ostlers bustled,
And lackeys ran, and travellers hustled
Into the coach for London bound,
No horse now whinnies or stamps the ground,
But the long yellow coach of fifty horse-power
Glides off at forty miles an hour.

In a hundred years will they laugh at us
Who went to town in a motor-bus?
Shall we seem as quaint as the Queen Anne squire
Who drove his chaise through the mud and mire?
However it be, we shall not care,
Having made the last journey, paid the last fare.

# CHAPTER XII

### THE HAPPY 'TRAITOR'

THERE are some names in my district you cannot avoid. They are part of the scenery. To the north of me we are in Stonor-land. In the reign of Queen Elizabeth, Francis Stonor was appointed as one of the " assistants to the Corporation of Henley "; and on July 22nd, 1560, about the time that the walls of my cottage were going up, Sir Francis Knollys of Greys Court, delivered a certificate to the Queen to the effect that among all the captains and able men of the County of Oxford, with armour and horses, was " Henry Stonor, Esquire, senior ensigne of iijc able fote men."

There is an account for " waste of torches " at the burial of Edmund Stonor, in 1475. They were ever a Catholic family. When two Henley townspeople complained to Miles Coverdale that the image in Our Lady Chapel of Henley was not removed, Master Miles busied himself to write to the authorities to the effect that the ordinances of King Henry VIII. were not being observed, and slyly hinted that Sir Walter Stonor, Kt. (together with the Bishop of Lincoln, Henley being in his diocese), the local King's Justice, was not performing his duty.

The road to Watlington, continuing from the Fair-mile past my house, leads up the Assenden Valley, following the course of the mysterious stream. After

passing Stonor village, and the park, it branches, left
to Watlington, and right to Turville Heath. The
ascent to the heath is by a semicircular road skirting
dense beechwoods, as glorious as any this district
can show. Shortly before beginning that four-
hundred-foot ascent, we pass old Stonor village, which
was formerly called Assenden ; but, if we are sensible,
we don't pass, we halt there a time.

Here are Chiltern cottages, Elizabethan, dormer-
windowed, brown-tiled, and flint-faced, to perfection.
Just beyond the village are the gates of Stonor Park.
The family mansion, spreading itself high on slopes
of the park-land, makes as noble a sight as any house
in England, with its dense background of beechwoods,
the superb contours of the glades and knolls, the ribbon
road winding up the valley, and the slim deer moving in
dappled sunlight beneath majestic trees. A public footpath terraces the opposite hillside, so that the old house
falls below one, dove-grey, seignorial, with hanging
gardens lifted against emerald sward and dark woodland.

To-day we will not pass inside the gates, set at such
a distance from the house as induces that requisite
sense of inferiority which grows with every hundred
yards of the approach. The landed gentry are ceasing
to be landed, and the Vere de Vere exclusiveness,
aided by high gates, small lodges, and long drives, the
true accompaniments of a ' seat,' is passing. It is
difficult to be Vere de Vere with a door on an arterial
road, and I observe many a gallant fight being made
behind the turning space for a baby car, and a door so
flimsy that the old butler seems afraid it will crack in
his hand. But in America I visited a ' seat ' that was

so feudal, with approach so prolonged, that I was asked at the lodge gates whether I would go by train or automobile across the estate, two hundred miles long!

This old England of ours, once so stubborn in the face of innovation, has now become so skittish that family seats are becoming as rare as bespoke boot-makers. I never pass the gates of Stonor Park without a nervous prayer for my Lord Camoys and the house of Stonor. So perfect, so untouched are that village, park, and uneconomic house, those shy deer and unaxed woods, that I feel like a connoisseur happy before an old master in an antique frame. A shiver of fear passed over me when I noted that the family priest no longer ' lived in ' but had been ' boarded out ' in a new ' antique ' house built opposite the gates. And, fresh symbol of modernity, the pylons, con-siderately fir and not steel, were carrying an electric cable that has tethered the village to an electric age.

Vain laments! Let us rejoice in this noble road bordering the wood that curves and ascends to Tur-ville Heath, an upland expanse of greensward, gorse, and hawthorn, so common in these Chiltern Hun-dreds. High on this plateau, 713 feet above sea-level, the air has a sharpness in contrast to the mildness of the sheltered valleys. In the last bend of the road we face a triple fork that will take us, left to Turville Park, right to Turville Court, and straight on across the open common to Turville Grange.

The Grange, with its warm Georgian face, is so inviting that we are tempted to go ahead. But it is not yet tea-time, and we will not thus early inflict our company on the hospitable Marquise d'Hautpoul.

Nor will we turn right to the Court, where attention may be torn between eyes and ears, between a collection of Sargents and old masters in the house, or the recitals by new masters in the barn, where a musical hostess has changed a threshing-floor into a dancing-floor ; for the rafters no longer reverberate to the Harvest Home roared from rustic throats, but echo with Ravel or Rachmaninoff, and the nice applause of the County, gloved and glowing.

Our way lies to the left down a magnificent nave of limes, back through a hundred years to look at the last home of General Dumouriez, Turville Park. The house, well guarded by its park, is undistinguished Georgian, built in 1741, flat-fronted, with that unromantic air which often marks enchantment hidden from view. When we have been ushered through the square hall into the morning-room, the mask falls. Out of those windows a noble lawn leads the eye to falling meadow and a vista of woodlands breaking, wave on darkening wave, until the sight fades in the blue haze where lie the Hog's Back and the Sussex sky. Across the meadow, westwards, beyond the thick wood, lies Nettlebed.

In the meadow there is a sudden recess, dug out of the ground. " What is it ? " I asked my host, the owner of the house. " The ice-house," he explained. The ordnance maps show many of these ice-houses, and there is an Ice-house Wood in the district. What is this ice-house, placed in the middle of a field, consisting of a small cavern dug in the sloping ground, and never far distant from the mansion to which it belongs ? It is the ancient counterpart of a refrigerator. In the winter, when there was a heavy fall of snow,

this bricked chamber under the earth was packed with
snow, and thus for many months there was a natural
ice-box providing cold storage for game and food.
I have counted no fewer than eighteen of these ice-
houses in the country around me, and the size of them
gives some idea of the extent to which a large country
house in the old days kept a store of food.

Turville Park provides another curiosity from the
good old days. In one of the outbuildings there is a
room with a copper, which I took to be a washhouse.
Actually it was the soup kitchen, from which the lord
of the manor dispensed soup to his labourers and the
poor of the village.

Let us return indoors. A hundred years ago it was
inhabited by Lord Lyndhurst, the Lord Chancellor.
He seems to have developed the week-end habit, for
after his labours in the House of Lords he ' ran down '
to Turville Park for the week-end, where he generally
had an important house-party. He announced with
pride that he could leave Turville Park and be at the
door of his house in Hanover Square within three
hours, by post-chaise. The journey to-day by car
takes two hours, owing to traffic regulations and congestion through fifteen miles of built-up areas which
in his time were green fields as far as Knightsbridge.
The day seems not far distant when the eighty-miles-
an-hour car will take the same time to achieve the
journey as the fourteen-mile-an-hour post-chaise.

We get a glimpse of one of these house-parties in
the memoirs of Baron Philipp von Neumann, the
engaging Austrian Minister at the Court of St. James.
He visited Turville Park, as a guest of Lord Lyndhurst,

on August 26th, 1847, paying a call on Lord Camoys at Stonor Park. " A fine park, but a bad house," he comments hastily. His first visit had been made in 1842, when he slept in the room in which General Dumouriez died. On the first visit he went by coach, on the second by train to Reading, a journey which was then sufficiently a novelty for him to remark on the extraordinary speed and comfort of the journey.

Lord Lyndhurst, while in no way so remarkable as the former tenant of Turville Park, had a singular career, for he was born in Boston, Massachusetts, in 1772, the son of J. S. Copley, the painter. He attracted the attention of Castlereagh, and became Lord Chancellor in 1827. He took a prominent part, as Solicitor-General, in the trial of Queen Charlotte. He began life as a man of almost revolutionary ideas, a republican and a Jacobin. He ended as a Tory of Tories, and never failed to support any reactionary measures.

His shade is now a faint one. It is General Dumouriez whose ghost still walks at Turville Park. He entered that house on March 14th, 1822, at 2.30 p.m. He died in it on March 14th, at 2.30 p.m., a year later, a man of eighty-four. He was buried in Henley Church, in a vault in the chancel, and *The News* of March 22nd, 1823, wrote : " This extraordinary man stood, at one period of his life, on the very pinnacle of triumph and glory. His feats as a warrior make up the more splendid pages of modern history. His name was a charm that gathered round it all the enthusiasm of millions ; but he died in exile, and deservedly, for he was a traitor to his country."

This was certainly the French view, held even to this

day, but the old General has stalwart defenders. His life-story is certainly a stormy and singular one. The Latin inscription over the south-aisle door of Henley Church, with the two large words *Champagne, Jemappes*, denoting his victories, gives little clue to the high adventure that had ended at Turville Park after eighty-four years of fighting, espionage, politics, and authorship.

He was born at Cambrai in 1739, and at nineteen saw battle as a volunteer in the French Army. Five years later, as a captain, he could show twenty wounds and the Order of St. Louis. Under the Duc de Choiseul he was in the secret service, going on missions to Italy, Portugal, Corsica, and Poland, but on the fatal Christmas Eve upon which the Duc de Choiseul was sent into exile, owing to the enmity of Madame Du Barry, Dumouriez's fortune crashed.

Later, he found himself a prisoner in the Bastille. On the accession of Louis XVI., in 1774, he was released, and an able military report resulted in his promotion. He took up residence at the castle of Caen. Here Fate seemed to have drawn the threads together. As a very young man he had fallen in love with his cousin, but the marriage was forbidden. The disappointed young lady took the veil, and Dumouriez took poison in an hotel at Dieppe. But he took too much and recovered, and sought his father's forgiveness. It chanced that the lady was now in a convent at Caen. The young captain again sought her hand, with a gallantry all the more remarkable for the fact that the poor young woman was now completely disfigured by smallpox. Her vows were annulled, and they were married.

So poor was he at this moment that he sold five

thousand books from his library to cover the wedding expenses. But promotion lay ahead, for, in 1777, Louis XVI. appointed him Commandant of Cherbourg, and he spent the next years fortifying that port and drawing up elaborate plans for the invasion of England viâ the Isle of Wight. It is sad to recall the unromantic end to Dumouriez's love-affair. The lady was a shrew and a hypochondriac. She made his life so unbearable that finally he was driven to seek a separation.

The death of Mirabeau, to whose party Dumouriez had attached himself, was a great blow, but he rose to be Commandant of Nantes, and, when Louis made his fateful flight to Varennes, he offered to march to the assistance of the Assembly. At the time of the outbreak of the Revolution, Dumouriez was fifty years of age, with a keen insight into affairs and a gift for detail. At heart a monarchist, he wanted to bind King and people together by a constitution. The King was suspicious of this reforming soldier, and ignored his advice.

Swiftly moving events carried Dumouriez high up in the Girondist party, and in March 1792 he became Minister of Foreign Affairs. A declaration of war against Austria following, he became Minister of War, resigning two days later when the obstinate King refused to come to terms with the Assembly. He went to the battle front, and on Lafayette's flight he assumed command of the army.

He was now hailed as a born leader of men. The events that followed seemed to prove it. France, attacked by Prussians and Austrians, needed a cool leader in the field. From a brilliant defence with Kellermann at Valmy, he went to a greater victory at

Jemappes, and found himself the hero of France. Speaking of his stand at Valmy, Napoleon said, years afterwards, " I was probably the boldest general who ever lived, but I wouldn't have dared to take post there."

With him in that battle rode the young Duc de Chartres, son of Philippe Egalité, afterwards King Louis Philippe. In one month Dumouriez swept the Austrians and the house of Habsburg out of Belgium. Mons and Louvain rose to heights of joyful frenzy after the occupation such as were only achieved again in 1918 when the German oppressors were expelled.

Dumouriez was now fifty-three. At home events were marching to a crisis. The doom of Louis was sealed by the discovery of the iron chest at the Tuileries, containing parts of his correspondence with the *émigrés* and with Austria. The execution of the King caused Dumouriez his first misgiving. The French Republic was now turning from defence to aggression. Danton declared for the annexation of Belgium to France. Events carried the General into a campaign against Holland. He had had stormy interviews with the French commissioners over their behaviour in Belgium. He was unhappy over events at home. He suffered a defeat at Neerswinden, and there was a scene with Danton. He now secretly decided to march on Paris, attack the Jacobins, disperse the Convention, proclaim the little Louis XVII. king, and re-establish the Constitution overthrown by the Paris rabble.

At first Dumouriez had accepted the Republic, but its cruelty, greed, and rapacity disgusted him. It had challenged England and Spain, and plundered Belgium, Savoy, and Nice. France was seething with inner revolt. Dumouriez thought he could march on Paris and overthrow the Jacobins. He promptly arrested the Commissioners of the Convention, who came to his headquarters to enquire into his conduct, and hurried them over the frontier into the hands of the Austrians. He had allied himself secretly with Coburg, the Austrian commander, an act of treason undoubtedly. He failed, however, to carry most of his army with him in declaring against the Convention and for the royal cause. Nothing remained but to cross the frontier. Most of his supporters shrank from this desperate step. With 458 foot soldiers and 424 horsemen, he crossed over to the enemy, taking with him the Duc de Chartres, the Duc de Montpensier his brother, and four generals.

From one end of France to the other Dumouriez was execrated as a traitor. Up till this date, April 1793, he had earned nothing but fame for his courage as a soldier, his energy as a man of action, his sagacity, statecraft, and high-mindedness. A good linguist, an impressive speaker, he had swayed men in office and armies in the field. But now the word ' traitor ' cancelled all his virtues, and henceforth the historians of his native land declined to admit extenuating circumstances or allow him any rectitude of character. They ignored the fact that he was not the only Frenchman who declined to bow the knee to Bonaparte. The future King of France had gone over to the enemy with him.

On October 19th, 1792, a martial trophy had been placed on the town hall in his birthplace, and ran : ' The Town of Cambrai is proud of having witnessed the birth of Dumouriez. January 26, 1739.' Six

months later the authorities issued a notice to the
effect : ' The Town of Cambrai shudders at having
witnessed the birth in her midst of the infamous and
wicked Dumouriez. Let passers-by share their horror.
Let all traitors tremble.' A proposal was made for
' the demolition of Dumouriez' birthplace on indemni-
fying the present possessor.'

In June 1793, Dumouriez crossed to England, but
he was politely deported after a vain appeal for asylum.
He landed at Ostend, and found a haven of rest at
Hamburg. He was penniless, and proceeded to write
for a livelihood. Book after book appeared criticising
the adventurer Bonaparte, and the anarchy which had
cost France over a million men.

In 1799 he visited Louis XVIII. at the court of the
Emperor Paul of Russia. In October 1800, Dumouriez,
then sixty, met Nelson at Hamburg, which had become
an asylum for many members of the French Court.
Nelson was travelling with Sir William and Lady
Hamilton. They met at breakfast, and the two distinguished men took a great fancy to each other.
Nelson begged him to accept a hundred pounds, saying
his poverty did him honour, and he had used his sword
too well to live only by his pen.

In 1803 Dumouriez was again in England, where he
had been invited to compile his treatise for the defence
of England. This year marked the height of the great
terror of invasion which had been growing in the
public mind since 1796. The Napoleon bogey now
frightened everyone. It seems likely Nelson had been
efficacious in recommending to the English Government the ex-Commandant of Cherbourg, who, as a

young man, had drawn up elaborate plans for the invasion of the Isle of Wight.

" I have wrote to Dumouriez," said Nelson in a letter to Lady Hamilton, " therefore I will only trouble you to say how much I respect him. I fancy he must have suffered great distress at Altona. However, I hope he will now be comfortable for life. He is a very clever man : and beats our generals out and out."

The indefatigable old general drew up a detailed scheme of defence, and a grateful Government conferred on him a pension of £600 a year. In the fierce struggle with Napoleon he bombarded the War Office with shrewd memoranda, much concerned by the slackness of the British ministers. He was the innocent cause of a dire tragedy. Napoleon, hearing that Dumouriez had as a neighbour near Baden the young Duc d'Enghien, was stirred to a white heat of rage. It seemed proof that Royalists and Republicans were working to overthrow the Consulate. Napoleon ordered the kidnapping of the hapless young Duc. Napoleon soon found that he had made a dual mistake. Dumouriez was not the Duc's neighbour, and the Duc was not plotting with Royalists in London. But Napoleon, having acted, let events take their course. The scion of the Condés was shot in the moat of the Château de Vincennes, and all Europe rang with denunciation of the crime.

Dumouriez had taken a pleasant mansion in Acton, London. The sluggishness of the Government in its policy against the agile Napoleon often drove him to despair, and his view was endorsed by the Tsar, who exclaimed in anger to some proposal of the British

envoy, " Act anywhere, provided you act at all ! "
Dumouriez was now in correspondence with Wellington,
whose career he followed with growing admiration. He
warned the Government of the necessity of a strict watch
on Napoleon at Elba, a warning ignored. The imperial
eagle escaped, and its shadow frightened Europe again.

When Louis XVIII. ascended his throne, he seemed
to forget the Royalists' champion, to the old general's
sorrow. He had expected to be given a Marshal's baton
or to be placed in the Chamber of Peers. " I think I
have merited the eternal gratitude of my nation, and
therefore the recompense of the King. They can,
without causing anyone in France to grumble, make me
a marshal." The King offered him the pay and rank
of a Lieutenant-General, which he proudly declined.

When Napoleon escaped, his pen was busy again.
He was now living at Ealing, and complained of the
costs of the journeys to London, for which the Government begrudged him his expenses. He had hopes
that Wellington would obtain a renewal of his Austrian
pension, given in 1800, which he had resigned later.
His hope proved vain. Nevertheless, he was happy in
England. He numbered the highest and the most distinguished in the land among his friends, the Prince
of Wales, the Duke of Kent, Nelson, Wellington, and
Canning among them.

While living in his pleasant house at Ealing he was
visited by his former comrade, the Duc d'Orléans, who
had once been a tutor in Ealing Academy nearby, and
among the pupils there, who looked with awe at the
famous exile, were boys destined to fame as Captain
Marryat, Lord Lawrence, Bishop Selwyn, Cardinal

Newman, and W. M. Thackeray. In later years the Duc d'Orléans gave him a handsome pension, which enabled him to keep a carriage. So the old gentleman was comfortable at last, the only regret being his King's neglect.

In March 1822, the General, alert in his eighties, moved to Turville Park, a house whose situation greatly pleased him. In his last letter he wrote, " At rest in a peaceful retreat, due to the generous hospitality of a fine people, sure of the friendship of men of distinguished rank, character, and intellect, I shall find nothing lacking from the happiness I shall be able to call mine if I know that the French people are themselves happy."

Dumouriez enjoyed life to the very last. A few hours before his death, which occurred exactly on the day and hour one year after his arrival at Turville Park, he walked to the window and looked out over the greensward and the woods, much as we see them now, and he stood long, regarding them in contemplative mood. A few minutes before his end his hands were seen to be clenched. " Que faites vous, mon Général ? " asked his companion. " Je me recueille " (I am harvesting myself), he answered. The priest said, " The General believed in God and in a future. He did harm to none, but good wherever he could. We will not have his last moments tormented with cruel questioning." He crossed his hands and touched his eyelids with holy oil, and the old warrior went forth on his last campaign.

And if *The News* shouted ' Traitor ' across the death chamber, a generous tribute followed him from a contemporary. " He died in exile as if to counteract the clamourous voice of popularity, which accom-

Park Place (about 1780)

panied his early career, with the calm stillness of
solitude which surrounded his bed of death. His
temper was singularly frank and generous, his affection
warm and cordial, his conversation full of strength and
spirit, diversified with a variety of knowledge and a
remarkable discrimination."

On October 8th, 1918, a young British soldier, a
student of history, marched with the British and
Canadian troops into Cambrai. The Germans, retiring, had heavily mined and utterly wrecked a wide
area in the centre of the town. The young soldier
proceeded through the débris to No. 24, Rue du
Petit-Séminaire. The birthplace of General Charles
François Dumouriez had survived for more than a
hundred years the decree which doomed it to destruction in 1793, but when the young soldier arrived at
No. 24, he found only a ruin amid ruins.

## II

Across Turville Heath, nobly isolated, and outlined
against the sky, stands Turville Grange. It looks very
old and dignified, with its white windows, its red-
brick façade, and its outer garden wall broken by a pair
of beautiful wrought-iron gates. On the right of the
house there is a wooden tower that brings an un-
English note to the scene, but not one that jars.
Denmark, Holland, and Normandy present such
objects. What is it ? A mill ? Actually it is our
hideous friend, the iron windmill-waterpump whose
ugly skeleton has been dressed in a French Empire
gown, as it were, by the late Marquis d'Hautpoul.

But let us ring the bell by the iron gates. It

announces you with a crash, and by the time you reach the house door, the butler is there. You feel that twenty windows have watched you up the path, and your reception has been decided by an inner conclave. Here again I fancifully detected the French note.

There is a great house in Paris where I am a happy guest, but familiarity has not yet overcome a certain terror of approach. The house and its courtyard are shut off from the world by an immense pair of gates in a wall that is a rampart to the street. When the bell is rung, a small gate automatically opens, and I crawl through, a clumsy camel passing the needle's eye. Just inside the gate there is a porter's lodge which gives no sign of life, but obviously its square window is a spy-hole.

I am now in a large cobbled courtyard formed by the house and its two wings. The main door is in a far corner of the courtyard, across which I sneak. Shall I get there unobserved? I have an awful feeling that I am watched from tiers and tiers of windows, by the noble duke and the noble duchess, by the countesses their daughters, the counts their sons, by the smaller brood of counts and countesses springing up in the nursery beds, by the secretary, the major-domo, the grooms of the chambers, the footmen, the valets, the chauffeurs, and, on the lowest floor, that numerous underworld ruled by the chef. Are my trousers well pressed, my shoes immaculate, and my gloves without holes? And why, oh, why, did I put on this old hat?

It seems a mile across the courtyard, and Jack approaching the castle of the Giant could not have felt more overwhelmed, more insignificant. There is only one way to enter this fortress with composure. I should have come in a Rolls-Royce with a bonnet as long as a recurring decimal ; the great gates would have swung open, and, with the superb arrogance of two chauffeurs and noiseless motion, I should have swept up to this door under its large glazed canopy.

But I have somehow got across the courtyard. Like a nervous swimmer in the deep end of a pool, I approach the steps with diminishing anxiety. My foot is on the first step, soon I shall be safe through the great glass doors when——

Crash ! Somewhere a great bell has splintered the silence ; a monstrous clamour announces to the world that I am standing on the doorstep. I feel that a hundred windows have eyes, that my tailor is not the best. That miscreant in the porter's lodge has been spying on me ever since I crawled through the wicket-gate.

But the ordeal is almost ended. A footman comes flying down the *escalier d'honneur*. The doors open. He relieves me of hat, coat, and gloves, but his silent dignity does not intimidate me, despite a background of men in armour, marble stairs, and Gobelin tapes-tries. Frequent visits to picture palaces harden one to this sort of thing. The inquisition and ordeal by courtyard are the real terrors.

The bell at Turville Grange does not crash on one in such a fearful manner, but it does evoke a Parisian memory with its French air. At Turville one is really very much on English soil, for the hospitable Marquise is Stonor born, in Stonor-land. She is truly on her native heath. From her windows she surveys a high landscape familiar to twelve generations of ancestors.

The Grange originally was a bakery. Once upon a

time, doubtless, small boys came here, trailing small sisters in boxes on wheels, and the bread was carried home in the lap of the boxed infant, in that easy un-hygienic manner in which bread is handled. The French again are unfeeling in this matter, or should I not write ' feeling,' since they are great bread handlers ? Almost any French street will present women and children carrying home long batons of crisp bread. I have seen cyclists using them, *à la Blondin*, as balancing poles, and once, on a never-to-be-forgotten occasion, I saw two boys engaged in a fierce baton fight with mother's bread, which gave delight to spectators and sparrows alike. Such a scene could only take place in France. Here we take our pleasures and bread sadly.

Nothing remains to-day of the Turville bakery. A pleasant house has grown about the vanished oven. It is a deceptive house, for it shows only a small though pleasant face to the world, and folds long wings behind it, with windows looking on to an enchanting English scene of lawns and rose gardens. Even those lovely iron gates owe nothing to Italy, as I surmised. They were an English present from a delighted and delight-ful guest, the late Queen Alexandra, who came for three days and stayed three weeks.

At the back of the Grange there is a fine panorama of Chiltern Hills, wooded slopes, chequered fields of pasture, and a windmill, at Ibstone, that looks as if it had been painted in by an artist specialising in old England. But the surprise is not the view, it is the magnificent industry of the Marquise, who has planted a woodland, a labour of love through twenty years. She must be a tree lover *in excelsis*. Through long years of Spring's burgeoning, Summer's leafiness, Autumn's fall, and Winter's iron anatomy, her memorial is secure.

Nor has the Marquise been content with tree-planting herself. She has virtuously called on the Royal Family's friendship and pressed them into service. The result is an inner Royal Park, which includes a veritable 'Windsor Park,' since the hands of the House of Windsor, be it those of Queen Alexandra, King Edward, Queen Mary, King George, the Prince of Wales, the Duke of Kent, the Princess Victoria and others, have planted them. The Prince of Wales must have a gardener's touch, for his tree has flourished above all other plantings of the Royal Family. It is a *Picea kosteriana* that has attained a height of twenty feet.

This lovely tree always seems to me to be going to a fancy-dress party. It is so much a costume piece, with its ferny boughs with their milky frills rising, pleat on pleat, like a crinoline. It is a tree not wholly at home in the English landscape, a kind of Polish countess about to dance a Chopinesque polonaise. These Royal *piceas* seem to be awaiting the soft wind of an orchestra to lift them tiptoeing into a ballet where, in a grand finale, their blue-green skirts will swirl out over the level lawn.

But it was not the Royal trees I was discussing with the Marquise as we wandered through the garden, the orchard, the woodland, and finally a shrubbery—a nurseryman alarmed by an over-populated shrubbery had made my hostess a present of one hundred shrubs which had been unostentatiously absorbed—it was old prints, particularly of Henley and its environs, which I sought for to illustrate this book.

" I think I can help you," said Madame d'Hautpoul.

She led the way into the drawing-room, and picked up a small leather-bound album.

"Look at those," she said; "I think they're beautiful."

I looked, and excitement possessed me at once. It was a small album of half-a-dozen steel engravings of Henley one hundred years ago. They were exactly what I sought, beautiful in line and tone, with that melancholy the artists of the early nineteenth century succeeded in imparting to their engravings.

"Who is the artist?" I asked, fascinated by their quality.

"I don't know—they're unsigned," said my hostess.

"But however did you find them?—they're wonderful!" I cried.

"I didn't find them," answered Madame d'Hautpoul with a quiet smile. "The Queen found them."

"Queen Mary—but how?" I demanded.

"Well, you know she loves antique shops, and has a keen eye for the genuine thing. She was rummaging in a shop near Sandringham, and found these engravings. In her kind way she thought of me at once, and she sent them to me," said Madame d'Hautpoul.

I turned the album over and over, gloating.

"What time does this household go to bed?" I asked.

"Why?" demanded my hostess.

"I'm tempted to do a little burgling. To think how I've run all over the place to find prints for my book, and here you have the very kind I want!"

"Well, there's no need to burgle me—I'll lend them to you," said Madame d'Hautpoul.

And thus it was I came by the five tail-pieces of these chapters.

# TOWN AND COUNTRY

Round Piccadilly Circus the traffic roars all day,
And thousands on the pavements pursue their lonely way,
Lonelier for the thousands, that still will ebb and flow,
Though none comes back at all there, and all for ever go.

Round every Chiltern cottage a country peace is heard,
The lowing of the cattle, the song of child and bird;
No one feels ever a stranger where everyone is known
By name from birth to burial, yet proudly walks alone.

# CHAPTER XIII

## A GOLDEN WEDDING

### I

I was busy on my knees pricking out the summer antirrhinums when there was a loud screeching of brakes at my garden gate. Only one car I know of has just that top note of a radio soprano gone static. It must be, I said, as I stuck my trowel in the earth, the A.M. and P.M. It was. I heard the engine die with a shudder, the slamming of a tinny door, and then the click of my raised latch.

" Good morning ! Good morning ! Good morning ! " shouted the P.M., coming down the path. The P.M.'s good mornings are always born in triplets.

" Ah ! You're busy. ' But half a proper gardener's work is done upon his knees,' " chirruped the A.M.

" I'm certain Kipling wrote that after *watching* his gardeners—if he'd done any kneeling himself he wouldn't have been so cheerful about it," I replied irritably, as I tried to straighten myself.

" We've just come from Fawley, and your old friends at the Smithy gave me this note for you," said the A.M.

I thanked her, and placed it on the garden seat, since my hands were dirty.

" Not ill, I hope ?—I haven't been up there for a week."

" Heavens, no ! " cried the P.M. " The old boy was digging in the garden."

The A.M. was busy examining a corner where I had been lately transplanting.

" That looks a fine bed of *Lilium candidum*. I suppose you know," said the A.M. sweetly, " the bulb of the Madonna lily is very good for baldness ? Poultenay, of course, always uses raw onion."

If the proof of the onion was in the pate, then the P.M. was a miserable testimonial.

" I've always wondered what monstrous fellow started this traffic in a bald man's faith," I said. " Whoever had the idea of desecrating the Madonna lily in this fashion ? "

" John Parkinson," replied the A.M.

" And who's John Parkinson ? " I asked, knowing I should receive an exact, detailed answer. The A.M. is an encyclopædia of gardening lore. She is the only woman who was ever known to get the better of Miss Whissitt in a wordy war over Narcissus Pseudo-Narcissus. You could almost hear her mind whirr as she dialled her memory, calling up her stored information.

" John Parkinson wrote the *Paradisus* and other works. He was physician to King James I., and of course was a contemporary of Gerard, who wrote the *Herbal*," explained the A.M. " He had a garden in Long Acre, and later he was a great friend of Charles the First's gardener. He was quite renowned for curing baldness. All his contemporaries used to recommend rubbing the head with onion and then standing in the sun. It was Parkinson who recommended the Madonna lily."

" Then," I said, turning to the P.M., " why do you

266

rub your head with the onion when you might gild it with the lily ? "

" Because, my dear sir," retorted the P.M. vigorously, " I'd rather see one more lily coming up in the garden than one more hair sprouting on my head. And I know which is the more certain. I've no faith in onions, lilies, or hairdressers. Amelia pesters me to death with her quackeries."

## II

When the A.M. and P.M. had departed, I opened the note. It was in Mrs. Harman's clear, spidery script.

THE SMITHY

*On the twenty-second of June it will be our Golden Wedding Day. We are having a family gathering and a few visitors. We should feel honoured if you could come and join us at tea, which will be at four o'clock. Hoping that you are well,*

*Yours respectfully,*
LAURA HARMAN.

This, of course, was much more than an invitation. It was a Golden Command. There was no possible engagement that could take precedence of this memorable event in the lives of my old friends. I accepted at once.

The twenty-second dawned, radiant with the loveliness of June. As I went up the hill, the woods were dappled with sunshine, and there was an afternoon stillness over everything. On a cottage window-sill a cat lay basking in the sun. As I came along the lane bordered with elms someone was sawing in a shed. Then stillness again as I passed the lych-gate of the churchyard. It was an afternoon perfect for lying on one's back in a field and wondering whether the clouds were moving at all. Perversely, I thought of Regent Street and all the red omnibuses, taxis, and people journeying in a faint haze of exhaust fumes, and of newsboys shouting papers full of the world's turmoil.

I found the blacksmith's cottage anything but tranquil as I entered. It seemed crammed with relations and friends, all smiling, talking, and trying to make themselves useful. The sitting-room, which I knew in winter's cosy lamplight, with a kettle singing on the hob, as well as in summer's open-windowed sweetness, was now completely transformed. A long table filled the room, with rows of chairs on either side. There was a gathering of tea-pots on the hob—many a neighbour must have helped out with a tea-pot on this occasion. The centre of the table was dominated by two enormous iced cakes, one the present of a married daughter, the other of a local resident, and all down the table were dishes of jam and great plates of bread and butter, and teacups, saucers, knives, forks, spoons, pots of flowers, and gay festoons of paper bunting.

It was a real farm-house tea, with everyone talking, and the old dames passing the tea-cups, and much coming and going with full plates and empty plates and jugs of hot water. What a scene of good cheer, like a chapter out of Dickens, with daughters and their husbands, and grandchildren, and neighbours, old, middle-aged, and young.

And there at each end of the table sat the hero and heroine of this bright occasion, and for a moment, as I looked at Mrs. Harman, with her rosy cheeks and bright blue eyes, with such happiness and vitality sparkling in them, I caught a glimpse of another festive table set fifty years ago, with its bride brought to this village by the stalwart young blacksmith.

The blacksmith just now would have passed for a bishop, so neat was he in his black suit, so benign with his patriarchal domed head and white beard. He regarded this celebration of his golden wedding with the utmost serenity. At eighty-four there is nothing much to get excited about. Time has become a pageant in which one has ceased to enact a part. As I looked at him now, I saw a figure of a dead era. The forges are passing from the village greens of England. If they do not fall into decay, then they are converted into petrol stations. When he was young and strong, the blacksmith rose with the dawn to shoe the squire's horses—there were eighty of them on the estate. Now there are not half-a-dozen. To-day another blacksmith pays a visit to the smithy once a month, and an odd horse is produced for shoeing. The squire's estate has shrunk too, and his woods have been felled. The village through which he motors is now no longer his, and on the edge of his most sacred coverts there are week-enders who have Elizabethened the farm-labourers' cottages with old oak, inglenooks, settles, tankards, grandfather clocks, and sundials.

Mr. Harman, sitting serene at the head of his table,

must regard us all as transitory visitors. How long his forbears have lived here it is impossible to say. There are records in the Fawley Church Register of his progenitors through nearly four hundred years. Doubtless he is descended from that favourite of William Rufus, Robert Fitz-Hamon, who first brought the name into this district when he was granted the fiefs of Queen Matilda. He was a great baron in that eleventh century. The yew tree that still flourishes in Fawley Churchyard was probably planted about the same time that Robert Fitz-Hamon planted himself in the neighbourhood and grew in dignity until he could style himself "by the grace of God, Prince of Glamorgan, Earl of Corbill, Baron of Glanville, Lord of Gloucester, Bristol, Tewkesbury, and Cardiff, Conqueror of Wales, near kinsman of the King, and general of the King's army of France." What a splash he would have made for himself in *Who's Who* to-day!

As I sat at my host's board, among his married daughters, grandsons, and granddaughters, there was one seat vacant. The long line of Harmans is broken for ever. When the blacksmith is gathered to his fathers in Fawley Churchyard, his male line, preserved down the ages, will be ended. The only son, a boy of twenty, lies in French soil, killed in the last month of the Great War.

The high tea is finished, the great cake has been cut, a simple toast has been made to our host and hostess on their Golden Wedding. "They said we started late," laughed Mrs. Harman, "for I was twenty-seven, and Mark was thirty-three, and that was considered quite old in those days. And it looked as if we weren't going to be married, for there we stood, waiting in the church, and no curate came. So they had to send for another. The curate who was to have married us forgot all about it, and sat at home reading, and came hurrying to the church when it was all over ! That was in London, and I suppose marriages didn't mean much to them."

There is now a scraping of chairs, a lighting of cigarettes and pipes, and a general move to the field in which the cottage is situated. Here we are all grouped under an apple tree, and our photograph is solemnly taken, in late afternoon sunshine, with Mr. and Mrs. Harman seated in the midst of their guests.

This is the crowning ceremony, and after more talk, congratulations, and handshakings, the guests leave, some for London, some for neighbours' cottages, and some for homes across the glowing evening fields. I depart with a momentous discovery. I had taken Mr. Harman aside and had gently probed his memory. You must decant an octogenarian's memory much as you do an old wine. Gently done, it will come sweet and clear ; clumsily done, its bouquet will be shattered by sediment. Cautiously I led him back down the years.

" When did you first start work, Mr. Harman ? " I asked.

" When I was little more than fourteen I was apprenticed to a blacksmith."

" Here, at Fawley ? "

" Oh no, sir, that was at Turville Heath. The old smithy's a private house now. When I'd been there about three years the blacksmith died, and I carried on by myself."

" But most of your life was passed here, at Fawley. You were born here ? " I asked.

The old blacksmith drew at his pipe, and taking it out of his mouth, looked at me with a roguish twinkle in his eye.

" I've lived here in this very house for the last fifty years, but I wasn't born in Fawley, sir. I was born at Lower Assenden."

" What ! In my village ! " I exclaimed.

" In your cottage, sir ! " he said with a chuckle.

Now I have talked with the old blacksmith through many an evening as he sat by the fire, nursing their enormous cat, but never before had I heard of this. He enjoyed the surprise he had given me.

" I was born in part of your house, sir," he explained, " for it was then two cottages—but which of 'em it was, I can't say. You see, I left when I was a month old."

This, I felt, was one more strand in our friendship. By a strange fate I own the cottage in which he was born and the cottage in which he has passed his life. I also own the smithy in which he has done his life's work. The word ' own ' sounds disagreeable in my ears. That smithy, I feel, belongs for all time to Mr. Harman. From early dawn to eve he has sweated by the furnace, his blows have rung out at the anvil, his strong hands and knees have gripped the fetlocks of cart-horse and hunter.

As I walked home that evening I pondered over my possession of his old smithy. It stands there, intact, with all its implements, on the edge of the village green. The smithies are dying out, falling into ruin, or being converted. What better memorial to the honourable race of blacksmiths, to Mark Harman in particular, could one devise than to preserve the smithy in which he has passed his life ? A resolution sprang into being. The smithy should be kept intact. The anvil, the trough, the bellows, the furnace, the long bench, and the tools hanging on the walls, with the door wide open and the window looking on the village green, should be there for all time, so that at any moment there might be a thudding of ghostly hoofs, a " Whoa ! " on the air, and a clink, clink of hammer on iron.

> *Under the spreading chestnut tree*
> *The village smithy stands——*

We have parodied the poem to death, but it speaks of a phase of village life through the long centuries since man compelled the noble service of the horse. The Fawley smithy has no chestnut tree, but long may it stand, the relic of honest labour and a sturdy past.

I had nothing of this in my mind while I talked to Mr. Harman. I was busy probing into his memories. He remembered when Fawley and the deer park were all corn-lands. Now it is mostly pasture, such is the decay of our land. The squires and the farmers had not been ruined by the imported wheat demanded by rapidly expanding industrial centres.

" Did the squire live in great style ? " I asked.

" Oh yes, he did himself very well—but he knew every cottage and the name of every person in it. He was always riding round. But Mrs. Birch, she was the woman for style, sir. I remember her coming into church—that was about 1860, when she lived at Henley Park—she was an old lady then, and she always walked down the aisle with two footmen in front, with powdered hair and knee breeches. One carried a foot-warmer, and t'other carried a Bible. There's been no one like that since."

No, indeed, and there never will be again. The grandees have gone for ever. Milord Brougham no longer drives across Europe with lackeys and postillions. A storekeeper's daughter may get herself a nondescript princeling for a husband and aspire to grandeur, but we can still hear the ring of the cash register above that of the champagne glasses. James and John survive, buckled and powdered, at a few palaces, royal or cinema, but they are on parade as curiosities of the past.

Mrs. Harman was the last to bid me good night. It is her custom to accompany her guests to the little iron gate that separates her garden from the village green. Here she will stand, white-haired and smiling, until the visitor has gone beyond sight. But this evening she went along the road with me a little, to take the usual evening constitutional.

" It's the Fawley air, sir," she observed, when I alluded to her alertness. " Do you know, when I came here a bride, they didn't think I was going to live, my lungs were so weak ! "

I laughed, regarding her apple cheeks and keen eyes. But while she may believe it is the Fawley air, I have another idea. Clearly she has never lost the zest for life. Her interests stretch far beyond the village. " Have you seen this about your book ? " she will ask, taking out of an envelope a cutting sent from America. " I see you are lecturing at Manchester to-morrow," she will inform me. Of all the books I have taken to the cottage there is none that she has not read with critical interest, and those who imagine that long residence in a small village results in severance from the outside world and its interests would be speedily shown their error in a ten minutes' chat.

As we walked along the lane, high on the edge of the plateau where the village lies with its commanding views, we came to the old square-towered church, and the Rectory opposite. This house had played a part in Mrs. Harman's life, for it was here she came in the service of a family from London which had taken it for a vacation. It was thus that she met young Mark Harman, the blacksmith, and was brought to live at the smithy. Looking at the Rectory, I called to mind another remarkable old lady, Mrs. Powys, who had passed much of her life in Fawley, and, over a century past, had died here at seventy-nine, alert to the end. But that is another chapter.

# MIDDLE AGE

*How quick the years are slipping by !*
*Spring blossom on the cherry bough,*
*A lark mounts up the April sky,*
*And I am nearly forty now !*

*How swift was love to set afire*
*The heart in other days of Spring,*
*The rapture and the fierce desire*
*To once experience everything !*

*How wide the world, what distant seas*
*Glittered 'neath Youth's enchanted heaven ;*
*Still on !—can any land appease*
*The wanderlust of twenty-seven ?*

*Youth fearless, restless, brightly armed,*
*Ride forth and find what I have found,*
*The whole world narrows to a charmed*
*Bird-haunted plot of English ground.*

*Of all this lovely earth one scene*
*I cherish most, this heritage,*
*Where Spring comes now, to make serene*
*These happier years of middle age.*

# CHAPTER XIV

## A GAY LADY

LET us call at Fawley Rectory, built by the Rev. John Stevens, the uncle of Mary Blandy, and meet Mrs. Caroline Lybbe Powys. We know much of her life, especially the local events and doings of Society between 1756 and 1808, because she left behind her a lively diary which she had kept from her youth onwards. In 1762 she married Philip Lybbe Powys, of an old family that had settled at Hardwick Hall, situated on the hillside beyond Mapledurham. She thus became mistress of one of the most beautiful estates on the banks of the Thames. One of her husband's younger brothers was Rector of Fawley, a fact which brought her to the Rectory later. We are given a brief sketch of her husband. " He's tall and thin. My father and all the tenants tell me there never was so beautiful a boy as the young Squire ; but I think (fortunately) the smallpox has given him now a good rough, manly face."

Mrs. Lybbe Powys loved life. She began to experience it to the full, going out and about in days when travel was physically fatiguing. In 1768, the Rector of Fawley, the Rev. Thomas Powys, received a young pupil at the Rectory, one, Master Pratt, the only son of Lord Camden, the Lord Chancellor who had so strenuously opposed the taxation of the

American colonists. He was nine years old when he arrived at the Rectory, and in after life never forgot his happy boyhood at Fawley, and used his considerable influence on behalf of his old tutor. Mrs. Powys described the Rectory as " one of the most elegant parsonages in England, commanding from a very good house a prospect uncommonly noble." That praise does not seem exaggerated.

In December 1776, Mrs. Powys was highly excited by events in Henley. The ' fashion ' was making it a centre, and a gala week had been planned. Lady Grandison, married to Sir Charles Montagu, had taken Phyllis Court. Her son, Lord Villiers, and his family, were living with them. " Their house is generally full, and to make it gayer than usual this Christmas, they talked of performing *The Provoked Husband*." This event created such a stir in the neighbourhood, wrote Mrs. Powys in her letter to a friend, that plans had to be made for an audience larger than Phyllis Court could accommodate.

Mrs. Powys was flattered to find herself taken up by the Grandisons. " When first Lady Grandison came we never went, as we imagined a family so deeply engaged in the fashionable game of loo could never wish an intimacy with one who never played at all, but my brother (the Rector) is very intimate there, who as a clergyman may, you know, easily keep clear of gaming, even with the approbation of the most polite."

The local excitement was immense. The famous Monsieur Tissier was to perform *Pygmalion*. A theatre had been fitted up in a barn and coach-house

in the neighbourhood, " hung with green baize, and
the whole to be lighted with wax." There were to
be two performances, and a supper and ball given by
Lord Villiers at *The Bell Inn*, and a grand ball by the
Freemans at Fawley Court.

The beds at *The Bell Inn* were all booked up, and
forty private ones were taken in the town. *The Red
Lion* was also full to overflowing, and the price of a
bed rose to four and six guineas for three nights,
such was the price of fashion. " A band of ten
musicians have been down at Sir Charles Montagu's
these ten days, the best band from Italy," recorded
the excited Mrs. Powys. " Lady Grandison was telling my brother yesterday they had above thirty set
down to dinner every day in the parlour. ' And
yet, Mr. Powys, you shall judge if my larder will not
hold out.' " Whereupon he was shown three does,
three brace of pheasants, eight hares, six brace
whistling plovers, twelve couple woodcock, ten brace
partridges, a pea fowl, two guinea-fowls, and snipes
and larks without number. The only alarm felt was
for Sir Charles and Mr. Garrick, who were both ill
with gout.

The great day dawned. Mrs. Powys, like everyone
else, was anxious about the weather, for she had to
make her way from Hardwick to Fawley. There had
been a heavy fall of snow on Sunday, January 5th, and
the usual track to Fawley proved impassable, but by
going some miles round by the Henley turnpike the
Rectory was reached.

Henley itself was packed with visitors. The theatre
proved the very glass of fashion. There were the

Villiers, of course, the Duke of Argyll and Lord Frederick Cavendish with Count Brule, and the Lord High Chancellor, Lord Camden, with his son from Fawley Rectory. The gay young Lord Barrymore was present, with Marshal Conway, from Park Place, who brought a great house-party; also, Sir Thomas Stapleton, from Greys Court. The ladies made a magnificent show, wearing their jewels.

The band struck up, the curtain rose, and the Rector's specially written prologue—he had a turn for verse—went amazingly well. The leading lady among the amateur cast was Miss Hodges. She was a most beautiful girl, recorded Mrs. Powys, and " had every advantage of dress, a pink satin suit of clothes, elegantly trimmed with gauze and flowers, all Lady Villiers' diamonds, valued at £12,000; four large bows making a complete stomacher, two of the same as sleeve knots, a superb necklace and earrings, her head almost covered, and a girdle of jewels, the ends hanging down a quarter of a yard."

This glittering vision carried all before her until the famous M. Tissier appeared in Rousseau's *Pygmalion*.

I had often marvelled at the passion for Pilgrim Cottage and its locality which, from the very day we entered it together, my secretary, Louis Tissier, had shown. When events took him back to France, first to perform his military service, and then to take up business in Paris, he was alert for every occasion when he might snatch a few days in his beloved English cottage. We did not know then, of course, that he was merely a reincarnation, and was visiting the scene of a former triumph in 1777, when he held all Henley

and its visiting aristocracy spellbound with his acting !
His modern legacy in the district is the fireplace he
built with me in the cottage, an occasion when he was
nearly bricked up for life inside the chimney into which
he vanished to give the work a few closing touches.
But this performance, extraordinary as it was, with me
acting chorus at the bottom of the chimney, fades beside
the fame of his performance on the night of January
5th, 1777. Here is Mrs. Powys's impressive account
of that memorable scene :

" When the curtain draws up, Tissier (the Prince)
is leaning on a table in the most melancholy mood,
dressed in a most superb habit. At the further end
of the stage was a canopy and curtain of gold and silver
gauze (which cost £10), behind which was concealed
his beautiful statue. He was, I suppose, twenty
minutes in all the attitudes of tragic woe, deliberating
whether he should draw the veil, so fearing the sight
of this too lovely object. His powers are certainly
astonishing ; 'tis said no one equals him. Some par-
tial *English* flatter themselves *their Garrick* might come
up to him. I own myself of that number : but then,
as not a perfect mistress of the French, I fear one's
opinion would go for nothing."

There followed the awakening of Galatea. Mrs.
Powys and the ladies of Henley were now a little nervous. Who knew how this Frenchman might go about
the awakening business ? Frenchmen are Frenchmen, from the land of *l'amour*. But M. Tissier seems
to have managed the business very well.

" She speaks, he kneels down, grasps her hand, and
while both seem under the most *indescribable* surprise,

the curtain drops. It was really the finest scene imaginable, and, you see, avoided every indelicacy."

It is highly probable some of the bucks were disappointed at so tame an awakening, but the Frenchman's acting relieved the tense emotions of the matrons.

" Most of the company had privately expressed their apprehensions of the well-known story in Ovid, for the sake of our sweet actress, who was so much admired, that I found most were of my sentiments of its not being the thing for a girl of fashion to appear in an affair of this very public nature."

All was well. Now for the ball and supper at *The Bell Inn*. Mrs. Powys did not go. It was already midnight, and she feared not being able to get through all the diversions of this gala week. But on Wednesday she went to the Freemans' supper and ball at Fawley Court. The grand old house was *en fête*. "Their usual eating-room not being large enough, the supper was in the hall, so that we did not come in thro' that, but a window was taken out of the library, and a temporary flight of steps made into that, from which we passed into the green breakfast-room, through the pink-papered billiard room, along the saloon, into the red damask drawing-room. Though none sat down, this room was soon so crowded as to make us return to the saloon. This likewise very soon filled, and as the tea was carried round, one heard from everyone, ' Fine assembly,' 'Magnificent house,' 'Sure we are in London ! ' "

The country mouse had no sense of inferiority that night. What rank and fashion, what chatter, what ogling ! " America, sir, and what do they think they'll

achieve now they've declared their independence ?
Egad, sir, a bunch of rebels. We should have dealt
firmly with 'em ! " " Mr. Coke is a most remarkable
man, sir. He intends to farm on a scientific plan at
Holkham." " *The School for Scandal* is a very pretty
piece, madam. By Mr. Sheridan the wit; I saw it
last week at Bath, where it's taken the fashion by
storm.'

There, in a corner, stands Lady Ailesbury, in a green
silk sack dress, holding court, with her handsome
husband, Marshal Conway, at her side. It is almost a
mob. There are no minuets, it is too difficult without
a master of ceremonies among so many people of rank.
But there is plenty of gambling, and Mrs. Powys is
somewhat shocked by the scenes at the loo table. A
lady of quality has borrowed ten pieces of M. Tissier
within half-an-hour of sitting down !

" Oh, what a disfiguring thing is gaming, particularly to ladies," wrote Mrs. Powys to a friend. " I
always observe even those who have it to lose have no
less a tinge of the rouge in their countenances when
fortune does not smile."

Meanwhile the orgeat, lemonade, capillaire, and red
and white negus are being carried around by the powdered flunkeys. At half-past twelve supper is announced, and the hall doors are thrown wide open.
The saloon is illuminated by three hundred coloured
lamps round the six doors, over the chimney place, and
the statue at the other end. Ninety-two sit down to
supper.

" Everybody seemed surprised at entering the hall.
The house had been amazingly admired, but now there

was one general exclamation of wonder. This, you may be certain, pleased the owners, particularly as many of the nobility there now never saw it before. The once so beautiful Lady Almeria, I think, is vastly altered. She and Lady Harriet Herbert had the new trimmings, very like bell-ropes with their tassels, and seemingly very inconvenient in dancing."

They were late home to Fawley Rectory, and next afternoon were breakfasting " at the genteel hour of three," when my Lord Camden and his daughter were announced, the young lady having arrived for Friday night's performance of the play.

" The Friday morn Henley town was just like any public place, such different sets of company walking about it. Never before was it so gay, or so much money spent there ; provisions rose each day immoderately. The gentlemen walked down. We were engaged in hair-dressing, of which fraternity five from London were at Lady Grandison's, three at Freeman's, and others in the town no doubt."

There was much bowing between the nobility out walking that morning. My Lord Villiers had sent tickets to my Lord Camden, since, having a little merit in the theatrical way, " 'twas impossible but they must too have such an orator as Lord Camden approve, if just, or blame with his unerring judgment "—though the damned fellow had backed the rebels in America ! " My Lord Camden, very pleased, returned a compliment as flattering. The graces are never wanting to persons of true politeness," observed Mrs. Powys.

They were all early at the theatre on Friday night, and the Powys boy found himself sitting behind sweet little Lord Barrymore, aged eight. That small boy may have got his taste for theatricals at this gala week. Later, he was to astonish Henley district with his own theatre at Wargrave nearby, and run through a great fortune in a few years.

The performance this evening again delighted the assembly. " Lord Villiers had a different and still finer dress, buttons and buckles quite in *ton*, viz. large to an excess ; all the very fine men wear two watches— Lord Villiers, Lord Malden, and Tissier had." At the very close of the play there was a surprise item. Messrs. Tissier, Churchill, and Englefield appeared. " The first an excellent figure as an old woman playing on the violin, the second, a girl with a brandy bottle, looking rather delicate, as Churchill is a pretty man, exceedingly fair ; she and her *pero* danced the *fricassée*, a most robust performance, an excellent burlesque on fine stage dances."

After this the company adjourned for supper, at which the chief topic was the highway robbery. Post-chaises had been stopped on the way from Henley to the stage-barn at Bolney Court. " Tho' the nights were dark we had flambeaux. The chaise behind ours was robbed. It would have been silly to have lost one's diamonds so totally unexpected ; and diamonds it seems they came after, more in number than mine indeed. It seems it was well known Mr. Hodges would not let Lady Villiers' jewels be kept at Bolney, so that each night her woman was sent in a hired chaise to bring them home, and we found only hired chaises had been stopped. On the alarm Lord Villiers sent a guard of six armed men for the Duenna, and so to the great joy of the company we soon heard of her being arrived in safety."

The roads around Henley were apparently none too safe. When the landlord of my local inn, *The Golden Ball*, astonished me one day with the information that Dick Turpin and Tom King had lurked there, and showed me their hiding hole, the highwaymen legends became very real. The number of rich people in the Henley district, together with thick woods, wide commons, and heaths, made it ideal for the gentlemen with masks and pistols.

Ten years after the attack on the post-chaise, Mrs. Powys makes mention of another robbery. " Mr. Powys and Tom went to Bletchingdon Park to shoot, and were robbed by a highwayman only four miles from Henley, on the Oxford Road, just about three o'clock. We hear the poor man was drowned the week after, by trying to escape (after having robbed a carriage) through some water which was very deep. He behaved civilly, and seemed, as he said, greatly distressed."

The wealth in the district constantly evokes expressions of admiration from Mrs. Powys. She liked to describe the elegant suppers, the wines and fruits, the dresses and jewels. The week of the Henley play must have cost Lord Villiers a large sum.

England at this time was in a distressing condition, the gaols were crowded, the roads were infested with starving, desperate men, Newgate Prison, George Dance's terrifying masterpiece of gloom, was going up, to be almost destroyed three years later in the Gordon Riots. A starving peasantry was adding to the misery of the towns. Hangings in public were the order of the day, a bright morning entertainment for a brutalised population. Capital sentences were inflicted for the most trivial offences. The law was administered with a cynical mixture of savagery and levity. On the Sunday preceding the execution of criminals at Newgate the ' condemned sermon ' was preached, during which a coffin lay on a table within an enclosure called the Dock, and round this coffin stood the prisoners condemned to die. The public were admitted at charges rising from sixpence to two shillings, the money going to the turnkeys.

In Abingdon market-place eight farm labourers, old inhabitants, were hanged for being concerned in rick fires, and twenty-seven fathers and sons were torn from their families and transported for life. Occasionally a voice was raised against the horror of these conditions, but Society, polite and kind in itself, had no social conscience.

Even kind Mrs. Powys thought of little else but the number of titles she encountered, the cost of the banquets, the splendour of the houses to which she was welcomed. " No servants but those of the Grandisons and Villiers ; indeed, they have such numbers no others could be wanted. Everything was sent from their house," she writes of the supper and the ball given at *The Bell Inn* after the play. " Soups and game as usual hot, the rest cold. We hear cost Lord Villiers £1,000."

In 1784 Mrs. Powys, with her husband and daughter, left their old home, Hardwick House, and came to reside with her brother-in-law at Fawley

Rectory. Her son, Philip, was now away from home, Marshal Conway having given him a commission in the army, Cornet of the 50th Foot. The Rectory was smaller, but the loveliness of its situation, crowning an ascent from the Thames valley of two miles of beech-woods, soon endeared the place to Mrs. Powys. The panorama extended from Windsor Castle to the Hog's Back in Surrey. It was the only house in Fawley possessing a water supply, a condition which endured for another hundred years, for it had its own well, 369 feet deep.

Life flowed pleasantly on at Fawley Rectory. There was ceaseless social activity in the neighbourhood, and there was a definite Henley season, in winter, when balls and theatricals drew the *ton* to the town. Royalty honoured the place from time to time. There was a flutter at Henley Park House in 1785, when the dowager Mrs. Freeman was suddenly surprised by her butler running up to her dressing-room, where she was confined with a cold, and announcing, " The King and Queen, ma'am ! " " Don't alarm me, William," retorted Mrs. Freeman ; " they are not coming here, but to Fawley Court, no doubt." But a footman followed immediately, saying carriages were coming up the drive, and he had lighted a fire in the drawing-room. " A smart breakfast, William," commanded Mrs. Freeman, throwing on a cloak.

She arrived downstairs just in time to welcome the King, the Queen, two Princesses, and a lady- and two gentlemen-in-waiting. How Mrs. Powys delights in her narration of this great event ! The Royalty stayed two hours and a half, talked a lot, and showed themselves very well informed of matters. Poor Mrs. Freeman must have felt the strain.

" The worst of these great visitors is that no servants must appear, and you are obliged to wait on them yourself," observed Mrs. Powys. Mrs. Freeman agitatedly made tea, served the Princess Royal, only to be told she had forgotten the King. This lapse was laughed over, but the hostess was really distressed by the fact that the lady- and gentlemen-in-waiting, who stood behind all the time, could not be offered any refreshment in the same room. The poor creatures had been called out early in the morning and would be late back at home. Had Mrs. Freeman had warning, she would have prepared a breakfast in another room for them.

Then the King very genially wished to see the house, and would not allow Mrs. Freeman to accompany them—" You shall not go out with such a cold." " To sit a prisoner in one's drawing-room and know the King and Queen are going in and out of rooms as they fancy ! " cries Mrs. Powys, who had her own fluttering moment.

The Royalty in the district excited everyone. It was market day in Henley. Two carters came thence to the Rectory, saying, " We can't stay, as the King and Queen are just behind ! " There was a commotion in the Rectory. On the heels of the rumour came a coach and six up the avenue. But it was only the Earl of Macclesfield paying a morning visit.

Poor Mrs. Freeman had to ' return ' the visit at the next Court day, and, as ever, found she had nothing to wear. Luckily her ' mantua-maker ' assured her there was no change in court dress, so she went in an old costume "flounces and trimmings, tho' quite out elsewhere, treble ruffled cuffs and long dangling ruffles as formerly."

A fortnight later there was a wedding, performed by the Rector, when he married Mr. Pratt, his former pupil, Lord Camden's son, to Miss Molesworth " and a fortune of £40,000." They all laughed exceedingly at setting out in two post-chaises, " to see the bride and bridegroom dressed with the utmost plainness in one carriage, and in the other that followed, the lady's-maid and the valet fine to a degree ; but this quite the *ton* now." So it was always thus, it seems, even in an age pre-instalment and pre-Woolworth.

Sudden visits seem to have been inflicted on the occupants of Henley houses. There was consternation at Park Place when the butler announced to Marshal Conway at dinner the Count Zekany and ladies. One of the ladies was the Princess of Hesse. " Then," recounted Lady Ailesbury, " I thought it was all over with me." The guests proved to be charming. But sleeping accommodation became a serious problem, for " foreign men and their wives seldom occupy the same beds, and, as the house was near full, this was of some consequence ; so she bid her husband whisper his friend, and find out what was to be done, and in this they complied with the vulgar English fashion, and Lady Ailesbury, sending the Duchess and Mrs. Damer up in the attics, made room for all their guests."

Little Lord Barrymore was growing up. He was now eighteen, and the theatrical performances of Lord

Villiers and the renowned M. Tissier had implanted a love of amateur acting. He converted a barn, and two years later he built a magnificent theatre, holding seven hundred, at Wargrave. It cost him £60,000, and his first wardrobe swallowed up 2,000 guineas. With the help of the Jews he raised money on an income of £4,000 a year, and a fortune of £100,000 on attaining his majority. It all proved too little. His favourite expression was " Damn the expense ! " He often spent £1,500 a night on his entertainments at Wargrave. Within three years he was almost bankrupt.

But on January 31st, 1789, all was gaiety and good cheer. The playhouse was packed with the neighbouring families. The play was *The Confederacy*, with young Lord Barrymore, then eighteen, in the leading rôle. The lavish hand was displayed in everything. " The cake, negus, and all kinds of wines were brought between the acts. The cake alone one night they say cost £20. The ball and supper on the Wednesday very elegant, as *The Red Lion* had orders to get everything possible. A service of plate was sent from London for the occasion. We hear his lordship is going to build a ball and supper-room adjoining his theatre."

In March of that year the whole nation was relieved to hear that the King had recovered from an illness. The Fawley family went to tea at Phyllis Court to see the illuminations in Henley, in celebration of the recovery. All the houses were lighted up. " We walked about in different parties from the neighbourhood, the whole made a very fine sight. Fawley Court looked vastly well from the bridge." The Rector, too, illuminated his house. The farmers and their wives were asked to dinner, there was a large bonfire, and a barrel of ale was given to the village.

In August that year Lord Barrymore grew even more lavish. The Powyses were at the play, which was timed for midnight—such was the simple country life. Actually the play began later, as the Prince of Wales had to be waited for. A box, a supper-room, and a ball-room had been built for His Royal Highness. The supper-room was circular, and it had a circular sideboard " at which no more than six of his lordship's servants attended, dressed in scarlet and gold with such uncommon cleverness that no one of the company but had everything wished for in an instant."

The Prince of Wales charmed everyone, " with such ease and grace he dances that he was sure to be known by his manner, tho' without star or any other signature of his birth," records Mrs. Powys, overcome in such exalted company, and then, recovering, adds—" What a pity such an accomplished young man, knowing so well how to make himself admired and beloved, can be wanting in duty to such parents as his, but time and his own good sense will very soon, I've no doubt, make him see the impropriety, even to his own future happiness, in this juvenile conduct."

He was already, at twenty-seven, married to Mrs. Fitzherbert, driven from Carlton House by his debts, and had authorised Fox, on his authority, to characterise the story of his marriage as a falsehood. One hundred and eighteen years later a sealed packet in Coutts Bank was opened by Royal permission, and was found to contain the marriage certificate. When the Prince died, and was buried at Windsor, as George IV., the miniature of Mrs. Fitzherbert lay on his breast, as commanded in an early Will.

Mrs. Powys in her pious wish for his reform was thinking doubtlessly of the Fitzherbert marriage, the defiance of his Royal parents, and the scandal of his conduct raised in a recent debate in the House of Commons. Her wish was never fulfilled. There followed, later, the Prince's lamentable quarrel with his wife Princess Caroline, so that when he drove through Henley, in 1814, in the train of the Allied Princes, the townspeople refrained from cheering him, so unpopular was his conduct towards the Princess.

The winter of 1789-90 at Henley reached the height of gaiety. The lavish Barrymore displays went from extravagance to extravagance. Four Henley balls had been given with great éclat. Lord Barrymore gave a masked ball to celebrate his majority, which the Prince of Wales attended, unmasked. There were four hundred and seventy of the nobility and gentry present, including the Duchess of Bolton. She and Barrymore had invented a special language for their set, done by arranging one vowel and one consonant to each word. Mrs. Powys enjoyed all this hugely, little dreaming it was the rake's progress. Lord Barrymore's theatre had now a cardroom, in which he had lost 2,800 guineas in one evening at quinze. The Rector, Mrs. Powys, and her sons were there, in black dominoes, and the Margravine of Anspach recited a ballad while masked.

In the spring of 1793 Lord Barrymore was marching

some French prisoners from Rye to Dover, when he called for his servant to give him a lift in his carriage which was following. After entering it he rested his shot-gun against his knees. It was accidentally discharged, shooting him in the head. He died forty minutes later, and was buried at Wargrave, in his twenty-fourth year, a swift ending to a swift career.

At the end of her diary in 1793, Mrs. Powys, apologising for its shortness, writes : " For though in my annual Pocket-book I always set down the visits of each day, yet here it would take up too much room, for in so excellent and agreeable neighbourhood it would be a constant repetition of dinners at each mansion within seven or eight miles round." What, one wonders, would lively Mrs. Powys have achieved in this age of motor-cars ! " Our most agreeable and social neighbourhood never suffer their friends to pass a day solo," she comments gratefully.

The death of Marshal Conway, in 1795, was a blow to the neighbourhood. Lady Ailesbury gave up Park Place. " Everybody bore so melancholy an appearance that it was hardly possible to keep up our spirits on the thoughts of losing so kind a neighbour." Lord and Lady Malmesbury followed at Park Place, and entertained on the same lavish scale.

Actors and actresses were not always in the high society they claim to be in to-day. A few made spectacular marriages, a Garrick moved in the fashion, but most of them were social outcasts and regarded as adventurers. Thus, when a touring company came to Henley in 1798, they " put £100 into the Henley Bank to answer any demands upon them. Rather unusual for strollers in general," adds Mrs. Powys caustically.

Life flowed pleasantly on. In January 1799, we find the Powyses at Park Place, where Lady Malmesbury gave a ball. " The house is superbly furnished with every elegance from Italy, France, and, in short, every country—fine pictures, pier-glasses, paintings of the Vatican Library, some curious tables, etc., that belonged to the unfortunate Louis XVI."

## II

There is one incident in Mrs. Powys's diary that I should not have noticed with such interest but for a personal experience a few days before reading it. " That evening we crossed the water to Fawley Court to see the night-blooming *Cereus*, a very curious plant," recorded Mrs. Powys.

A very curious plant indeed. My own acquaintance with it occurred on a visit to Lady Jekyll's, at Munstead House.

" Look at my plant," said my hostess, as I came down for dinner. " It's going to bloom to-night in honour of your visit. It'll start to bloom now, and will go on till midnight. After that it will collapse and die."

I looked at the strange plant standing in the hall. It was over six feet tall, with a thin stem supported by a bamboo. Its dry prickly leaves were of a cactus variety, pear-shaped. On the end of one of these leaves, looking most unnatural in their positions, protruded two blossoms, enormous and trumpet-shaped.

They were still half-closed, waxy-white, with pink-tipped petals.

" You'll see it will have opened quite a lot after dinner," said Lady Jekyll.

" It blooms to-night at midnight ? " I asked, fascinated. There was something slightly sinister in the thought.

" It blooms to-night at midnight," repeated my hostess.

We solemnly walked in to dinner, and a chant seemed to follow us. " It blooms to-night at midnight."

Towards half-past ten I went out into the hall to look at the plant. Its blossoms were now enormous. The two trumpets had expanded, each turned almost angrily from the other. The petals had opened, and they had assumed, in their outward curl, the menacing shape of tentacles, like those of an octopus aroused to aggression. I stared at the malignant blooms, entranced. There was a chilly horror about their waxen forms. In each yawning funnel, at the root of pistils that might have been fangs, there was a splash of blood. The flowers hung there, transient, aware, as if awaiting in the silence of that dim hall their incautious prey.

I went back into the drawing-room, awed by this mysterious plant slowly gathering its strength for the ultimate orgasm at midnight. Midnight approached. My hostess bade me good night. For a few minutes I lingered at the foot of the stairs. There was a tense stillness. The clock over the fireplace ticked nervously, the shadows watched, and over all arose an indescribable odour, acrid, fetid. The cereus was living, it had a consciousness that seemed to pervade the air. It had made the large dim hall at once its scene of triumph and its death chamber.

" It will bloom at midnight," cried an inner voice. " It will die at midnight ! " came a whisper out of the shadows. Should we wait to see the climax ? Like a serpent it was still uncoiling itself. In a revulsion of horror I let my friend take me up to bed, leaving the drama to be played out down in the dark hall.

I awoke in the night. The room was dark. Something had broken my sleep. " It will die at midnight," whispered a voice. Had it died down there in the dark hall ? Nervously I switched on the light. It was 4 a.m. Angry with myself, I switched out the light, and tried to sleep. But I could not sleep. Was that fearful bloom dead now down in the hall ? Was it all over ? Had it bloomed in malignant lust, achieved its nocturnal orgasm, and died exhausted ?

I could not sleep. Finally, I weakened to the attack of imaginative curiosity, rose out of bed, opened my door, and stealthily crept along the corridor and down the stairs. There was no light, there was no need for light. At the foot of the stairs it stood there, a sinister presence, spectral in the darkness. But as my eyes sought it out in the fascination of horror, I experienced a new thrill. It was there, but its great trumpets were drooping, heavy, inert, mere shrunken flesh, repulsive as a hanging corpse.

For a long moment I gazed at it, revulsion mingling with pity. Its strange, sinister life was over. It had bloomed at midnight, and had died.

Stealthily I crept back to bed, like one who had been called to a final scene and had returned from the chamber of death.

### III

The cereus that Mrs. Powys saw had bloomed on the night of June 24th, 1800. Mrs. Powys was now sixty-two, but her zest for life was unabated. On the following January 8th she lost her mother, aged eighty-nine. At sixty-five we find her attending a ball and supper at Lord Malmesbury's, and getting home at four in the morning.

Every year she went with her husband for the season at Bath. She had a quick eye and ear, and every good story went into her diary. She was delighted with an account of George III.'s visit to Mr. West at Culham Court nearby. Mr. West had rolls brought, wrapped in flannel, from Gunter's the confectioners in Berkeley Square, London, thirty-four miles away, by relays of horsemen; whereupon the King exclaimed, "Ah, Gunter, Gunter! I am glad you deal with Gunter, West. Nobody like Gunter!"

At sixty-seven Mrs. Powys notes, "I rode my donkey for the first time, which Mr. Powys has just bought me," and a few days later she and her husband set off for Staffordshire, in a post-chaise hired at a guinea a week from a coachmaker in the Fairmile.

The years were now taking their toll. Mr. Powys died in April, 1809, and in October her brother-in-law, Dean Powys, died. This meant farewell to Fawley Rectory. She moved down into Henley, and occupied a solid red-brick mansion, in Queen Anne style, in

New Street, a street at least five hundred years old. It still stands, known as Ely House now, having taken the name from a Bishop of Ely who was born there in 1820. It possessed, in Mrs. Powys's day, a large walled garden, and from her back windows she had a fine view of the Thames, now blocked out by the boat-houses. From the front, as now, she commanded a view of the river up to the bridge, and she could sit in the window and watch the old broad-wheeled wagons draw up, and follow all the life of the cheese fair held by the wharf at the bottom of the street.

A Powys was still at the Fawley Rectory, for Mr. Freeman of Fawley Court presented the living to Mrs. Powys's second son. He was the father of six children when he went to the Rectory, and the following May was presented with triplets. As Mrs. Harman often remarks to me, " The Fawley air is wonderful ! "

Mrs. Powys's end came at seventy-nine, and occurred while on a visit to the Rectory. She had ceased to keep a diary for the last nine years, but there is evidence that she was active, and out and about until the end.

Sometimes, in the grey dusk, when I am walking along the winding lane on the ridge that leads to Fawley, I think I see her shade and wonder if I have caught her on her way to an elegant party at my Lord Villiers', or returning from a call on dear Lady Ailesbury at Park Place. Then, a few more steps, and the shade becomes a reality. Rosy cheeks and bright eyes under snow-white hair show me it is Mrs. Harman, on her way home from the churchyard. She has been paying a visit to the church in which her husband

rang the bells for fifty years, and to the village War
Memorial, where her flowers are often placed in
memory of that only son killed in the last month of the
war, and with whose death the Harman line fades
from the church register, where it has been known
since 1568.

# VILLAGE WAR MEMORIAL

The lamps are lit in Henley Town,
  And mistily flows the stream,
But there's one lad no more returning
  To his home and his firelit dream.

The houses lean together still,
  And the gables shadow the street,
But there's one voice no more will sound there
  By the bridge where the lovers meet.

The owl cries in the Fawley Woods,
  With the moon o'er Remenham Hill,
But there's one lad goes not a-courting
  By the race of Hambleden Mill.

The lamps are lit in Henley Town,
  And it's dawn in far Nazareth,
Where a simple lad lies a-sleeping
  In a slumber that draws no breath.

# CHAPTER XV

## THE REGATTA

### I

FROM Fawley the beechwoods descend steeply to the Marlow-Henley road and the banks of the Thames, on which are situated Greenlands, Fawley Court, and Phyllis Court, united in the events of the Civil War, when Royalists at Greenlands, and Parliamentarians at Phyllis Court, bombarded each other, and poor Fawley Court received a hammering in between them. That cannonade has long faded down the vista of time, and all I hear to-day is the report of the starting cannon down by Temple Island. For it is Regatta week, and a band in the Stewards' enclosure on the meadow opposite Phyllis Court, now a country club, wafts its music downstream, while a band on the great green lawn of the club returns the compliment, alternatively.

The colleges are all represented, and bronzed athletes from America, Germany, Italy, and France are carrying their respective flags in this international contest. Along the old river wall of Phyllis Court, covered with scarlet roses, lines of deck-chairs stand on either side of a canopied space, where the distinguished visitors, Royal if possible, and at least ambassadorial if not, will be roped in, and wrapped round with the local gentry.

I have just greeted the A.M. and P.M. The latter

has taken out of the press a Shantung silk suit whose lines were fashionable at the last Delhi Durbar. But the dear old Brigadier-General makes a striking if tropical note. This is the week of weeks, when he strings a monocle about his neck, and carries a rhinoceros-hide walking stick with a boar's tusk handle.

The A.M. is very neat, with her neck fenced round with lace and whalebone. She knows everything about rowing, and answers at once what crew is paddling downstream, and what ' time ' Jesus made in the Ladies' Plate. Her two cavaliers are stout gentlemen who wear absurdly small caps on large heads, and ties of the pinkness of an apoplectic baby. But hush! they are gods of the Leander Club, whose entrance is so narrow that only a slide in a varsity boat can carry one through.

I have just caught Sir John Lavery hidden away in a corner by a great elm busily painting a summery picture of the terrace, dappled with sunshine, parasols, and frocks. Lunch is now ready, and my hospitable friend, Captain Finlay, has asked us to dine in his private sitting-room. His hospitality being larger than his table, and twelve guests having grown to twenty-six, we will behave nicely and wait for the second sitting.

## II

Meanwhile, in a quiet corner, let us evoke the past. The river has not changed, and after a drought the lawn shows signs of the foundations of Sir Bulstrode Whitelock's Fillets Court, which was part of the Manor of Henley held in 1307 by Piers Gaveston, and later by the Marmions. Sir Bulstrode's father had bought it in 1622 for some £3,000, but never lived in it. It was then an old house, but had escaped the legend of Queen Elizabeth having slept there. Queen Anne, however, the Consort of James I., did sleep there.

It was the custom in those days for kings and queens to travel with their own bedding and furniture. We know that Queen Elizabeth went forth on her country house visits with her luggage conveyed in a hundred two-wheel carts, each with six horses to drag them. Courageous lady, she complained to the French Ambassador that, after a week's journey, she was unable to sit down with comfort for several days ! No wonder she carried about her own bedding.

Queen Anne also took care to ensure the maximum comfort in a hard age. She did not risk the coach ; she came in a barge from Windsor. There is a record of a payment by the Lord Chamberlain of £7 17s. 4d. to Giles Phettiplace, a gentleman usher, " for allow-ance of himself, one yeoman usher, three yeomen, two grooms of the Chamber, two grooms of the Wardrobe, and one groom porter, for making ready a house at Henley, called Phillips Court, by the space of eight days in the month of August, 1604."

The old house was left by Sir Bulstrode to his third son, William. In 1688, Lord Lovelace, living nearby at Hurley, was the instigator of a plot to bring over Prince William of Orange. Lord Lovelace collected a party of seventy horsemen to ride to Torbay to meet the Prince, and among these was Sir William White-lock's son, Bulstrode. There was a skirmish at Cirencester, and young Bulstrode was killed.

On December 13th, 1688, the Prince of Orange reached Henley on his triumphal route from the West, and he slept that night at Phyllis Court, whose hospitality must have been shadowed by the death of Sir William's son. There arrived that same evening a number of peers and the Bishop of Ely, who came with a declaration of the Lords drawn up at Whitehall after King James had retired from London. The peers supped with the Prince, and afterwards he held his first court in England there, receiving the addresses from the City of London and the Lords.

After the gaieties of Lady Grandison, and her son Lord Villiers, who had married Marshal Conway's niece, the old house seems to have been pulled down, the principal part in 1788, and more in 1837, and the present Phyllis Court erected. A descendant of the Whitelocks visited the derelict old house in 1784, and found there some painted glass with the Whitelock arms, and a portrait of Queen Christina of Sweden, which she had given to his ancestor, Sir Bulstrode, the ambassador. The bowling green in front of the house, now part of the lawn, and a portion of the old moat still exist.

From the windows of this second Phyllis Court one looks out now on the Royal Regatta. Lady Grandison, playing loo, and Lord Villiers learning his lines for his part in *The Provoked Husband*, could never have been disturbed as we are disturbed by the frenzied cries of partisans as the crews approach the winning-post. For Henley Regatta did not begin until 1839. It has continued since, though the death of the house-boat has curtailed much of its picturesque glory. But it is still a week of carnival. On the final night there is a fair in the meadow, and a display of fireworks. Then, on the Sunday, a silence falls. The lusty youths depart, and the Regatta is only a memory.

But it would seem that some of them leave souvenirs behind. A friend of mine who employs a sewing woman was astonished to learn that her services would not be available in April. She went to work in a Home run by a charitable lady, and in April her whole time was demanded.

" But why in April ? " asked my friend.

" Well, ma'am, you see April's our busy month with the Regatta babies."

" The Regatta babies ? Whatever do you mean ? The Regatta's in July and——"

But a brief calculation checked further argument.

### III

An overpowering lady has risen from the luncheon table, where a few places are now vacant. She is bearing down upon the A.M. and P.M., who are becoming desperately hungry, and are in a rage with Lady Almina Lushington-Crowfoot. The Mervyn-Morpeths of Pages Bottom, and the Lushington-Crowfoots of Russells Water, have been waging a local battle for a hundred years, having nothing in common except their hyphen and their pride.

Lady Almina is very massive, and, like a liner, her wash in passing is formidable. Having decided that Sir John Lavery had the largest name among the lions gathered at the feast, she annexed him. The A.M.

and the P.M. had made an attempt on Sir John (Did
he know that Sir Edwin Landseer used to visit their
great-aunt when she lived at Fairies Hole ?), but Lady
Almina, with a gesture had given them her backwash,
and they were pushed off like little tugs. Following
this, Lady Almina had eaten enoimously and leisurely
at the table, knowing quite well her rivals were
famishing.

She has risen at last, releasing Sir John, and proceeds
across the room to administer that final lash of courtesy
which denotes the social ringmaster.

" There *are* two places ! Sir John was so interesting I was simply held entranced. He's just been painting Lloyd George. I must say he made that regret-
table man sound most attractive."

" Sir John is naturally the master of flattering portraits," hisses the A.M., desperate for the vacant place.

" How kind of Captain Finlay to ask so many ! "
coos Lady Almina. " Why, the racing has started
again ! "

The noise of cheering comes through the window.
Lady Almina smiles sweetly, and turns away. The
A.M. is shaking with rage. The P.M. has secured a
place, but next to him Miss Whissitt has suddenly
seated herself, exclaiming, " What a lovely day—but
thunder—*n'est-ce pas* ? "

Yes, there is a rumble outside. There is also an
ominous rumble inside the A.M. That monstrous
Lushington-Crowfoot woman knew Miss Whissitt was
snatching her place.

Strange, these little feuds, this quiet stiletto work
between people who are really so nice. Among the

amenities of the district I must count my neighbours. They are friendly and very hospitable. They live in pleasant houses, whose interiors frequently match the beauty of their exteriors. There is every social grade, but I have never found one lacking in courtesy, from the squires behind their gates to the labourers behind their tankards. I see around me the English at their best, reserved, well-bred, conforming to long social traditions, but not imprisoned by them.

Lady Almina is only a late edition of Lady Grandison, and Mrs. Harman, transferred across a century, from the Smithy to the Rectory, is Mrs. Lybbe Powys full of the zest of life at seventy-nine.

I can travel in the space of a few minutes from London to Paris, Brussels, Hamburg, Berlin, Prague, Rome, Vienna, and Moscow, by the mere turning of a knob, or by lifting the telephone receiver, such are the miracles of the twentieth century, but I can also walk a mere hundred yards into *The Golden Ball* and talk with men whose ancestors cut their bows in Remenham Woods, and carried them at Crécy, Poitiers, and Agincourt, and I do not think the race bred by this country soil has deteriorated. They row faster at Henley Regatta to-day than ever they did since 1840. They run, ride, box, and swim faster. It may be they work less ; it is certain they drink less. Do they live longer? I think it must be so. Within an area of two square miles I know seventeen octogenarians.

I hope the Whissitts, the Mervyn-Morpeths, and the Lushington-Crowfoots will not die out. They give a slightly comic note to the landscape, but they also supply a tradition of quiet manners and education.

They are no fools, as the invading week-enders, slick on the Stock Exchange, or suave at the Bar, may think them. You mention some incident in history, with local associations, and they unlock a surprising store of knowledge, of solid reading. They have a quiet derision for the writers of snippets in the gardening press, for they are very wise in a long tradition of gardening. In potting, planting, pruning, and grafting, they are unrivalled. The A.M. and P.M. perform miracles under fifty feet of glass, with a coke bill that sorely tries their pockets. No one has been known to catch out Miss Whissitt in floral nomenclature. She is at home with *Clethra Delavayi*, otherwise sweet pepper bushes from China, or *Eucryphia pinnatifolia*, a lovely white flowering shrub from Chile, which had long gone unnamed in a neighbour's garden.

But lunch is finished at last. One must really show some kind of interest in the Regatta. You will observe that, to-day, the male of the species is as gorgeous as the female, for the lawn is bright with variegated college blazers, and the terrace overlooking the river is a human herbaceous border. The water, too, is mottled with colour, to which the boys from Radley College, navigating punts and canoes, contribute with their cerise-and-white-striped ties and straw hats.

Eton College, too, is much in evidence, for a special train has brought two hundred boys from Eton. Their tremendous excitement over the race just coming up, Eton College *v.* Trinity College 2nd, is due to the fact that, if they win, there is another excursion from Eton to-morrow, and if they lose, crew and excursionists vanish from the scene to-day.

But the schoolboy crew that excites attention is called Kent School. It comes from the U.S.A., shepherded by a fat black Father, who is their physical and spiritual coach. A schoolboy crew ? By what right are these young giants classed as schoolboys ? Six-footers, with what chests, what biceps, what thighs, all bumping the scale around twelve stone ! " Kent Preparatory School. Yessir ! Preparatory ! Sure, there isn't one of us over seventeen. No, sir ! "

They bring strange names, strange accents, and strange habits. They bellow at their deaf old Father, he bellows back, the cox bellows through a megaphone at the crew, and when the crew win they throw the cox into the river.

" Can they do anything with a slimy bottom ? " asks the voice of Lady Almina Lushington-Crowfoot, rising above the strains of *Annie Laurie*, as we wait for the next race. This must be rowing jargon. I listen intently.

" You put a quarter of an ounce of copper-sulphate crystals in a coarse bag and drag it to and fro," answers her companion. " A quarter of an ounce to a thousand gallons is strong enough to cure any confervoid. My *Nymphœa* flourishes now ! "

For a horrid moment I suspected the lady of being a nymphomaniac. Why crystals in a coarse bag ? Whose bottom is slimy—St. John's or Merton's ? Whatever is confervoid ? Where is Miss Whissitt ? She will know.

I found her, in the shade of the copper-beech.

" Confervoid ?—oh, it's that green, slimy growth you get in pools and garden ponds. Why do you ask ? " said Miss Whissitt.

"I overheard Lady Almina asking what could be done with a slimy bottom."

"She should put copper sulphate in her pool; it kills confervoid. Oh, there's a race coming up—it's Brasenose and Jesus. I do want Brasenose to win!" cried Miss Whissitt.

"Why?" I asked. "Is your family Brasenose?"

"Oh no, but they're such a handsome crew, *n'est-ce pas*?"

I felt tempted to enquire if she would like to stroke them, but refrained.

Brasenose won; after which we all flocked in to tea.

## SUN BATHERS

In the heat of the day when the bees are winging
From flower to flower, and in the plain
The wheat sways not, and a low voice, singing,
Veers from the garden and goes again,
Why do I lie so long in the sun,
    With my work undone?

Folly to ask! for in idleness
Love grows apace as I watch the light,
Vine-leaf shadowed, that falls to caress
Your hair of gold, your throat so white,
Your silk gown clinging as close and thin
    As an almond skin.

When the still noon drowses with scent of flowers,
And the sheep lie down in the elm tree's shade,
When no bird sings, and the heat overpowers,
I pillow your head and am half-afraid
Lest Death might come in the guise of Sleep,
    And my dear love keep.

And yet I know, when the day, declining,
Brings cool winds for my fevered brow,
You will wake and mock at mine eyes repining,
And, laughing lightly, will ask me how
The night shall be spent, in dance or song;
    And my work waits long.

315

# CHAPTER XVI

## SHADOW

### I

WHEN by crawling through a hole in the hedge I first stumbled on Pilgrim Cottage, shut up and dozing in the noonday sun, with a humming of bees over the lavender beds, and the soft ' plonck ' of an apple falling from a burdened tree, I was too excited by my discovery to consider whether it was situated in a district I should like.  A man falling in love does not greatly care whether his adored one lives in a Kensington square or a Derbyshire coalfield.

As I write these words, I am lying on a daybed in the garden, taking my sunbath, with only a fat speckled thrush, and a young blackbird not yet black, for company.  The bird-table is quite near, but they have long ceased to find me a scarecrow.  To-morrow I must leave this garden for Venice, *en route* for Athens and Constantinople, and for the first time in my life I am not excited by the prospect of travel.

It has been a long dream to see the Acropolis at Athens, and walk in the Olympian fields, to follow in the wake of Jason's Argonauts, to pass the plains of Troy, and sail—

*Where the narrowing Symplegades whiten'd the straits of*
    *Propontis with spray.*

The dream is now to be fulfilled, and yet I am

317

reluctant to go. Why? I ask myself. And looking around me I know why. The old tiled roof, so crazy in every curve, the vine-covered walls, the small windows looking east, south, and west on woods of beech, elm, larch, and fir, and on green curving hills, tell me I shall see nothing more pleasing to the eye, more suggestive of content. Indoors there are a hundred books waiting to be read, a hundred tasks to be completed. I can be busy for ten years. I want to lay a new floor, to make latches for the doors, to carpenter a new bookcase, to put on old clothes and mix mortar and point the chimney stack, to tie two ladders together and examine the roof, to renew a fence, replant a hedge, replan the beds, and, generally, to entertain more friends, and write a new book.

This last task is always deferred. The country for me is no place in which to write. I am a grand potterer. Week after week slips by without a line written of the promised book. It is vain that I have pinned up over my desk the exhortation *Nulla dies sine linea*. There is always a job in the house or the garden, or something to be seen in the vicinity. Moreover, I know now that my dream of seclusion is dead. I have become a house of call, for I am on the way to Oxford, to Burford, to Stratford, to Worcestershire, Gloucestershire, to the Midlands, and to Wales.

I pretend to be upset by all these callers, who find me nicely placed for lunch or tea, a break in the outward or return journey, but deep in my heart I know I am glad to see them, since they postpone this task of writing, which I heartily dislike. " What ! " they exclaim, " you dislike writing—oh, not really ? "

But indeed I do, for I never believe I am going to get through with the book, and, like a nervous diver, I shiver and defer the dreaded plunge. I defer so long that often the summer is gone, and I depart to my rooms in London, where I draw the curtains and burn the midnight oil.

Exceptions there are, and these books on my rustic adventure have been written mostly in the garden, as, clad only in white hat and dark glasses, I lay sunbathing. Like the garden dial, they record only the sunny hours, and I have a foolish fancy that I may thereby capture in them a scent of flowers, a sound of birds' voices, a glimpse of leaf-shadowed lawn and quiet, open-windowed rooms.

I was unhappy at the thought of leaving Pilgrim Cottage, but I was happy to think that all through August and September the place would not stand empty, the windows curtained ; that in the garden the snapdragons, hollyhocks, gladioluses, and dahlias would bloom for others, the apples redden on the bough, the chestnuts darken, the rich pageant of Autumn pass not unseen.

It chanced, one July day, that a friend, the Marchesa Malacrida, sat in my garden, and exclaimed, " Oh, if only I could spend weeks here ! " People often talk like that, and yet they cannot stay anywhere more than a few hours. Was she one of those ? It amused me to say—" Well, I'll lend you this place for September, if you like. I've already lent it for August."

She looked at me a little startled.

" You don't mean it ? " she asked.

"Of course I do! I shall be away all August and September. It seems a pity for no one to enjoy it."

"But you could let it!"

"I could, but I wouldn't. I can't lock up all my papers and books. I should hate to present the tenant with an inventory, and afterwards haggle over a burnt lounge or a cracked dinner-service. I should feel, too, that the cottage would resent being turned into a hireling, and Henrietta would never forgive me the lèse-majesté."

"Henrietta—your housekeeper?"

"No, Henrietta, Queen of England, my Van Dyck in the study. She's a Bourbon, and that long nose of hers makes me careful. No, whoever comes here must be a friend. He must walk in, with no just impediment when he takes my bride of quietness."

We were distracted just then by Amy, the Marchesa's cocker spaniel. I must explain that Amy is no ordinary dog. She has inspired numerous poems, and one of these, surely among his best, was written by Humbert Wolfe. It occurred to me just then that a nice coincidence would be achieved if Nadja Malacrida and Amy, her spaniel, took possession of the cottage. The last time I had vacated it another beautiful lady, with Cox, her spaniel, had spent August in it. My own cocker, Beau, had behaved beautifully, and shown no jealousy.

When my guest was departing, with Peter her husband, and Amy—they had all worked hard in the garden digging—she said to me, as I closed the door of her car—"Do you really mean it?"

" Certainly I do."

" With Amy ? "

" Amy is an essential clause in the agreement," I replied.

" But you know she's a habit of going off," said the Marchesa.

She had been off twice that day, and Peter and I had to seek her, threatening and whistling. The woods had proved too alluring.

" That will be your responsibility. I think Amy will soon feel settled," I answered.

Two days later the telephone rang.

" Do you still really mean it ? " asked the Marchesa's voice.

I assured her I did. The cottage was looking forward to her sojourn.

" The electric light has come, and the electric cooker. There's a power plug in each bedroom, to supplement the radiators."

" But I shan't want heating in September ! " she exclaimed.

" England is England—you never know," I replied.

" I believe you're saying that just because you're going to Greece ! "

" Perhaps I am feeling a little malicious," I replied. " You enjoy a holiday in sunshine abroad much more if you know it's grey and cold at home. You feel your travelling has not been in vain."

" How monstrously right you are ! " said that lovely voice.

II

So on September 1st Nadja Malacrida arrived, with Amy, and began the simple life. There were long sunny days, and she lived in the garden, reading and writing and sleeping. Every night and every morning she telephoned Peter in London, who could only get down for the week-ends.

I was a little amused and incredulous of this mood of Nadja Malacrida's. She, who was one of the modern young people of the West End, who had the gift of holding a *salon*, was one of the best-dressed women in London, a perfect hostess, quick-witted and charming, and so lovely to look at—it was difficult to imagine her in a simple country setting, alone. But how little we really know of the dual natures of our dearest friends. The Nadja Malacrida I knew was the delightful hostess of Grosvenor Street, happy at her long dinner-table in the midst of her guests. She had written plays in collaboration with her husband; the B.B.C. had discovered she had a lovely speaking voice, and she had given readings of selected poetry at the microphone. And now she was a country mouse, and I, who had imagined it was a temporary phase, discovered she had a genuine passion for the country.

Meanwhile, I had been sailing in the Ægean, and on my return from Greece a letter awaited me in Venice. It was in her handwriting.

PILGRIM COTTAGE,
*Sunday Night.*

*An apple has just fallen ' plop ' outside the window, the doleful cow is mooing her unrest to an unsympathetic*

322

*world, in the distance the sound of home-going motorists comes like a faint hum, and reminds me that there really is a world outside the garden of your almost-too-good-to-be-true cottage.*

*I've been here a week, and I still gasp with wonder and surprise every time I open the green door—am I making you hideously home-sick? But I can't help it, for I want you to know how utterly happy I am here, and how grateful, grateful beyond all words, I am to you for this delicious fairy-tale experience!*

*The weather has been consistently fine—it's rained, but never so as to prevent our doing what we wanted to, and my walks abroad have been sheer delight—I'd no idea your county was so beautiful—I, who adore woods, am filled with rapture each day anew, and find something fresh and lovely every time.*

*I'm having a delightful time, too, among your books, and am just finishing the complete perusal of Maugham's plays—how well they read. . . . Good night to you, and a million blessings for this happy time, and all nice thoughts.*

Another letter, bearing the Henley postmark, also awaited me. It was from a firm of local estate agents. I was in negotiation with them for the purchase of Greys Court, on behalf of a friend. This ancient house is on high ground on the other side of the beechwood that cuts the skyline seen from my garden. My walks had often taken me within sight of its grey Elizabethan façade. It had suffered various changes, including Georgian and Victorian additions, but its ancient form was still discernible, and here and there towers and walls had survived from the feudal castle. One could still trace the large court, and its line of fortifications.

It belonged to Walter de Grey, Archbishop of York from 1191 to 1216, and in 1348, in the reign of Edward III., Lord Grey had an order to crenellate and fortify his castle. Four of the towers, now in various stages of ruin, and the moat and embankment, probably date from this time. The east tower has walls four and a half feet thick, and four storeys surmounted by battlements. There is a long curtain wall between the towers, and these are probably all the work of Lord John de Grey.

The property, granted to his father by Henry VIII. at an annual rental of a red rose at midsummer, was in the possession of Sir Francis Knollys in the time of Queen Elizabeth, and he erected the Queen's Gate for her visit, on coming from Henley. In the line of the curtain wall there still exists the magnificent barn in which Oliver Cromwell's men stabled their horses, and nearby is a small house, probably a dower house, now called Bachelors' Hall, with a stone lintel over the door on which is inscribed *Melius nil cœlibe vita*—" The bachelor life is best," an inscription which appears to date from the middle of the eighteenth century.

The old mansion itself has a north front, and on the east side there are three gables still retaining several sixteenth-century windows, with stone mullions and transoms. The well is a curiosity. It is over two hundred feet deep, and in a building over it there is an enormous donkey-wheel which raises and lowers two buckets. The donkey treads within the wheel, in the manner in which a dog turned a dog-spit.

One other curiosity was part of the property, and it has caused endless discussion regarding its authenticity. This was a large chest, some seven feet long by three feet high, with a spring lock, which could only be opened with a curious key and in a special manner. It was carved inside and out with mythological and scriptural subjects, in the manner of an Italian *cassone*.

It has been claimed that this chest was the original of the ballad of *The Mistletoe Bough*, but Marwell Old Hall, Bramshill, and Minster Lovel have all been said to possess this chest, in which Lord Lovell's daughter was imprisoned while playing hide and seek on her wedding night.

Greys Court remained in the possession of the Lovells until the attainder of Francis, Lord Lovell, in the reign of Henry VII. It then passed to the Dukes of Bedford, who owned Marwell. There is a connecting link, therefore, between these various claimants to the original chest. Whether legend or truth, whether the original chest or not, Greys Court proudly exhibited the fatal chest.

Such then is the history of the house I was attempting to buy, and concerning my offer for which a letter from the agents in Henley awaited me. I did not want this house for myself. The idea arose in the mind of a friend, as we were sailing up the Dardanelles. She knew the estate, but circumstances made it difficult for her to enter into direct negotiation. I think we had been discussing the beauty of the Chilterns, perhaps perversely, considering our cruise through the

325

blue Ægean in a halcyon August. However it was,
I undertook the negotiations for the purchase of the
estate so near to my cottage. The price limit was
fixed, and I felt certain of success. Excitement was
added to our quest, after our return to Venice from
Greece, by a small daughter, who on a visit to the
Church of St. Anthony at Padua put her small hand
on the shrine of the saint, and wished. She kept her
wish a secret, of course, but we divined it.

"We shall get Greys Court," laughed her mother.
" St. Anthony never fails ! "

The days slipped by in Venice, and my friend left for
home. Letters passed between me and the agent.
My friend, having walked over the property, again
wrote : " I must buy it, if only to save St. Anthony's
face ! I count on you as St. Anthony's ambassador."
Finally, I was on the eve of success at a price well
within our limit. There was nothing more to do but
to wait until my return to England, when the purchase
could be decided upon. There was no hurry ; the
estate had been in the market for some years.

September drew towards its close. I received a
letter from the Marchesa, and learned she had gone
rustic with a vengeance.

PILGRIM COTTAGE,
*September 20th*

*It's past my ' Half Way ' now, and already the
return to London and all that town life entails looms
grimly before me. But it has been the greatest delight,
this month down here ; and so much have Peter and I
fallen in love with this part of the country that we*

*are scouring the neighbourhood for a small place of our
own ! So you may have us as neighbours yet ! I
must say I never dreamt that one could find country so
unspoilt and people so amiable at a distance of thirty-
five miles from London—I've done all the walks round
about, and never tire of the views from every side as one
approaches the village. And, of course, the cottage
still remains the wonder it was when I first set eyes on it.*

*The apples on the ' red ' tree are nearly gone ; but
you will still see your russets on the bough, I hope . . .
I do like the Henley people. I am not a bit surprised
you love your place. And your housekeeper, of course,
is a joy ! Bless her. She's made me so comfortable.
After which I must say good night and au revoir.*

*Yours,*
NADJA M.

And then something happened which belongs more
to the realm of fiction than fact. I was sunning myself
on the balcony of my garden in Venice, a little walled-
in garden, where I had only to stretch forth a hand to
pluck a ripe fig, and where a cool murmur rose from
the cherub's fountain head, when a letter arrived by
air mail. It was from Nadja Malacrida.

PILGRIM COTTAGE,
*September 25th.*

*You have been so very kind to us that, in this
grasping world, you will probably not be surprised to
hear me, like Oliver Twist, asking for more. Which
is all obscure and not over-grammatical, I'm sure.
But here are the facts. You are the direct cause of*

327

*our falling in love with this part of the world, and with one particular house in it, and Peter has to-day made an offer for the Greys Court property!*

*If it is true that you are not coming back till the 8th of October, could we trespass on your amazing hospitality until the 4th or 5th? This would help Peter enormously, as he is living in a maelstrom of architects, builders, land-agents, surveyors, and what not.*

*Do you know Greys? It is all so exciting that I hardly dare allow myself to think of living there. But I have a sort of feeling that if one wants a thing sufficiently one sometimes gets it.*

*How are you—are you still in Venice? I do hope this will catch you before you leave.*

At that moment Giuseppina called me in to breakfast, but I left it untouched. After the first shock I had to adjust myself to these tangled circumstances. It became increasingly plain that, as the friend of both intending purchasers, I could not honourably negotiate for either; whichever succeeded, I should be in an invidious position with the other.

I immediately telegraphed and wrote to the Marchesa, explaining I had been bargaining for the estate on behalf of another friend but that I should not enter into a renewed contest. To my other friend I also wrote, explaining my position, and asking to be relieved from further negotiations. They must fight it out without me.

A few days later I left Venice for Turin and Paris. A breakdown of the Rome express brought me, three hours' late, to Paris at midnight, on October 4th.

The faithful Louis Tissier met me with my letters. I opened these in the taxi. The first, a telegram, was from my friend—" I have bought Greys." Then I opened a letter. It was from the Marchesa Malacrida.

PILGRIM COTTAGE,
*October* 1st.

*It is certainly the most amazing coincidence, and we were not less flabbergasted by your letter than you were at mine. But I am very much afraid we shall not get the place, for this morning we were informed that someone else has just made an offer far larger than ours, and I imagine she will get the prize. Incidentally, I am so desperately in love with Greys that I am quite heartbroken. I adore it, its possibilities, and its country. And this, when, as the agent says, Greys has been spurned and neglected for years! I am sorry for you, but quite frankly far sorrier for myself, as I was quite decided that I was going to live at Greys for the rest of my life. And, of course, now I feel that nothing else will do!*

*However, I have loved my month here. I feel so very much better for it, and my love for the Chilterns and this part of the world certainly dates from my stay in Pilgrim Cottage. When you are back, do ring me up and come and see us, that is, if you can be dragged away from the cottage for an hour or so. You see, I've got to live near here! I like the country, the people, even Henley as a shopping centre! What is to be done about it?*

*I send this to Paris, and look forward to seeing you very soon. Your garden is looking exquisite in its*

*early autumnal finery, and awaits you eagerly, I know.
And there are still some trees with their apple harvest
on them. And it's warm and mellow and kindly, and
altogether beautiful.*

*Welcome back when you come, and may the ghost
of my happiness haunt you just a little in the future.*

NADJA.

I sat back in the taxi, thinking how gallantly she had
taken her defeat, when I noticed a curious expression
on my friend's face.

" Is there anything wrong ? " I asked.

" I suppose you haven't seen to-day's paper—with
that ? " said Louis, quietly, offering me *The Times.*

*Car's Crash Over Embankment. Marchesa Mala-
crida Killed.*

My heart seemed to stop still. Then, in the dim
light I read on.

The Marchesa Malacrida was killed yesterday
when her car, which she was driving, skidded,
crashed through a fence, and plunged down a
40-foot bank on the hill just over Henley Bridge.
The groundsman of a nearby cricket ground saw
the car turn over and over as it fell down the bank.
He ran to the scene, and found the Marchesa a few
yards from the wrecked car. She was dead. The
road at the bottom of the bank was littered with
suitcases and hat-boxes. The car was going up the
hill when it mounted the path at the side of the road,
tore through the fencing and fell down into a lower
road. A spaniel which was in the car, ran away

when the crash occurred, and was found later, terrified but uninjured.

The Marchesa, who was 35, a niece of the late Annie, Lady Cowdray, was on her way back to London after a stay at Pilgrim Cottage, the property of Mr. Cecil Roberts, the author.

I read no more, and closed my eyes. When I opened them we were rounding the Arc de Triomphe, flood-lit at the crest of the Champs Elysées. Yesterday! Only yesterday. Nadja Malacrida dead. Leaving my cottage. Was this a nightmare?

The pressure of my friend's arm in mine told me it was not. That last sentence of her letter rang in my head : " May the ghost of my happiness haunt you just a little in the future."

### III

Somehow I got through that night, thinking now of her radiant beauty, of her parents, her husband. In the morning I decided to hurry over to England, but after a telephone call I found it was useless. They were burying her that noon in the little cemetery on the hillside opposite my cottage, the cemetery whose yews and cypresses stood so dark against the vivid green when I looked out of the dormer windows.

A day later I was home, and when I rose in the morning the flooding sunshine of that early October day filled the landscape with the beauty of russet and gold. Never had I seen a day so heavenly with its vivid tints sparkling in the crystal air. I walked across from my tragedy-shadowed cottage to the still cemetery. The flowers lay on her grave in all their lovely freshness. Could they be for her? On Wednesday only she had left the cottage, bidding my housekeeper farewell, and waving back as she drove out of the lane. A few minutes later she was dead. It was now only Saturday, and I stood by her grave, covered with flowers in the fresh loveliness of this golden morning.

I looked at the beechwoods in their autumn gold, afire where the sun caught them. I looked up the valley where the hills shone now the mist had uncovered them. On a cypress branch a spider's web scintillated with its dewy burden. A distant car, and a blackbird's voice, told of the living world. Through a frame of branches Pilgrim Cottage gleamed beneath its thinning poplars. The glory of this October morning caught my breath. The scent of roses and lilies rose in the sharp air. From horizon to horizon not a cloud was visible in the pale-blue sky. Surely, surely there was no death? Not the ghost of her happiness, but she herself would be walking in my garden when I returned?

Folly to imagine such things, as well I knew, but the heart in sorrow rebels against the pitiless fact. I left the place where her wish had been so tragically fulfilled. "I love this valley—I'd like to be buried over there," she had said lightly one morning, standing in the garden, and looking towards the dark screen of cypresses.

Too soon, too truly, her wish had been fulfilled.

## IN MEMORIAM: N.M.

No sound, not even leaf-fall, breaks the spell
Where moonlight moves the shadows down the lawn .
    Oh, watch you well,
Tall poplars, burnished windows, dark, clipped fir !
    Is there no sign of her ?

Indoors, the log-flame whispers in the grate,
The clock ticks softly on the open desk ;
    Relentless Fate,
Save Time, and dying flame, does nothing stir ?
    Is there no sign of her ?

I call her name within the silent house,
And touch the book wherein she marked the page ;
    She cut these boughs
Of russet beech, this purple lavender—
    O lovely signs of her !

Surely within my garden she will come,
Drawn to its scene by so much happiness ?
    False voice be dumb !
While blossom breaks or bird sings, everywhere
    There is a sign of her !

# CHAPTER XVII

## OCTOBER SUNSHINE

THAT autumn girded itself for a pageant. A few red apples still mocked me from the topmost bough. The russet tree bore a fabulous crop, and, after hampers had been despatched to friends in London, there was still the problem where to lay those apples. They lay along the landing upstairs, in orderly regiments whose red and khaki jackets shone resplendently by day, and gleamed ghostly in the moonlight when I went up to bed. Apple pies, and apple jam and apple chutney would reduce their ranks, but I knew they would march well on into the spring, when the boughs would be heavy with the snowdrift of blossom.

I made all ready for the siege of winter. Not that winter is ever hard in this sheltered valley, but there is pleasure in the contemplation of long dark nights, of the log blazing in the grate, of the curtains drawn, the lounge pulled up to the fire, the quiet and leisure for reading, the smell of buttered toast, the singing of the kettle, the soft gleam of silver and china, the bright patchwork of tea-cosy and lace tea-cloth.

Outside in the garage the gardening tools have been housed, and the bulbs covered down in their winter quarters. One's breath rises mistily, and it is no place or time for tinkering. The frost begins to grow up the window panes at four o'clock. One must take a torch to post a letter at the village post office, or to call in at

*The Golden Ball*, where a fire blazes in the parlour, and sends light dancing over the ceiling and glinting on the feathered darts awaiting the deft hands of plough-man and carter.

But pleasure is not wholly confined to life within doors. The leaves are long in falling, and there will be golden days of surprise, when the wooded landscape will smile, the air blow with a summer softness, and the hips and haws hang in red clusters above the fleecy mantle of Traveller's Joy, of which " the floures thereof come forth in July : the beauty thereof appears in November and December," as old Gerard observed centuries ago.

We must be early afoot these days, to catch the morning sun, and be home before the fall of darkness. There is a beauty in wintry fields and woods no less enchanting than summer's glory. The anatomy of nature is now best seen ; the elm and the beech stand forth in their nakedness, miracles of ironwork against the lavender sky, and in the valley shines a village or a stream we have never glimpsed in summer's flounces.

And how little we have seen ! We had intended to go rambling afar, and we have stepped but a short distance from Pilgrim Cottage. Over those hills and beyond those woods lie villages whose beauty and wealth of legend we have not tapped—a vintage of the years that may yet prove the best at our feast.

But we must end. The lights are lit in Henley Town. The log burns brightly in the grate, the tea-table is set, and the slippers are warming by the fire. This evening we will take our ease, and perhaps, God willing, go—

*To-morrow to fresh woods and pastures new.*

THE END